PENGUIN BOOKS

THE ENGLISH HOUSE
THROUGH SEVEN CENTURIES

Olive Cook has written a number of books on architectural and topographical subjects, including *The English Country House, An Art and a Way of Life, English Cottages and Farmhouses, The Wonders of Italy* and *Breckland*. Interested in all forms of visual expression, she is also the author of a book on the prehistory of the cinema, called *Movement in Two Dimensions*. She was married to Edwin Smith (1912–71) who trained as an architect but who made his reputation as a photographer. He was praised by Cecil Beaton as 'an understanding and loving connoisseur of his subject' and Sir John Betjeman called him 'a genius at photography'. He had special feeling for the domestic shell, whether grand or humble, and an amused and sympathetic eye for the casual detail of either. His photographs do far more than complement the text of this book: they are an integral part of the whole presentation, giving it an exceptional and exciting sense of unity. Among the many volumes illustrated by Edwin Smith's photographs the following make a special contribution: *English Parish Churches, The English Garden, The Wonders of Italy, England, Ireland, Great Houses of Europe, Pompeii* and *Venice*.

Note to Reprinted Edition

This book attempts to tell the story of the English house primarily as a work of art. But this does not mean that it is intended to be no more than an account of changing styles. The development of the house as a work of art reflects an attitude to life which, while peculiar to these islands, is at the same time an expression of the idea underlying the whole of Western civilization. This idea, very broadly speaking, is based on the apprehension of man's individuality as the source of his highest achievements and greatest felicity. There is evidence that this idea, and with it the civilization it inspired, is moribund. Although it is not yet possible to view the tendencies of our own age objectively, the course followed not only by architecture but by all the arts indicates that tradition is everywhere being flung aside, and philosophical and political trends confirm that the sense of unique, irreplaceable personal identity which nourished the traditions we are uprooting is giving way to the conception of collectivity. The story unfolded here throws a clear light on this process. For the success with which in the past builders combined utility with the most vivid manifestations of individuality is particularly striking in a form of art which, of all others, is the most sternly conditioned by needs which have nothing to do with aesthetics and which has now become little more than a statement of those needs.

Britain's isolation from the main-stream of development on the Continent and the unusual variety of materials resulting from the complicated geology of the country have enhanced the idiosyncracy already encouraged by the prevailing intellectual climate; and because of the relative internal peace enjoyed by these islands since the Norman Conquest, the material embodiments of a long and continuous tradition lived on into the present century in astonishingly large numbers. There, before 1945, change was largely a matter of renovation, addition and slow growth in which past and present were one. But today, because of the economic consequences of a radically altered ideology, the new is not only springing up beside the old: it threatens to engulf it. It has long since become apparent that the day of the large country house is over. And now the survival of the smaller traditional house and cottage is jeopardized by the further inevitable results of that same ideology, the rank growth of population, widespread car ownership, an exaggerated regard for utility, a wave of industrialization on a far greater and more destructive scale than that of the last century and, in short, by a way of life into which the homes of our forebears no longer fit.

In order to give perspective to the theme of these pages and to stress its urgency, this history of an art, emerging in the Middle Ages and enduring until the close of the nineteenth century, has been prefaced by a glance at the prehistoric darkness and the Roman period, out of which it was born, and concluded by a brief reference to what is taking its place. Because of the point of view adopted, every kind of house has been included in this survey, although the choice is necessarily personal and very far from comprehensive. For the same reason an eccentric example has sometimes been preferred to a more typical instance of a particular style. Although the arrangement is roughly chronological, it has occasionally seemed more expedient and more informative, especially pictorially, to group different phases of a development together, even at the risk of some repetition and overlapping. The title of the book is not to be taken too seriously, for although the majority of the houses photographed and described are English, some of the examples come from other parts of Britain. They have been introduced as parallel and evocative developments in altered conditions and as variants of forms originating in England.

I originally wrote this book in response to a suggestion of the late Leonard Russell and to him I owe the opportunity of getting to know an endlessly fascinating subject a little better. His idea was that such a general account might complement the major work on the English House by Nathaniel Lloyd, since the publication of which in 1931 no full scale study had been attempted. The book which resulted from Leonard's suggestion makes no claim to supersede Lloyd's *History* but the inclusion of new material and the continuation of the story up to our own day may justify the venture and perhaps the wide canvas may give perspective to the numbers of brilliant explorations of specialized aspects of domestic architecture which have been published during the decade which divides the first and the present edition of these pages. Although I might now write differently about some of the houses mentioned, my conclusions and standpoint remain unaltered for nothing has occurred which could lead me to modify them. So I have not revised the text for this new edition except to correct obvious mistakes. And although the condition of some of the buildings illustrated may have deteriorated while not a few other houses, among them the Vineyard, Saffron Walden, Great Cressingham Manor and the former Vicarage at Methwold, have been rescued from decay, it seemed best to leave a text untouched which when it was written corresponded to the images shown in the photographs. In describing the locations of individual houses the traditional names and the traditional boundaries of the counties have been retained.

Olive Cook

I

The Theme Foreshadowed

PRE-NORMAN BRITAIN

Interior of a Neolithic house at Skara Brae, Mainland, Orkney

This house is one of seven discovered in 1850 after a storm had blown away the top covering of the sand under which they had lain concealed throughout the centuries of recorded history. The Stone Age village was later excavated by Professor Childe, who found that the houses were connected by galleries and that each was provided with a central hearth and inbuilt furniture. The houses probably date from about 2000 or 1800 B.C. and may be contemporary with Maes Howe, the remarkable prehistoric tomb above Loch Harray a little distance from Skara Brae. Some archaeologists, among them Dr Glyn Daniel and Professor O'Riordàn, suggest that the builders of both the tomb and the village were the descendants of trading communities from Spain and Portugal who left their homeland some time in the third millennium B.C. and travelled from Brittany, the west coast of France and Normandy and spread from Ireland and Wales to Scotland and the Orkneys. The photograph shows the combination of monolithic slabs and cut stones which characterizes the building methods of these people. The fine quality of the masonry is partly due to the availability of the Orkney flagstones which were easily split into smaller pieces, but also to an innate sense of form, a conception of the house as something more than a convenient shelter.

It is usual to begin the story of the English house with the emergence of the period styles at the time of the Norman Conquest; but the Conquest was only the most recent of innumerable invasions and immigrations which had already conspired to blend foreign and native traditions in these islands. And viewed in the light of later developments the survivals of human dwellings dating from prehistoric and Roman Britain are of extraordinary interest. They hint at the possibility of continuing traditions and, even more fascinating, they reveal patterns in domestic building which reappear centuries later with little or no evidence of direct influence. While there is no exact repetition, the similarities are sufficiently arresting to suggest that they mark specific moments in the ceaseless oscillating movement to which all life is subject and which dominates man's effort to create order out of chaos.

Surprising affinities with subsequent practices can be observed in the most exciting of all surviving prehistoric houses in these islands, those at Skara Brae in the Orkneys. Covered and preserved by shifting sands for thousands of years, this village was exposed in 1850 when a storm of exceptional ferocity tore the grasses and top layers from the high dune in which it lay buried. Seven houses and four older structures were discovered. Each house consists of a single large room with a central hearth and a passage connecting it to its neighbour. There are the remains of an effective sewage system. But the most astonishing characteristic of these houses is that they are provided with built-in furniture, shelves, a shelved dresser, cupboards and beds which immediately recall the built-in furniture of the seventeenth century found in farmhouses in the Lake District. Yet this Skara Brae furniture is perhaps closer in feeling to the slate shelves, mantelpieces and lavatory seats of some Welsh houses, for it is formed exclusively of local stone, the same Caithness flagstone of which the dry-stone walls are made. One of the houses exhibits a further totally unexpected feature: an impressive attempt at constructing pillars with rude capitals to support an architrave and frame doorways and recesses. These pillars are truly architectural and their appearance in the dwelling of a Stone Age farmer marks the emergence of a sense of something more than mere function, of a groping towards that combination of form and ornament which characterizes the finest domestic design.

In actual time Skara Brae belongs to the period of c. 1800 B.C., when the south of Britain had already entered the Bronze Age but the knowledge of metal had not reached these northern villages, and there could be no more forceful illustration of the Neolithic way of life than these stone beds and dressers. Skara Brae is thus an early and unforgettable example of the effect of region on domestic architecture. Just as the Elizabethan manor of Chastleton incorporates the oolitic limestone on which it stands, or Sawston Hall embodies Cambridgeshire clunch in its walls and Cambridgeshire bog oak in its staircase, so these primitive habitations reflect that intimate relation between house and setting which endured until the nineteenth century. They are fashioned of the very stuff of the country. They

9

The long house

The photograph on the left shows the principal room of one of the seven houses in the late Iron Age village of Chysauster, near Penzance, Cornwall. Each of these houses is roughly rectangular in shape and the rooms are built within the thickness of the wall and open into a central courtyard. The interest of the Chysauster houses in the present context is that each consists of two apartments: a living-room, furnished with a hollow granite basin used as a mortar, and a byre for cattle. This custom of housing men and beasts under the same roof was general among pastoral peoples in wild or mountainous regions and has persisted until the present day. The arrangement is seen in the traditional crofter's cottage on Lewis, Hebrides (top right), thatched, warmed by a central hearth and windowless. Such dwellings were called 'black houses', not only because they had no windows, but also because it was customary in the Hebrides to strip off the soot-impregnated thatch once a year, in May, for manure. One of the objects of the roof, which was originally without a smoke-hole, was to encourage the accumulation of soot. Today most 'black houses', if they are still in use, are occupied entirely by cattle. Although many centuries divide this crofter's dwelling from that at Chysauster, the method of construction, the massive dry-stone walling, is the same in each case. The cottage from Ballinaboy, Co. Galway (centre), is characteristic of the one-storeyed dwellings found everywhere in Ireland; it again incorporates the principle of the long house, the end nearest to the camera and furthest from the hearth, referred to as the 'bottom end', being reserved for a cow. But though the byre is part of the rectangular house, there is no direct access from the main room to the feeding walk as in the long houses of Dartmoor. In many Irish examples the former byre has been converted into a bedroom, store or dairy. A similar conversion took place at Warbstow, Cornwall (bottom), where the byre and the hayloft of a two-storeyed long house dating from the early eighteenth century were turned into a dairy and bedroom during the Victorian period. The upper window on the left was once the opening into the hayloft and was reached by an external staircase. This house is of cob, protected by slate-hanging (*see* page 146).

also introduce the theme of the house remote from the centre of fashion and new ideas. Except for the grandest mansions such houses do not show innovations until they are one or more generations out of date: a Westmorland farmhouse may well appear to be of the seventeenth century when in reality it was built in the Georgian period, and a late seventeenth-century house, such as Eyam Hall, Derbyshire, may still wear the look of an Elizabethan manor.

The type of house revealed at Skara Brae seemed to have no immediate successors. The celebrated street of Iron Age houses at Chysauster, near Penzance, on the other hand, discloses an arrangement which occurred again during the Roman occupation and is still found in some districts today. Each of the Chysauster houses consists of two apartments: a living-room and a byre for cattle. In a Romano-British farmhouse excavated by Colonel Pitt-River at Iwerne in Dorset – built of flint and rubble just like the cottages which are characteristic of that landscape today – the family and their livestock were sheltered under one roof in exactly the same way. The Dark Age history of this type of house is obscure, but the long house was widely known over medieval Britain, and in parts of Cornwall and Devonshire, in the north, in Wales and in Ireland the tradition of housing animals and humans under the same roof outlived all the changes which in southern and eastern England led to the separation of byre and dwelling.

These primitive oblong houses seem akin to the rectangular houses which emerged towards the end of the Middle Ages. The cross-walk dividing the animals' shelter from the family apartments in Devonshire and Lakeland long houses recalls the screens passage of a hall house; and the characteristic Irish homestead comes very close in its arrangement to the medieval rectangular hall house. The likeness is particularly striking when represented by a house such as Truthall, near Helston, which is low and continuously roofed. The typical Irish dwelling is one room thick, and the door, placed near one end of the principal central room, the kitchen, is directly opposite another door. Small apartments lead off this main room at one or both ends, and there may be two attic rooms in the roof. Before the introduction of chimney flues the hearth was in the centre of the main apartment, as in the older hall houses. A central fire was not unknown even as late as the nineteenth century, for Charles Lever, the novelist, describes one he saw in the Brannock Islands. The parallels between this kind of house and the English rectangular house are, however, purely fortuitous; for the long house is the product of a continuing tradition, while the rectangular house, as will appear later, is the result of a combination of two distinct types of dwelling.

In any consideration of recurring patterns in domestic architecture, the centuries of the Roman Occupation are peculiarly stimulating to the imagination both because the civilization then established produced so much that was echoed by later developments and because the abrupt decline of that civilization was inaugurated by a period of chaos and destruction dramatically like that upon which we are now entering. Only the fringe of this vast and complex subject of analogies can be touched upon here. The reintroduction in our own era of the luxuries of the baths and central heating, which became an essential part of the plan of most villas in the last phase of Roman rule, is an obvious instance of repetition. The themes of the town house within a garden, contrasting with the true town house as a unit in a composition filling the street frontage, and of ribbon development along arterial roads, creating urban sprawl, were also first stated in Roman Britain.

A comparison of the effects of the first impact of classical art on domestic building in Britain with that of the second great wave of Mediterranean influence which culminated in the Palladian house inevitably reveals countless resemblances, for the ultimate source of inspiration was the same. The absorbing interest of such a comparison, however, is that the British genius for manipulating and transforming classical design, which is expressed with such zest in a composition such as the three-storeyed porch of Kirby Hall, which combines an utterly free interpretation of the Orders, exotic pillars and scrolly brackets, with a curving gable, and which reached its full flowering in the unique harmony of the eighteenth-century house, is already manifest in the remains of Roman Britain. The exuberant Venus mosaic at Rudston, Yorkshire, for example, and the mosaic figures of the seasons at Chedworth, near Cirencester, are reminiscent in their quality of caricature and enthusiastic infidelity to classical models of the robust interpretations by Elizabethan and Jacobean craftsmen of Renaissance motifs. They invite comparison with such works as the carved screen at Audley End with its rollicking terminal busts or with the coloured plaster friezes in relief of the stories of Diana and Orpheus in the Great High Presence Chamber at Hardwick, which are also strangely related in both colour and feeling to the Orpheus pavements of Cirencester and the south-west which were a speciality of Romano-British taste. An abstract mosaic like that from Littlecote Park, Ramsbury, now in the Ashmolean Museum, bears as little affinity to the Venus pavement as do the reliefs at Hardwick to the sophisticated plasterwork of Charles Stanley or Joseph Rose. Just as Adam's saloon at Kedleston, though inspired by the Pantheon, is unmistakably English, so this mosaic, while based on Roman models, could never be confused with Mediterranean work. The bold contrasts and brilliance of the typical Roman mosaic have undergone a significant metamorphosis. The colours, in common indeed with those at Chedworth, are as restrained and muted as those of the English landscape on a cool, cloudy day. This Ashmolean mosaic includes three semicircular shapes filled with an unfolding fan device within an ornamental border. They precisely correspond to the favourite shape and the commonest design for fanlights over eighteenth-century doors.

It seem incredible that a civilization so long established as the Roman, covering a period, after all, about equal to that which divides the reigns of Queen Elizabeth I and Queen Elizabeth II, could have been wholly effaced; that all the manifestations of a classically inspired way of life were obliterated after the withdrawal of Roman government. We do indeed know that the massive ruins of deserted Roman cities still excited wonder three centuries after their builders had vanished. The remains of Aquae Sulis, Roman Bath, are the subject of one of the most moving of early English poems, that first of many meditations on old stones, called 'The Ruin':

> Well wrought this wall: Wierd broke it.
> The stronghold burnt . . .
> Snapped rooftrees, towers fallen,
> The work of Giants, the stonesmiths
> mouldereth.
> > Rime scoureth gatetowers,
> > rime on mortar.
> Shattered the showershield, roofs ruined,
> age under-ate them.
> Bright were the buildings, halls where springs ran,
> high, horn-gabled, much throng-noise,
> these many meadhalls men filled
> with loud cheerfulness. Wierd changed that.
> > Hosts who would build again
> shrank to earth. Therefore are these courts dreary
> and that red arch twisteth tiles,
> wryeth from roof-ridge, reacheth groundwards . . .
> Broken blocks.

The Romans themselves are less than ghosts to the writer of this poem: he has

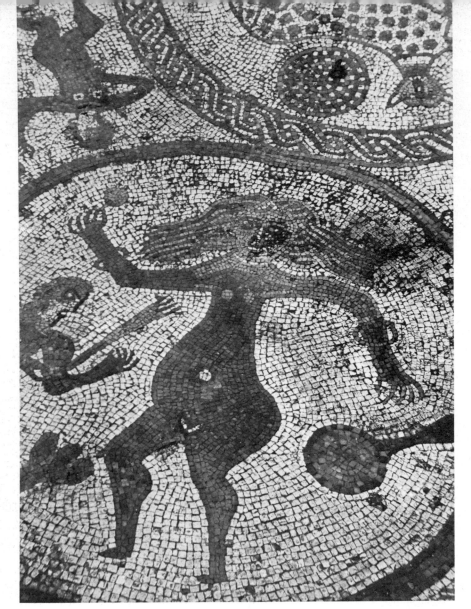

no knowledge of them and to him their remains are 'the work of Giants'. But there is evidence that if the race who had left their shattered monuments was no more than a legend, the men who came after them were not blind to the building practices displayed in the fabric of these ruins. At Trinity Church, Colchester, courses of re-used Roman bricks lace the flint masonry of the Saxon tower in exactly the same way as Roman bricks strengthen the near-by flint walls of Camulodunum. The Saxons did not themselves make bricks: they were content to use those which, because they had been manufactured in such vast quantities, so plentifully survived the Occupation. But the combination of the two materials, flint and brick, later became common in all those districts where flint is abundant. Thus the great drum-like bastions of Burgh Castle, one of the forts of the Saxon Shore, its immensely stout walls now besieged by corn filling and surrounding them, are intimately and touchingly related to eighteenth- and nineteenth-century cottages in the neighbouring villages because they are all fashioned of the same local flints bonded with brick. The Roman bricks do indeed differ from the later ones. They are strikingly thin, resembling tiles more than bricks, commonly measuring about $18 \times 12 \times 1\frac{1}{2}$ inches, though they vary in size. But the use to which the manufactured material was put is more important and more immediately impressive than such distinctions. A most interesting aspect of this first introduction of bricks into Britain by the Romans, the bearers of classical

Detail from the plaster frieze of the
High Great Presence Chamber,
Hardwick Hall, Derbyshire

The great coloured plaster frieze,
some twelve feet deep, of which this
detail shows Diana and her maidens,
was the work of Abraham Smith,
c. 1595. Just as the mosaic pavement
(opposite) was inspired by Roman
example, so this unique plasterwork
was based on the imagery of a master
more conversant with classical motifs
than the English artist: it derived
from a design by Martin de Vos. But
in both cases the vigour and originality of the copy impart new life to
outworn themes. Other subjects of
the Hardwick frieze include Venus
chastising Cupid, as well as Orpheus
and Ceres, all embowered in a forest
where men and dogs hunt among
smooth-stemmed trees and giant
foliage.

ideals, is that when classical forms were again beginning to influence architecture
in these islands, the fashion was accompanied by the widespread popularity of
brick, which had not been made again after the Occupation until medieval times
and was then only used sporadically.

There is no real connecting link between the brickwork of the Romans and
that of Tudor England. Yet recent excavations appear to show that some threads
of continuity may have linked the declining order of Roman Britain with that
which was to take its place. It is possible, for instance, that the manufacture of
cylinder-blown glass may never have died out. Window glass was widely used
in Romano-British dwellings, even in native settlements and in sites as far north
as the Scottish Lowlands. But formerly the only evidence for the occurrence of
window glass in Anglo-Saxon Britain came from such sources as Bede's reference
to Benedict Biscop's appeal to Gaul in 674 for glass-makers to teach the art of
making glass windows to monkish craftsmen in Britain and St Wilfrid of
York's mention of the insertion of glass in windows previously fitted with linen
or a fretted slab. During recent decades discoveries at Glastonbury, Thetford,
Old Windsor and Southampton of glass manufactories of pre-Norman date,
each site revealing fragments of window glass of the type made during the
Occupation, suggest that the Saxon glassmen were following and upholding a
skill introduced by the Romans.

Yet it would be rash to assume that this comforting hint of continuity rested on more than conjecture. The Saxon glasshouses may well have been founded by foreign glass-makers brought to Britain in response to demands like that of Benedict Biscop. It is still less likely that the hall house, which, probably stemming from Saxon practice, became the characteristic form of dwelling for a landowner of the early Middle Ages, was a survival from Roman times. Thus the anticipation of this type of structure in Roman Britain is among the more striking manifestations of those haunting parallels which excavation is continually bringing to light. The labourers on the larger Romano-British estates were usually housed in a barn-like building standing on one side of the farmyard. The most impressive example to have been discovered is probably the enormous dwelling which forms part of the famous villa at Bignor; it measures 128 by 56 feet, thus exceeding in overall size the largest medieval timber hall so far known in the British Isles, the twelfth-century building measuring 110 by 60 feet excavated at Cheddar by Mr P. A. Rantz for the Ministry of Works in 1963.

The interior of the Roman labourers' dwelling was divided into nave and aisles by timber columns; and occasionally a partition, not unlike the screen of a medieval hall, ran across one end of the vast apartment. Stores, implements, livestock and workers were all housed in the building. Sometimes, when the farm was only a modest establishment, as at Clanville and Castlefield in Hampshire and at Ickleton in Cambridgeshire, the aisled hall provided the only domestic accommodation.

The advanced form of timber construction which was the pride of English domestic architecture in the late fourteenth and succeeding centuries, the building in which a well-carpentered timber frame took the main stresses, filled with wattling and clay daub and rendered with a coating of lime-wash or plaster, was clearly an established feature of the scene in Roman Britain. Although actual remains of Romano-British timber buildings are rare owing to the perishable nature of the material, the precision with which the Romans built has caused marks to be left in the soil from which archaeologists have been able to reconstruct their methods. The upper storey of the fine villa at Chedworth was timber-framed and its roofs were constructed with tie-beams and king-posts. The ground floor of this villa was stone-walled, but less important dwellings, like that of which traces have been found at Ditchley, were entirely timber-framed. The timber wall-posts were set on a 'groundsill' and this practice, reintroduced by the Anglo-Saxons, became the basis for all timber house construction in the Middle Ages. The roofs of the Romano-British timber-framed buildings were stone-slated, as they were not to be again until the Middle Ages.

The possibility of a persisting tradition of advanced timber construction during the Dark Ages is remote, for the commonest type of primitive dwelling, the round hut, formed the basis of domestic building habits for several centuries after the eclipse of imperial civilization. The rejection of the round house in favour of the rectangular, which must certainly have followed on the adoption of sophisticated Roman ideas in building, was however repeated by an independent development which probably neither took place nor became widespread until long after the Romans had departed from Britain.

In all districts where timber was available the circular hut was constructed of posts interlaced with brushwood and covered with sods. In the centre of these pole huts was a hearth made of slabs of lias, gravel or sandstone or of baked clay, and near the hearth was a pole supporting the roof. Such were the celebrated dwellings whose fragmented foundations were laid bare near Glastonbury about half a century ago. Although archaeologists have reconstructed the appearance of these round houses, their remains are much too scanty for even the most imaginative spectator to create a strong visual image. But there are in these islands certain treeless wastes where stone counterparts of the pole huts were built and still stand entire, preserving the very essence of remote living

An outhouse near Recess, Connemara, Co. Galway, and (below) beehive huts, Slea Head, Dingle Peninsula, Co. Kerry

Although primitive construction in timber has, from the nature of the material, almost entirely disappeared from the English scene, there survives an archaic tradition of building in dry-stone in humble storehouses and shelters still erected in Ireland and found also in Wales, in the Orkneys and occasionally on Dartmoor, timeless structures which might be ascribed to any period within the last three centuries and which repeat forms once used as dwellings and once carried out in timber and brushwood. Outhouses such as this Connemara example are used for a variety of purposes, as pigsties, hen-houses and fuel stores. The circular form and the single, lintelled opening, though here of wood instead of stone, are identical with those of the beehive huts or clochàns on Slea Head. The corbel principle behind these structures, whereby courses of flattish stones of roughly uniform size are so placed that each course projects slightly further inwards as the wall grows higher, the roof being a continuation of the wall, occurs in the Megalithic tombs of prehistoric times, and some of these clochàns may date from the Neolithic period, although such dwellings were still being built in the early Christian centuries. Most clochàns measure from between 12 and 15 feet in diameter, although a few large, oval structures could give standing-room to as many as fifty persons. Instead of being fully corbelled, the roof of the outhouse is furnished with a covering of loose straw and turf piled up in a conical shape on horizontal beams and then roughly thatched with rushes and marram grass.

conditions. More than a hundred beehive huts lie scattered, singly or in clusters, on the savage promontory of Slea Head in Co. Kerry, scarcely distinguishable at first glance from the boulders which crowd about them and of which they are fashioned. It is not possible to date these structures with any accuracy; some of them are contemporary with a near-by Iron Age fort, while others belong to the Early Christian period. The long persistence of the circular form is proved by the fact that many of the modern outhouses of the little farmsteads on the Dingle Peninsular and in Galway exactly resemble the clochàns on Slea Head. The idea of the pole hut was similarly perpetuated, for in his *Evolution of the English House* S. O. Addy illustrates a charcoal-burner's hut in Old Park Wood, Sheffield, which is constructed in the same way as the conical houses of our forefathers. But this hut and its like have long since vanished.

Some of the Irish clochàns are more oval than round and one or two are almost rectangular. They are corbelled structures consisting of courses of flat stones of roughly uniform size so placed that each course projects slightly farther inwards as the building proceeds upwards, the roof being a continuation of the wall. The famous Gallerus Oratory, of the eighth century, also on the Dingle Peninsula,

Cruck-built house at Lacock, Wiltshire, and (right) The Gallerus Oratory, Dingle Peninsula, Co. Kerry

The similarity between the upturned-boat shapes of these two buildings is at once apparent and points to the conclusion that the timber-framed structure represents the survival of an ancient tradition preserved in its stone form in the treeless expanse of the Dingle Peninsula. Professor E. Estyn Evans does indeed suggest that the primitive wattled dwellings of Ireland, which were contemporary with the Gallerus Oratory, were supported by crucks, or pairs of curving timbers joined together at the top.

The celebrated Oratory is assumed to date from the eighth century and is particularly interesting as a perfect example of a dry-stone walled, corbelled building on a rectangular plan which evolved independently of Roman influence. The workmanship is immensely superior to that of the clochàns in the same district (page 17); the stones have been chosen with immense care and so ingeniously fitted together (without the aid of mortar) that after the passage of about 1,200 years the interior remains bone dry. The massive cruck truss of the Lacock cottage may date from the early fifteenth century, although the building has been much altered since then.

though part of an eremitical monastery and probably not a dwelling, is a perfect example of the kind of rectangular house which evolved from the circular clochàns. Like them it is corbelled and dry-stone walled, though of immensely superior workmanship. The stones have been chosen with the greatest care, many of them are partially dressed and they have been fitted together with such ingenuity that even after the passage of 1,200 years the little building is completely weather-tight. There is no line of demarcation between the side-walls and the roof, so that the Oratory is like an upturned boat or a neatly stacked pile of turf. Exactly the same impression is created by the timber counterpart of the Gallerus Oratory, the cruck-built house; it resembles a boat and its walls and roof are continuous. To construct it two pairs of bent trees were set up on the ground to overlap and carry the longitudinal ridge-rafter or roof-tree; poles or branches were fastened horizontally from one pair to another and the frame thus fashioned was covered with thatch. The ends of this inverted V-shaped house were filled with wattle and daub, leaving an opening for the door.

The transition from the circular to the oblong plan was clearly effected in Ireland independently of Roman influence, for Ireland lay beyond the sphere of

Roman invasion and Roman government. The cruck-built house likewise does not appear to have been initiated by Roman example despite the fact that the couples of bent trees which formed the structural bases of such a house were anciently known as forks and were called by their Latin name *furcae*. Vitruvius, writing before the conquest of Britain, refers to this type of dwelling as obsolete, describing it as the most primitive form of building. 'First men erected forks,' he said, 'and weaving bushes between them, covered the walls with mud.'

The rectangular space between two pairs of crucks, a length of about 16 feet,

Cottage at Didbrook, Gloucestershire

The evolution of the timber-framed house is summed up in this little house, much altered in the course of the centuries. A tradition of immense antiquity, probably going back to pre-Saxon times and perhaps ante-dating the Roman Occupation, is represented by the most prominent feature of the design, the inverted V-shape made by the two long timbers, or crucks, rising from the stone plinth on which the cottage is set and meeting at the apex of the original roof. This roof reached right down to the ground like its stone counterpart, the roof of the Gallerus Oratory (page 19). A horizontal tie-beam and collar-beam seen above the door and in a line with the low lintel strengthened the crucks. Later on a third and longer tie-beam was introduced projecting immediately above the base of the crucks. The remains of this tie-beam are still clearly visible, though the part between the crucks has since been removed. This tie-beam enabled a new roof of a lower pitch to be built and also made possible the erection of vertical walls, thus providing more head-room inside the cottage. Finally Cotswold stone replaced the original wattle and daub walls, the roof was pitched still less steeply and the old structure with all its alterations lay embedded in the new casing.

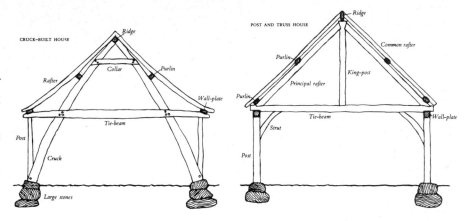

was known as a bay, and this became an accepted unit of measurement. Medieval houses were often assessed for taxation by the number of their bays, forks or gavels (the original form of the word 'gable'). For cruck houses were still being built in the Middle Ages and much later and examples can still occasionally be seen. The primitive character of such structures is emphasized by the fact that they are rarely found in East Anglia and the south-east where timber framing was most highly elaborated. The distribution of cruck-built houses, in fact, as Mr J. T. Smith points out, coincides to a marked degree with that of British place-names of pre-Saxon origin.

I know of no complete extant example of the earliest form of the cruck-built house, but there is a haunting reminder of the all-roof type of structure, an unexpected survival of ancient procedure, at Clifton in Oxfordshire. Here two gigantic adjoining gables, perhaps at one time two separate dwellings, jut out from a picturesque, patched, altered and utterly irregular thatched house, conforming to no known plan. Each of these gables reaches to the ground and is supported by straight timbers inclining towards one another to meet at the ridge. The thatch covering extends from the ridge to the ground. The remains of former tie-beams can just be made out in the masonry, which may have replaced wattle and daub in these gable-ends. Cruck builders discovered that if a tie-beam placed about half-way up the cruck was extended at either end, it made possible the erection of vertical walls. This was the first step in the evolution of the splendid timber-built houses and timber roofs of the later Middle Ages.

It is this more developed form of cruck construction which can occasionally still be seen in barns and cottages, especially in the west midlands and parts of Yorkshire. A well-known example occurs at Didbrook in Gloucestershire, where the original crucks have been preserved within a larger and later post and truss house (in which the timbers of wall and roof are separate) and both are now encased in Cotswold stone. The tie-beam, which marked the width of the original roof and the juncture between that roof and the walls, was cut off between the crucks for internal convenience when the house was altered. The crucks of this Gloucestershire cottage are almost as straight as the gable timbers at Clifton. Other examples, more sophisticated and obviously of later date, such as can be seen at Weobley in Herefordshire and Lacock in Wiltshire, boast a more architectural character and exhibit beautiful symmetrical arches, closely resembling the stone ogee arches fashionable in the fifteenth century and contrived by halving a carefully chosen curving trunk or branch. But this refinement on a tradition of undateable antiquity and the story of the timber construction which flowered from this tradition belong to another chapter.

2

Variations on Three Units

The development of domestic architecture during the centuries immediately following the Norman Conquest represents a fortuitious rather than a conscious process, a combination of slowly maturing traditional methods and foreign elements which was entirely overshadowed by ecclesiastical building. Whatever the motives which led to the erection of the thousands of religious works which still proclaim the aspiring, dynamic spirit of the medieval period – the desire to raise a lasting monument to the glory of God, personal and family pride, local patriotism, aesthetic interest or mere superstition – there can be no doubt that these buildings, monasteries, cathedrals, chantries, collegiate and parish churches embody the most splendid and inventive achievements of the age, all the most daring explorations of new ideas of construction, all the boldest as well as the most poetic conceits. No medieval house, however venerable its fabric, however romantic its associations, makes that dazzling impact of high genius which impresses such features of ecclesiastical art as the spire and chapter-house of Salisbury, the nave of Ely or the ruined choir of Bolton forever on the memory. The secular architecture of the Middle Ages was altogether subordinated to this great endeavour in the religious field. The attitude of mind which fostered such a situation could not be more eloquently attested than by the fact that in every nobleman's house the chapel or oratory was considered a more urgent necessity than comfort, convenience or privacy.

Whereas stone had replaced timber for ecclesiastical building by the beginning of the thirteenth century, the medieval house was commonly constructed of traditional mud or wood. Stone houses were so rare that, according to T. Hudson Turner in his *Domestic Architecture in England from the Conquest to the End of the Thirteenth Century*, they were named in deeds to indicate boundaries. Building in mud must have been widespread: C. F. Innocent found documentary evidence for the general use of this material for the walls of London houses in the year 1212. As for timber, the ancient ancestry of the cruck-built house has already been mentioned; and it has been pointed out that the box-frame or post and truss method which replaced cruck construction was known in Roman Britain. The transition from the earlier to the later procedure in the Middle Ages, which is so vividly illustrated in the picture of the cottage at Didbrook shown at the end of Chapter One, was doubtless first achieved by church builders. It cannot be closely followed in other examples as, apart from a number of aisled halls, usually disguised externally beneath the alterations and additions of later ages, very few medieval timber-framed houses still stand which can be dated before the fifteenth century. The essential distinction between the two operations was briefly described a page or two earlier: whereas in the cruck-built house walls and roof are indivisible, in the post and truss house the timbers of walls and roof are separate, thus providing for infinite diversity in the height and width as well as the length of the house. The general method of erecting the framework was this: groundsills were laid on a base of stone, flint, rubble or brick and upon these were set pairs of stout wall-posts. The posts supported the wall-plates upon which were set the massive principal rafters, notched into place and carrying at the apex

Of the mid-fourteenth-century aisled hall of Tiptofts Manor, two of the three original bays and one aisle survive in a remarkable state of preservation. The roof structure is exactly the same type as that at Cherhill (page 22). There is no ridge-piece, the rafters being pegged together where they intersect. A crown-post, treated as a column with capital and base, upholds a central purlin which strengthens the collars tying the pairs of common rafters. The crown-post sends out four branching struts, two to the central purlin and two to the collar immediately above the massive, cambered tie-beam on which it rests. This tie-beam is morticed not into the wall-plate, as in fully developed post and truss construction, but, because this is an aisled hall with the roof coming down to within a few feet of the ground, into a stout purlin parallel to the wall-plate. A graceful oaken pillar (shown in the photograph opposite below), from which spring curving braces, strengthens both purlin and tie-beam. The moulded capitals and braces and the filleted shafts of column and king-post, the cusped spandrels and moulded tie-beam all bear witness to the carpenter's growing aesthetic sense and mastery of his craft.

the longitudinal ridge-piece. Each pair of principals was further strengthened and prevented from spreading by a horizontal beam morticed into the wall-plates. The so-called truss formed by these span-bridging timbers was reinforced by an upright king-post rising from the centre of the tie-beam to the ridge, or by either a crown-post or two upright queen-posts supporting a collar-beam. Between the wall-plate and ridge-piece and parallel with them a so-called purlin ran from principal to principal and carried the common rafters. Across these common rafters were nailed laths to take the outer covering, which in the Middle Ages was invariably thatch, although wooden shingles provided an occasional alternative and tiles were mentioned in an Ordinance of 1212 prohibiting the use of straw for roofing in London. The wall-posts were shaped from tree-trunks and set inverted, a practice which is thought by some authorities to have been a means of preserving the timber by allowing the sap to dry out. But the real advantage of the custom was that the butt end of the tree was thick enough for the tie-beam and wall-plates to be laid upon and jointed to it and coupled with each other. Subsidiary and smaller uprights, or studs, were fixed between the main posts, and the spaces between them were filled with wattle and daub. Upright rods of hazel or ash were sprung into prepared grooves in the timber frame and small sticks were woven in and out of them in the manner of basketwork. The daub, commonly composed of clay, water, straw or cow hair and cow dung, mixed with lime wherever it was available, was applied to both sides of this hurdling. The clay from which the daub was made was usually dug close to the site of the house and this explains the frequent existence of small ponds in the vicinity of timber-framed houses. The extraordinary number and random geographical occurrence of these ponds, dotted about over nearly the whole of England, is an indication of the ubiquity of the timber house in the medieval period.

In an age when England boasted at least sixty great forests there was no shortage of hardwood and oak was the preferred material for frame building. Oak becomes

Abbas Hall, Great Cornard, Suffolk, and (below) the hall, Tiptofts Manor, Wimbish, Essex

By comparison with the work at Tiptofts, the ponderous timber construction at Abbas Hall looks extremely rough, although it is of roughly the same date. A floor was inserted in the open hall some time during the sixteenth century to give the house two storeys, and thus the bedroom in which the photograph was taken sets us on a level with the upper part of the structure. It is of the same crown-post type as the Tiptofts roof, and the view of it shown here corresponds almost exactly with that of the Wimbish hall below it, with the former aisle column bursting through the floor and crowding the low-ceilinged space with its formidable struts and braces.

The photograph of Tiptofts was taken from a gallery beside the huge brick chimney which took the place of the former, open central hearth in the Elizabethan period. The space between the free-standing column and the end-wall was once occupied by the screens passage, and the wall shows traces of the openings which led into the buttery and pantry. The two-centred arch of one of these openings, now filled in, can be glimpsed through the gallery balustrade.

harder as it dries and therefore encouraged the medieval tendency to work with unseasoned timber. The inevitable process of shrinkage was sometimes reduced by allowing the stripped trees to float for several months in running water; and in any case the leisurely progress of medieval building permitted a certain amount of time for the oak to dry off. The advantages of seasoned timber were not ignored in the Middle Ages, for L. F. Salzman quotes from a letter written by John Thoresby, Archbishop of York, in January 1355-6 in which he requested that the wood for a building he had commissioned should be felled during the winter so that it might dry off during the summer months for use in the following year.

The basic type of box-frame construction just described was elaborated in response to varying practical needs and influences which will become apparent as the story of the English house unfolds. It has been pointed out that very few early medieval half-timber houses survive with the exception of a number of aisled halls of a kind which had existed in Britain before Saxon times. These aisled halls formed one of the basic units upon which all future developments in domestic architecture depended. They consisted of a single enormous apartment divided, like a church, into nave and aisles by lines of timber columns. The reason for the aisles was technical. It was impossible to bridge the huge span between the low walls of the earliest hall houses without nave arcades, and the full width was needed for the multifarious purposes of the one-roomed house. The immense twelfth-century structure excavated at Cheddar was mentioned in the previous chapter. The arcade posts of this vast building were 2 feet square and probably rose to a height of 50 to 60 feet. But it is not easy to visualize the original hall on the present Ministry of Works site, which does nothing to warm the imagination, and for a vivid idea of the appearance and atmosphere of this great single-room dwelling and the many others like it, it is more profitable to visit some of the numerous surviving medieval barns, such as those at Great Coxwell and Pilton, whose lofty roofs and cathedral-like expanses of timber columns spring from the same tradition as the hall house.

Originally, as in Roman Britain, animals were stalled in one of the aisles of the hall, but later this space was used for the accommodation of servants and storage. There were doors opposite each other at one end of the hall and these were left open to provide a draught for the central fire. Just inside each door a wooden screen jutted out to prevent sudden gusts of wind from blowing the fire in all directions. These short screens eventually became a continuous structure reaching from wall to wall, pierced by two doors. When they were fully developed these screens, judging from those still to be seen at Haddon Hall, Lytes Cary, Little Sodbury Manor and Penshurst Place, relied in style upon church example. The screen dividing the Great Chamber on the first floor from the oratory over the porch in a Berkshire house, Ashbury Manor, a much more modest building than those just named, instantly recalls a parish church parclose screen, such as that at East Harling in Norfolk, though the work at Ashbury Manor, as is generally the case with medieval domestic architecture, is simpler in detail and workmanship with its six trefoiled panels and quatrefoiled spandrels than the delicate and intricate carving in the Norfolk church.

When it became fashionable, during the second half of the fifteenth century, to build a rood loft above the chancel screen in churches, a similar feature was at once introduced into the domestic hall and became popular as the minstrels' gallery. Apart from well-known survivals such as that at Penshurst Place, one of the earliest and most interesting examples, exceptionally large for the size of the hall, occurs at Woodlands Manor, Mere.

Behind the screen ran what was called the screens passage, which must have been so excruciatingly draughty that it is not surprising that the doors at either end of it should have later been protected by porches which developed into magnificent architectural features. From the far side of the screens passage opened the pantry and the buttery, which at first were probably no more than shacks leaning against the gable wall. The kitchen was usually a separate building approached from a passage between the buttery and the pantry, though cooking was also done on the fire burning on the floor towards the upper end of the hall. At this end of the great apartment there was a raised, paved space, which came to be known as the dais, where the head of the household and his family could dine and retire from the dirt and disorder, the litter of food scraps, straw and rush that turned the earth floor of the rest of the hall into what was disdainfully referred to as the 'marsh'.

This simplest type of house was still being built without extensions as late as the end of the thirteenth century, for Fyfield Hall in Essex has been shown by Mr J. T. Smith to have consisted originally of no more than a two-bayed aisled hall. The style persisted with additions and modifications into the fourteenth and even into the fifteenth century, and Mrs Wood lists well over thirty examples which still stand, even though they have been disguised and sometimes mutilated by later alterations and are usually unrecognizable externally because they have been encased in brick, stone or weatherboarding. Many more are possibly awaiting identification, especially in the eastern counties.

Much of the character of these early aisled halls can still be strongly experienced in a house near Sudbury, Abbas Hall, despite the insertion of a floor, a chimney-stack and a Tudor fireplace. The low, dark bedrooms of the present house have been contrived in a forest of timbers of gigantic size which, at first confusing, resolve themselves into the structure of the upper part of the former aisles, massive arcade plates and the tops of huge, rough pillars, and into the members of a tie-beam and crown-post roof bursting with struts and braces. So closely massed are the enormous timbers of this roof that it is difficult to move among them, but it is not only because they are seen at such close quarters that they inspire so crushing a sense of weight: it is the rude, unpolished aspect of the workmanship which is daunting. Yet compared with the simple construction of the Didbrook cottage, this roof seems a complicated and skilful piece of work. It is in fact a coarse version of the commonest type of those open timber roofs which in parish church architecture were to develop into such glorious and peculiarly English compositions as those which soar above the naves of Needham Market, Trunch, Pulham, Knapton or March.

The roof of Tiptofts Manor, Wimbish, shows a finer feeling for design, though its date, the mid fourteenth century, is not much later than that of Abbas Hall. Only two of the three original bays of this aisled hall survive, but these are miraculously preserved in atmosphere if not in every detail, and the great height of the noble structure makes its full impact unimpeded by the intrusion of a horizontal division. One of the aisles, that on the side from which the hall is now entered, vanished when the house was given a new front, although a pillar from the former arcade can be seen embedded in the later wall. Its slim, free-standing companion opposite is a Decorated column carved in dark, hard oak with filletted shafts and a boldly moulded capital. From it spring curving braces to support the purlin and a tie-beam cut with a camber to counteract the tendency to sag. The spandrels are cusped and the lower part of the principal rafters dividing each bay are wave-moulded. An octagonal crown-post with four branching struts rises from the tie-beam to carry a central longitudinal purlin which strengthens the collars tying each pair of closely set rafters. There is no ridge-piece in this roof: the rafters are halved and pegged where they intersect. The central pair of principal rafters rest on hammer-beams, but this may be a later alteration to obviate the necessity for aisle columns and so gain more space.

Apart from the interest of its superb roof, it is still possible in the hall at Tiptofts to see where openings led into the buttery and pantry. One of these openings, a two-centred arch with ornamented spandrels, is still in use; the second has been filled in. During the sixteenth century, when a chimney was added to the hall,

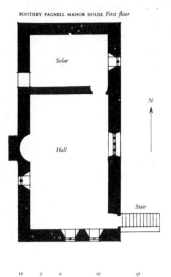

BOOTHBY PAGNELL MANOR HOUSE *First floor*

Solar

N

Hall

Stair

10 5 0 10 20

Two-storeyed Norman houses

Hemingford Manor, Huntingdonshire, built *c.* 1150 (top left), the
interior of the first-floor hall of which
is shown underneath; Boothby
Pagnell Manor House, Lincolnshire,
c. 1200 (top right); and the Jew's
House, The Strait, Lincoln, *c.* 1170
(bottom right), are examples of the
third component which determined
the development of the English house.
They introduced the two-storeyed,
rectangular theme into domestic design
for the first time. Built of stone and
with the hall and another room
opening from one end of it, on the
upper floor they incorporated an
arrangement totally different from
that of the aisled hall. The photograph
of Boothby Pagnell shows the external staircase by which in such houses
the first-floor entrance was usually
approached. The door of the Jew's
House at Lincoln is, however, on the
ground floor, probably because the
lower part of this town house was
used as business premises. Immediately above the door, resting upon its
hood mould, rises the chimney-stack
of the hall fireplace. A typical
Norman wall fireplace flanked by
shafts with cushion capitals survives
at Hemingford (bottom left). Both
this house and Boothby Pagnell
Manor House retain the two-light
round-arched windows which usually
lit the first-floor Norman hall.
Whereas the covering arch at
Hemingford is adorned with the
popular chevron motif, and the door
of the Jew's House is still more richly
ornamented with an uncommon open
heart pattern, the plain window arches
at Boothby Pagnell herald the simpler
Early English style. The ground floor
of the Norman stone house was
generally used for storage, and for
purposes of security was originally
lit only by narrow loops.

living-quarters. The windows are in general round-headed and set within a containing arch, but at Moyses Hall the arches enclose square-headed windows. They
are unquestionably of the same date as the house and are of particular interest as
extremely early instances of this design.

The focus of the little house was the large first-floor room, or hall. The smaller
apartment, or solar, adjoining it provided privacy and such comforts of civilization, perhaps a garderobe in one angle, as were then available. The great chamber
was generally entered by means of an outside stair rising parallel to the wall, as
in the manor house at Boothby Pagnell. At Isaac's House, Norwich, the stair
was enclosed in a forebuilding. An internal stair led down to the well-nigh
impregnable ground floor. But if the lower floor was used as a workshop or
for the transaction of business, as was sometimes the case with town houses, there
was a street door at ground level. The rich door of the Jew's House, Lincoln, is
the most conspicuous object in The Strait. It survives almost entire except that
in the jambs only the capitals remain. The doorway arch exhibits a comparatively
rare Norman ornament, the open-heart, a motif which occurs more frequently
in France than in England. Another curious feature of this house is that an enclosing arch above the doorway carries the chimney of the first-floor fireplace,
an arrangement found also in a house of the same date at Cluny. While the opening in the roof of the timber-framed aisled hall, through which the central fire
sent up its curl of smoke, was capped by no more than a small clay chimney-pot
or pottery louver, like those now in the Chichester Museum, these sophisticated
Norman houses, with their wall fireplaces, were graced by tall cylindrical
chimneys such as those still to be seen at Boothby Pagnell and Christchurch.
Some of these were open while others were topped by a conical cap like those
which still taper above twelfth-century houses at Cluny and Bayeux.

If they are not in ruins, turned into museums, or preserved as empty shells,
these Norman houses have usually been so much altered and enlarged in the
course of their long lives, that although, as in the Jew's House, Lincoln, the
original character of the exterior may still compel attention, this exterior no
longer corresponds to the internal arrangements and the building exists as a relic
rather than a vital organism. There survives one Norman house, however, in
Huntingdonshire, where despite later accretions the builder's plan emerges with
astonishing clarity and meets the demands of present inhabitants as adequately
as, from about 1150 onwards, it satisfied those of a long succession of past owners.
At Hemingford Manor past and present mingle in an atmosphere which, in its
magical essence, is still that of Norman England. The miracle has been partly
brought about by the surprising fact that the landscape in which the house is set
has scarcely altered since the first owner and builder Payne de Hemingford looked
out on it from the splayed, round-headed windows. The manor house confronts
a flat, willowy expanse where backwaters separate Houghton meadows from
the main stream of the Ouse, and stands islanded by the river and by a green moat
swept by overhanging trees. Immense yews throw shadows on to the walls, the
rough stone of which has been plastered over, in accordance with medieval
usage, to make a scintillating, irregular surface like that of a palette-knife painting.
The south window, with its twin lights and chevron-ornamented arch, stands
out in relief against this richly textured wall like the piped decoration on an iced
cake. Near this window, in the angle of the house, a modern opening marks the
position of the doorway formerly approached by an outside stair. Another
Norman window looks towards the east, and yet another, on the opposite side,
opens from the hall into a bedroom which, with the kitchen below it, was
probably added to the house in the eighteenth century. The hall, or great chamber, remains the most important room at Hemingford Manor; it is still the
centre of the life of the house. It is no longer exactly as Payne de Hemingford
left it, for the wall separating it from the solar is now taken up by a gigantic
sixteenth-century chimney, the leaning mass of which nearly fills the width of

the original house. Yet in spite of its prodigious size this structure contributes less to the memorable atmosphere of the room than the chimney-piece it supplanted, a fine architectural composition in the west wall, a shallow arch with a bold keystone head flanked by pilasters with scalloped capitals. This and the deep window embrasure, revealing the impressive thickness of the wall, set the mood of the apartment.

The main stream of English domestic planning derives from various combinations and elaborations of the three types of dwelling just described: the tower-like keep, the rectangular Norman house, with its upper-floor hall, and the aisled hall. The theme of the tower has an independent history besides playing a part in diverse amalgamations. It is perhaps even more associated in the imagination with the Middle Ages than the Great Hall; and in the medieval mind it certainly persisted as a dominant image long after the need for defence which gave it birth had vanished, satisfying the strong predilection of the age for verticality and for symbols of authority. Free-standing residential towers may sometimes have owed their existence to a restricted site, as the most economical means of obtaining the required accommodation, as at Okehampton, where the tower house was actually built on the stump of a Norman keep. And towers were a necessity for several centuries in the wilder and more disturbed parts of the British Isles, in the northern counties, in Ireland and in Scotland. But the necessity became a fashion, the extravagant development of which, especially in Scotland, the country above all of tower houses, will be discussed later in these pages. For the moment it is the association of the tower with the two-storeyed house and the traditional hall which is of interest.

A combination of the first two of these units, creating a new L-shaped plan, can be seen in the thirteenth-century Little Wenham Hall, Suffolk. The first floor, approached by an external stair, is occupied by the hall, while a chapel with traceried windows opens at right-angles from it. Above the chapel, rising over the rest of the little building in the form of a square tower, is the solar. The ground floor, like the bottom storey of the Norman house and the castle keep, is low and vaulted. The union of tower and hall was, however, a more commonly occurring design. At Longthorpe Hall, Northamptonshire, a massive square tower was added early in the fourteenth century to a hall of about 1260, probably by Robert Thorpe, Steward of Peterborough Abbey and son of William de Thorpe, who is thought to have built the hall. The ground floor of the tower is vaulted and was used as a store, while the first floor comprises the Great Chamber and a tiny room contrived in the thickness of the west wall which may have been a garderobe. A narrow staircase concealed in the south wall leads to the third storey, a room in which all the original stone window seats survive and where, in the window recesses, the draw-bar holes for securing the shutters can still be seen. The stone seat of the garderobe in the south wall has also been preserved. The Great Chamber was inaccessible from the ground floor and was entered by steps from the adjoining hall. It is now reached by a passage on the level of the floor inserted in the hall during the seventeenth century.

The Great Chamber at Longthorpe is distinguished by a unique series of mural paintings which reveal the religious climate in which medieval domestic architecture evolved even more compellingly than the ubiquitous chapel. These decorations are conditioned by the same habit of mind as that which informed the great didactic schemes of wall and glass painting displayed in Gothic churches. The fact that they were commissioned by a man who was not connected with the church and was not a great lord indicates that such paintings were a normal and fashionable feature of fourteenth-century houses. The theme of the murals is the contrast between the worldly and the spiritual life as exhibited in a number of biblical scenes, episodes from the lives of the saints and various moralities. Immediately on entering the room the visitor is hugely confronted by an image of the Virgin, mysteriously commanding though half obliterated, clasping the

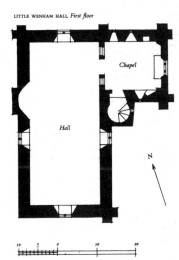

LITTLE WENHAM HALL, *First floor*

Window from Longthorpe Tower, Northamptonshire, and (below) window at Hemingford Manor House, Huntingdonshire

The deep embrasure of the window at Hemingford, seen from the inside of the upper-floor hall, shows the great thickness of the walls and reveals a curious and unusual feature, the lobes protruding from the soffits of the lights. There was originally no glass in the windows of twelfth-century houses, and these projections probably helped to keep shutters in place. Between the stone window seats, parallel with the splayed jambs, where two persons might sit withdrawn, is a stone foot-rest or step, only just visible in the photograph. This could alternatively be used as a seat for a single person.

The window from the hall of Longthorpe Tower illustrates the persistence in the thirteenth century of the two-light opening, but the proportions have become more slender and the arches are pointed instead of round-headed. The quatrefoil in the window-head is cut in the stone and is an example of 'plate' tracery. The dividing shaft is a simple version of the Early English cylindrical column with plainly moulded capital and base.

Child and reclining on a high couch of ecclesiastical design. Above her the Wheel of Life depicts the seven stages of man's transient pilgrimage on earth and below her the Apostles walk in pairs with a woman representing the Church and holding a scroll. Beneath them again runs a dado of exquisitely drawn birds, most of them of the kind native, or once native, to the near-by Lincolnshire fens: bittern, curlew, shelduck and goose. A tonsured figure sits in an armchair in a window embrasure instructing a child, and a vision of Christ dazzles a hermit and a basket-maker. But at first the eye scarcely registers either these personages or the enchanting birds, so instantly is it drawn to a dramatic representation of three kings brought face to face with their own skeletons and the realization of the vanity of earthly rank and wealth. Equally arresting, both in subject-matter and execution, is the strange device above the fireplace, the Wheel of the Five Senses, typified by a monkey, a vulture, a spider's web, a boar and a cock. The Wheel is controlled by a gigantic kingly figure, perhaps the Almighty, standing behind it, and making an impression even more memorable than that intended by the artist by reason of the surprising colour of his complexion. It is blotched and swarthy. The colour of the undercoat for the flesh tints was black, and where it has worn away the faces of the figures have assumed the dusky hue of Moors, while the reds and ochres of the rest of the paintings still glow with a fiery intensity although they can only be the ghosts of the original pigments.

The plan resulting from the fusion of hall and tower appears to have remained fashionable over a long period. Richard Stonyhurst, author of *De Rebus in Hibernia Gestis*, records the survival in Ireland in 1584 of long halls built 'of clay or mud and thatched' attached to stone towers containing solar chambers. At Broughton in Oxfordshire a hall was built in the fifteenth century on to a fourteenth-century tower; and even as late as the sixteenth century Pengersick Castle, near Helston in Cornwall, was designed as a hall (now destroyed) abutting on to a three-storeyed tower and taller angle turret with a door into the hall from the solar on the first floor.

But the most fruitful play upon the once separate components of the emerging

Little Wenham Hall, Suffolk, and (right) Longthorpe Tower, Northamptonshire

At Little Wenham Hall, dating from *c.* 1270–80, the two-storeyed plan of the Norman house and the tower house, exemplified by Castle Hedingham (page 29), are combined in an L-shaped house. The long arm of the L contains a hall above a vaulted basement which, like that of Boothby Pagnell Manor House, is reached by an outside staircase, of wood here instead of stone, while the shorter arm takes the form of a tower with a chapel on the first floor and a chamber above it. The ground floor is lit only by narrow lancets for purposes of security. The three-light chapel window indicates by its size the importance of the chapel in the medieval house and shows also how in the course of the thirteenth century 'plate' tracery developed into geometric tracery completely filling the head of the window. Little Wenham Hall is constructed mainly of brick mixed with flint and septaria, and is one of the earliest instances of the use of brick, as distinct from the re-use of Roman brick, in the Middle Ages. At Longthorpe the massive tower was added to the thirteenth-century hall in the early fourteenth century.

34

Interior of the Great Chamber, Longthorpe Tower, Northamptonshire

The remarkable murals in this principal, first-floor room of the Tower were hidden under successive coats of limewash until 1945, when the tenant discovered evidences of painting. The whole amazing scheme of decoration was recovered and restored by Mr E. Clive Rouse. The subjects seen here are the Nativity, immediately above the window arch, with the Seven Ages of Man in the arc outlined above the scene. On either side of the window opening are pairs of Apostles, while below them can be seen part of a dado of Fenland birds.

Old Soar, Plaxtol, Kent (right)

At Old Soar, dating from c. 1290, a wing based on the plan of the two-storeyed Norman house was set across the end of an aisled hall. The gable-end of the two-storeyed structure, with the solar on the upper floor, can be seen to the left of the photograph. The hall was replaced by a brick house in the eighteenth century. The projection in the foreground of the picture, with its simple, two-light lancet window, is the upper-floor chapel, with a vaulted chamber with external access beneath it. The chapel is entered through a door in the south-east corner of the solar.

house plan was the combination of the hall and the two-storeyed dwelling. In some instances they are not actually brought into contact but are joined by a passage. This is the case at Woodlands Manor, Mere, a basically fourteenth-century house built by Thomas Doddington when he left the Quantocks to marry the Wiltshire daughter of the lord of the manor, John Guphaye. The house comprises two structures each under its own roof connected by a short passage not more than 5 feet long. The north building is a version of the Norman two-storeyed house with a chapel on the upper floor, formerly entered by an external stone stairway on the north wall and still reached from within by steps going up from a pointed arch in the passage. The room below the chapel, probably once used for storage, later became a kitchen with an outside door. Its three windows were inserted in the sixteenth century. The second building stands parallel to the chapel and contains the fine hall with its minstrels' gallery, the porch and the little room over it, once a columbarium, and a sixteenth- or seventeenth-century addition now used as a kitchen.

At the thirteenth-century manor of Old Soar in Kent, the hall and the two-storeyed block assumed a relationship which was to become standardized. The manor has lost its hall, and where it stood an eighteenth-century red-brick farm-house now dwarfs the little grey ragstone medieval survival in its wonderfully unaltered setting of steep woods and orchards. But the corbels of the former hall arcade, embedded in the west wall of the existing building, testify to the manner in which the two structures were associated. The two-storeyed unit was set across the end of the hall house, and a spiral stair, which has been preserved, led from the north-east angle of the hall to the upper chamber of the two-storeyed block, which could also be approached by an outside stair. This apartment is furnished with a fireplace in the centre of one of its long walls, and two small rooms open from its north-east and south-east corners. One served as a garderobe, the other was a chapel. The hall was used for dining and for the accommodation of servants, while the upper chamber of the cross-block, the solar, with the chapel leading from it were for the private use of the owner, with pantry, buttery

and place for storage on the ground floor. The plan thus mirrors a way of life
involving a principal and a dependent household.

In general, house design was furthered by combinations of two of the originally isolated structures, particularly by the merging of the aisled hall and the
two-storeyed dwelling. But occasionally tower, upper hall house and hall came
together in a single composition. These, for instance, are the familiar components that underly the deceptively haphazard aspect of Stokesay Castle, the
picturesque irregularity of which is enhanced by its romantic site in the wooded
valley of the River Onny and by the calm reflection of its fretted, faded fabric
in the remains of its own broad moat. The north end of the house, with its later
projecting half-timber storey, was built as a free-standing tower before 1270,
the suggested date of the hall, which, according to Mr J. T. Smith, was once
aisled. The cross-wing, containing the solar, was added to the south end of the
hall in 1291, at the same time as the conspicuous, curiously shaped and battlemented south tower. The older tower, the structure of the upper part of which
seems to bear out the theory that stone towers were preceded by timber buildings
such as are shown in the Bayeux Tapestry, was entered from the hall by a rough
wooden staircase, but the solar block was cut off from the hall in the interests of
privacy and the only access was by an external stair.

The cross-wing was a more important factor than the tower in the evolution
of the house and the advance which followed on its fusion with the aisled hall is
well illustrated by a house in East Anglia which is rather earlier than Stokesay
Castle and superficially utterly different in character, although in plan it is
actually closely connected both with the Shropshire house and with Old Soar.

Northborough Hall, Northamptonshire

The type of manor house which emerged from the union of the hall and the two-storeyed, separately roofed cross-block is well illustrated by Northborough, built *c.* 1330-40. The porch protected the entrance into the original open hall and led directly into the screens passage. Inside the passage the three original ogee-arched doors can still be seen which once led into the buttery, pantry and kitchen. Medieval kitchens were usually in separate buildings owing to the danger of fire, but in the triple-door arrangement which was fashionable in the fourteenth century, the centre door led into a passage to the kitchen. The heads of the two hall windows are filled with blocked flowing tracery showing the ogee and heart shapes found in church windows of the period. The dormer was inserted during the seventeenth century when the hall was divided horizontally to give an extra floor. The bold crockets adorning the gable-end of the hall are a rare survival, and still more interesting is the chimney at the apex of the gable, dating from *c.* 1340. It is hexagonal and crenellated, with a ball-flower cornice and an ornamental gable on each face.

Thirteenth-century doorway, Little Chesterford Manor, Essex

This is one of two service doorways which originally led from the screens passage into the buttery or pantry. The opening is typical of the period, a two-centred arch with a roll-moulded hood. The original purpose of the hood was to throw off rainwater, externally. Here it is used purely ornamentally.

St Clere's Hall, St Osyth, Essex (opposite)

When two cross-blocks were combined with the hall, one at each end of it, a symmetrical, winged arrangement resulted which became the standard H-plan of the English manor house. St Clere's, built in the fourteenth century, is one of the least altered examples of a house conceived from the beginning as an aisled hall with separately roofed cross-blocks at either end. On the right can be seen the lean-to or 'outshut', which provided extra storage space and which might also have represented the service departments, the buttery and pantry, if the family wished to use the *(continued opposite)*

space next the screens as a dining-room. In a house of this kind the aisled hall was the heart of the home. The wing to the right contained the buttery and pantry on the ground floor with a bedchamber above it, while the corresponding wing on the left, farthest away from the entrance, comprised the solar on the first floor, for the private use of the family, with below it a parlour, used as a bower for the daughters of the house or as a reception room.

CHARACTERISTIC HALL HOUSE

Solar above

Parlour

Dais

Fire

Aisle   *Aisle*

Front entry   *Back entry*

Pantry   *Buttery*

Chamber above

Little Chesterford Manor originated as a two-storeyed house built in the style of Hemingford Manor in about 1225 of flint rubble strengthened with clunch and limestone. A recently exposed doorway in the upper chamber doubtless gave on to the former outside staircase. Another door of Tudor design and the windows of this room are part of later alterations, but the low ground floor, its stout walls knurled by rough flints gleaming in the dim light from two tiny original windows, remains structurally much as it was when a timbered, aisled hall was added at right-angles to the house just before the end of the thirteenth century. Two stone arches lead from this ground floor of the cross-block into what was once the hall, but which is now scarcely recognizable after horizontal subdividing to make extra floors and rooms. Only two posts of the aisle are still visible and the roof timbers only emerge here and there from ornamental plaster ceilings.

At some time during the fourteenth century a block similar to the earliest two-storeyed wing was erected at right-angles to the opposite end of the hall. The wing at farthest remove from the draughty entrance now became the solar, while the apartment below, at first a storeroom and wardrobe, became the parlour, a room for the reception of guests, or, known as the bower, set aside for the use of the daughters of the house.

Whether it came into being purely in response to a desire for greater comfort and convenience or was prompted by a sense of design, this addition of a second cross-wing to the hall house created a symmetrical H-shaped dwelling which, with significant modifications, was to determine the pattern of manor-house architecture for many decades, indeed until the close of the sixteenth century in outlying districts. The more important houses were now conceived from the start as three-part buildings, at first, like Northborough Manor, built in about 1330, and like St Clere's Hall, St Osyth, as a great hall with separately roofed cross-blocks at either end, and then, with the passage of the years, as ever more closely integrated amalgamations of the three components. At the same time there developed a conscious, romantic taste for past conventions which resulted in the deliberate designing of a house such as Great Chalfield Manor, Wiltshire, on the early medieval plan of a great hall balanced by a cross-wing at either end, at a period (1480) when these three units had all been brought under a continuous roof-line. These tendencies were the dominant influences in domestic plans of the later Gothic age.

The gatehouse of Oxburgh Hall, though certainly less vulnerable than that of
either West Bower Farm or Lower Brockhampton, is in reality not much more
effective as a piece of fortification. Sir Edward Bedingfield obtained licence to
crenellate his house in 1482. The king's 'licence to crenellate' originated in a
decree of Edward I that no castle might be erected without the monarch's
permission, for at that period a strongly fortified castle housing a large number of
men could constitute a threat to the state and the purpose of the law was to control
that menace. But by the time Oxburgh Hall was built the licence to crenellate
had become a symbol of power and status which was only translated into defensive imagery as an outward sign of the recipient's importance; sometimes, indeed,
as at Pattenden Manor, Kent, the evidence of the licence is expressed no more
conspicuously than by the use along the wall-plates of the hall, or perhaps on the

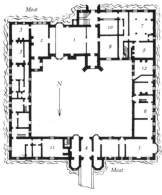

OXBURGH HALL *Ground floor*

1. Great hall	*5. Library*	*9. Buttery*
2. Dining-room	*6. Breakfast room*	*10. Knapery*
3. Withdrawing rooms	*7. Kitchen*	*11. Laundry*
4. Entry	*8. Bakery*	*12. Servants' hall*

screen, of the favourite late medieval motif of miniature battlements. Sir Edward was not so discreet: the machicolated arch connecting the polygonal turrets of his gatehouse may be ornamental rather than defensive, the fanciful battlements and the moat may be no more than striking details in a deliberately pictorial composition, but the structure nevertheless rises to a height of seven storeys. The discrepancy in size between this immense edifice and the rest of the symmetrical mansion springs only in part, however, from Sir Edward Bedingfield's desire to impress his contemporaries: it also testifies to his conscious pleasure in a design of marked originality and in an exaggerated allusion to a convention which had been a necessity in the immediate past. The sense of romance at Oxburgh is heightened by the reflection of turrets, crenellations, stepped gables, oriels and slender chimney-stacks in the glassy moat, and probably by the fact that, apart from the gatehouse, a good deal of the fabric was rebuilt in the early nineteenth century at a time when the taste for the Picturesque had not yet hardened into the insistence on archaeological correctness which so often destroyed the vitality of Victorian work. It was then that the ranges were roofed with the pantiles which now seem so integral a part of the composition. The harmony of the design and the impact it makes are due as much to the colour and character of the material as to the shape of the building. It is the weathered red brick of the walls which so instantly conjures up the romantic's view of the Middle Ages and brings to mind lines like those William Morris used to describe a moated medieval castle:

On the bricks the green moss grew,
Yellow lichen on the stone,
Over which red apples shone;
Little war that castle knew.
Deep green water filled the moat;
Each side had a red-brick lip
Green and mossy with the drip
Of dew and rain.

Brick had of course been common in Roman Britain, but there are no records of brickmaking between the time of the Occupation and the Middle Ages. One of the most frequently mentioned features of Little Wenham Hall (p. 34) is that, except for the flint and septaria base of the walls and the stone buttresses, it is built of brick and that it probably represents the earliest use of locally made brick in England since the departure of the Romans. They are of a creamy, greenish-yellow hue, with here and there a touch of pink or red, and they are of the Flemish or Low Country type and may have been made by Flemish immigrants. The arresting use of brick at Oxburgh Hall, however, as at Herstmonceux, was a direct result of the influence of French brick building on the English knights who had been engaged in the wars against France. On their return to England, they built houses for themselves which were based on French fashions in material as well as style. Sir Roger de Fynes, the builder of Herstmonceux, had served in France, and Lord Scales, the author of Middleton Towers, Norfolk, with its orielled gatehouse, had been seneschal of Normandy for several years. It is significant that the very word 'brick' only came into use in these islands during the fifteenth century. Before that time bricks were not distinguished from tiles and were referred to as *tegulae*. The new material stimulated the creative imagination of builders and although their boldest flights of fancy are associated with the sixteenth century rather than with the Middle Ages, there were other notable

Tattershall Castle, Lincolnshire

The castle began as a fortified stone dwelling-house with a curtain wall strengthened by towers, built by Robert of Tateshall in 1231. It was rebuilt in 1434–45 by Ralph, 3rd Baron Cromwell, Treasurer of England under Henry VI, with the addition of the Great Tower, which now stands alone. This is 110 feet high and is remarkable both for its design and for its brickwork. It was planned to look like a fortress in an age when the fortified castle keep had become obsolete. But despite the thickness of the walls, as much as 22 feet in the basement, the tower was planned as a magnificent residence, and nothing shows this more than the size of the two-light windows on every floor. The dovecote occupies the south-west corner turret on the second floor of the tower. It is lined with wattle and daub. Pigeon houses or dovecotes were a common feature of medieval manors and monasteries, for pigeons formed a considerable item in medieval diet, but though nesting-places were sometimes provided in the gable-ends of houses, barns or parish churches, dovecotes were usually detached buildings. Lord Cromwell had served in France through most of Henry V's reign, and the brick buildings he had seen there prompted his choice of this material for his great
(continued opposite)

tower house. The deep-red bricks measure about 8 × 4 × 2 ins. The splendid use to which the material was put is shown by the view from the principal room on the first floor into the south-west angle turret, and, above all, by the vaulting of the lobby from which the principal apartment of the third floor is entered. It is a rare example of brick stellar vaulting (quadripartite vaulting with intermediate and lierne ribs producing a star pattern). The spaces between the ribs have been filled by quatrefoil tracery carried out in cut and moulded brick. The principal boss shows the Tateshall and Cromwell arms.

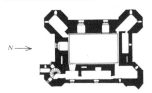

TATTERSHALL CASTLE *first floor*

fifteenth-century compositions in brick in addition to those which have been mentioned.

The most surprising example of all is Tattershall Castle, Lincolnshire. It was once a very large-scale brick version of the hall house and tower house design, but now the tower stands alone in the Fen landscape, a powerful, unforgettable image in its isolation. It was built between 1434 and 1452 by Ralph, Lord Cromwell, Lord Chief Treasurer of the Exchequer, under the supervision of his agents Thomas Croxby, John Southell and John Combe, with brick supplied by one Baldwin from kilns at Edlington moor. The name of the mason has been lost. With its frowning battlements and heavy machicolations, it looks as menacing as any true fortress; but the size of the arched windows piercing even the lower floors of the huge six-storeyed building at once refutes the idea of defence. There was no thought of the serious employment of the elaborate military devices exhibited in the composition of this tower: they were the mere trappings of a castle used to adorn a magnificent and spacious house. Inside the tower there was a hall for Lord Cromwell's personal use on the first floor above a guard-room; there was a solar on the next floor and above that apartments intended for the ladies and children of the household. The corner turrets throughout contained garderobes, and additional chambers were contrived in the thickness of the walls on every floor. Though it is now an empty shell, the delicacy of the brick vaults with their carved bosses and the beauty and variety of the sculptured fireplaces still bear witness to the sumptuous character of Lord Cromwell's great tower house, while an emblem everywhere repeated, a purse with the arrogant motto 'N'ay je droit', vividly recalls its owner's office and personality.

The arrangement of the rooms inside the tower made it a private mansion which could be independent of the rest of the castle, and this recalls those free-standing residential towers which are such conspicuous features of the landscape in the Border Country and in Scotland, and which have already been mentioned in passing. The simplest form of this type of dwelling, as exemplified by the

45

famous fourteenth-century island castle of Lochleven, at once reveals that it is a special form of hall house modified by the insecure conditions of the north. It is in fact the hall house up-ended, comprising a great hall on the first floor, entered by an external stair, with storage and service accommodation below it and a solar above it. This vertical version of the hall house outnumbers every other kind of dwelling of the later medieval period in Scotland and makes a unique contribution to the domestic architecture of Britain. Although the unsettled state of the country led to the persistance of such towers as an economical type of defended house long after fortresses had become no more than ornamental in the south, the tendency to elaborate the structure in the service of both convenience and aesthetics soon declared itself and eventually resulted in a house of such charm and such commodity that it was preferred for its own sake when the protection afforded by its plan had long ceased to be necessary. Externally the austere tower, articulated by no more than a parapet projecting very slightly on a corbel table, was enlivened in the fifteenth century by the French fashion for boldly putting parapets on huge corbels and for angle turrets corbelled from the exposed corners of the building, and these proliferated in time into the fabulous array of conical towerlets, dormers and machicolations such as crown Armisfield in Dumfriesshire. Increased space inside the tower was achieved first by the introduction of chambers in the thickness of the walls, as at Elphinstone Tower, Midlothian, and then by variations on the original square or rectangular plan. A favourite design was the L-shape, of which one of the earliest and most attractive examples is Neidpath on its high promontory above the Tweed, despite the fact that it has never recovered from the loss of the timber which once softened its bleak situation. It was sold by that dissolute Duke of Queensbury known as 'Old Q',

Borthwick Castle, Midlothian

Built *c.* 1430, this Scottish castle is a tower house which at the same time incorporates the hall house design. The two formidable rectangular towers shown in the photograph correspond to the cross-wings of the hall house. Between them, deeply recessed, lies the central block containing the hall on its first floor with service rooms to one side of it and a withdrawing room on the other. The castle was built by the first Lord Borthwick.

Neidpath Castle, Peeblesshire

The gateway and the door reached by
the fan of steps were seventeenth-
century alterations to the fortress
dating from the fourteenth and fifteenth centuries. The keystone of the
portal shows the strawberry plant, or
fraise, of the Norman-French Frasers,
the first owners of Neidpath, and the
coronet and goat's head of the Hays
of Yester, who acquired the castle
through marriage into the Fraser
family. Neidpath consists of two
tower houses: a tall narrow structure,
taking up one arm of an L-design
behind the building seen in the photograph, and Sir William Hay's massive
rectangular tower. The expanse of
windowless wall points to the continued need for defence in the unsettled conditions north of the Border.
The parapet walk, clearly visible in
the photograph, once continued on
north and south sides of the tower.
But it was roofed in during the
seventeenth century to form galleries with turrets. The interior
shows the characteristic tower house
plan, which is like that of a hall house
arranged vertically instead of horizontally. The first floor is taken up by
the entrance, formerly approached by
an outside stair, with a room leading
off it containing a trap-door giving
access to a dungeon and garderobe.
The Great Hall is on the second floor
with a private room adjoining it, and
the third floor consists of two
bedrooms.

an act of vandalism which moved Wordsworth to write his well-known sonnet
on Neidpath.

An even greater flexibility of plan animates Borthwick Castle, Midlothian.
Dating from about 1430, this remarkable building incorporates one of the most
brilliant exploitations of the hall house design. Strength and impregnability
were still matters of urgency in Midlothian when the castle was planned, and
externally it is overwhelmingly stark, an effect which is emphasized by the
surroundings, a desolate valley threaded by the Gore and Middleton Waters.
Two colossal, absolutely plain square towers project from the main block, rather
like the cross-wings of a horizontal hall house, except that here the central
elevation, instead of dominating the structure, is proportionally so narrow that it
lies like a deep, dark chasm between the towers. This arrangement enables the
hall house plan to be carried out both vertically and horizontally, for the first
floor contains kitchen, great hall and solar in the sequence they occupy in the
traditional English hall house, while the vaulted chamber below the hall is used
for storage and that above it is a private chamber with an oratory over it. The
vertical and horizontal themes are elaborated by numerous wall chambers,
stairways and garderobes.

Great Dixter, Northiam, Sussex

The hall at Great Dixter dates from between 1450 and 1466 and is a superb example of the unaisled great hall. We are looking towards the former dais end. The tiny opening in the end-wall is a reconstruction by Lutyens of the squint, through which the lord of the manor could observe all that went on in the hall after he had retired to the solar, reached by a stair through the door seen on the left. The bay window is also a reconstruction by Lutyens, but the canted posts on either side of the recess gave evidence of its former existence. In the roof structure hammer-beams alternate with tie-beams. Great Dixter was the home of Nathaniel Lloyd, author of the standard work on the history of the English house.

The nucleus of all the buildings so far described in this chapter is the hall house with its upper-end and lower-end chambers, whether arranged horizontally or vertically. Though the great hall itself could now only be regarded as part of the essential accommodation in an important house, it continued to be used as a centre for the administration of justice and assemblies of tenants. The great significance of the hall in the medieval way of life is demonstrated by the persistence of the word 'hall' to designate the great house in a village community long after the hall itself had ceased to exist except as an occasional architectural relic, long after it had become horizontally divided to create space for upper rooms, and even after it had been transformed, first into one among several living-rooms, and then had dwindled into the mere vestibule of recent times, partaking more of the character of the former screens passage than of the noble apartment from which it derived its name. Indeed, in many a converted hall house – at Abbas Hall and Pattenden Manor, to name only two examples which figure in this account – what was once called the screens passage is now called the 'hall'. The first stage in this metamorphosis could be associated with the disappearance of the aisles, even though the immediate result of this was the enhancement of the formal and aesthetic character of the great hall. In early medieval houses, as we have seen, the hall was aisled because in the home which consisted of nothing but a hall, its great span could not be roofed without supporting pillars, while the aisles thus formed provided essential storage space. But once the two-storeyed Norman house and the aisled hall had been merged into a single building, the need for great width and arcade alike vanished and an unaisled type of hall made its appearance. Its high walls were pierced by important windows, its open timber roof was of ever more ingenious construction and its whole splendid character was the creation of craftsmen whose skill was continually increasing and the fruit of tastes which were fast growing more sophisticated.

The hall roof, Woodlands Manor, Mere, Wiltshire

The hall at Woodlands Manor is of the developed type without aisles, and the fifteenth-century roof is a splendid example of the arch-braced, collar-beam type, which had first become popular in the previous century. The arched braces, reminiscent of crucks, spring from the side-walls to support the collars, thus giving an impression of great height; and there is no tie-beam. Massive braces alternate with lighter trusses. The raking struts of the main arches, branching out to support the principal rafters, add to the richness of the design. Both the braces and collars of this finely wrought roof are moulded, while the tiers of cusped windbraces supporting the rafters between the purlins are not only functional but supremely decorative.

Although for power of invention and for richness of ornament the timber roofs of unaisled medieval halls can seldom, except in unusual instances like the magnificent anachronistic example in Edward IV's palace at Eltham, be compared to the finest church roofs, they are based on the same varieties of design and show the same advance from the simple crown-post and ridge roof to the elaborate hammer beam type. The crown-post roof, such as that seen at Tiptofts Manor (p. 24), gave place to the queen-post type. In a roof of this construction the crown-post is replaced by two upright queen-posts resting on the tie-beam and supporting the collar immediately above it near the ends. The effect is as if the aisled hall structure had been raised to the roof. At Church Farm, Fressingfield, Suffolk, the arrangement is two-tiered, with a crown-post in the upper tier and queen-posts as well as a crown-post in the lower tier. The late fourteenth- or early fifteenth-century hall at Woodlands Manor, Mere, exhibits a type of roof which had lately become fashionable: the arch-braced, collar-beam style. The cambered collar-beams, high-set, each with two branching struts, are supported by large braces springing from the wall-plate, reminiscent of crucks, and indeed primitive cruck construction may have influenced this variety of roof. The absence of a tie-beam enhances the impression of height and space. Between the purlins and rafters supports known as wind braces have been inserted and made decorative with curves and cusps. Margaret Wood makes the interesting suggestion that such braces may derive from the arch braces of the aisled hall, and this is borne out by the occurrence in some unaisled halls, at Trecarrell, near Launceston, for instance, of straight wind braces.

The main arches in the roof at Woodlands Manor are moulded with a slight but wholly delightful irregularity, so that the timbers look like the swaying, ribbed stems of giant rhubarb. The grooves were cut with no other tools than the

chisel and gouge, for it was not until the seventeenth century that moulding planes like those mentioned by Moxon in his *Mechanick Exercises* (1679) came into use; and it is this absence of uniformity which imparts such liveliness to the texture of these medieval timbers and calls attention to the ingenuity of the early carpenters.

Another roof of the kind seen at Woodlands Manor crowns the granite hall of Cotehele, a house beside the Tamarin in Cornwall built on the quadrangular plan with a powerful gate; which in this case was more than a mock fortification, for Sir Richard Edgecombe, the builder, wished to be prepared against the attacks of a neighbour who had already driven him once from the site. Although begun in 1485, Cotehele was only completed in 1540, and by that time the great hall open to the roof was decidely old-fashioned. It is an instance not so much of the romantic enthusiasm for the past which inspired many sixteenth-century designers as of the inevitable conservatism of remote districts. In the Middle Ages Cornwall lay on the edge of the known world, an almost legendary land, encompassed on two sides by a dangerous coast, a situation which fostered isolation and regional habits including the preservation of the Celtic tongue. At Cotehele there are three purlins on the slope of the roof, and between these and the main rafters arched wind braces make a complex pattern of four tiers of interlacing arcading.

A roof of quite another character distinguishes the hall of Great Dixter, Sussex, built between 1450 and 1465. It exhibits an enormous cambered tie-beam cut from a single great oak tree, reinforced by curved and cusped braces on a massive scale and itself supporting a noble octagonal crown-post with moulded capital and base; and this design is combined with hammer-beams – beams projecting at right-angles from the wall, supported by curved braces and with arched braces springing from them. The purpose of these hammer-beams was to strengthen

The roof of Gifford's Hall, Stoke-by-Nayland, Suffolk

The hammer-beam roof, already half in evidence at Great Dixter, appears in its fully developed form in the hall of the house built by the Mannocks in the time of Henry VII. It is of the type so richly exemplified in many East Anglian churches, such as Trunch or Palgrave. The structure here is a double hammer-beam roof in which a second range of hammer-beams ties the principles more firmly to the wall. The vertical strut rising from the hammer-beam to the principal rafter is not set on the hammer-beam but morticed into it, and ends in a lavishly carved pendant. The whole composition is articulated by carved designs, pierced tracery and heavy mouldings.

the arch-braced roof by tying the principal rafters, embedded in their outer ends, more firmly to the wall. The faces of the hammer-beams at Great Dixter are decorated with heraldic shields, the arms of the Etchingham, Dalingridge and Gaynsford families. The central rafters are still blackened by the smoke from the former open fire than burned on the floor in the middle of the hall. The exceptionally strong sense of continuity conveyed by this noble room is intensified by a charming detail: a woodpecker's nest, cut in half when the braces of the huge tie-beam were fashioned, has been preserved ever since then in the woodwork. Another roof of a similar type, combining tie-beams and hammer-beams, can be seen bursting from the plaster ceiling of a later date in the rectory at Market Deeping, Lincolnshire. The hammer-beams here are finely carved with pairs of downward-glancing animal and human figures.

This and the roof at Greater Dixter show the most uncomplicated form of the hammer-beam type. From it evolved the double hammer-beam roof, where the original hammer-beam projected much farther and a second one was introduced to strengthen the junction of the two parts of the arch-brace in a construction without a tie-beam. This style of roof, for which East Anglia is especially famous, was popular throughout the late fifteenth and sixteenth centuries. The overpowering roof of Gifford's Hall, near Stoke-by-Nayland, Suffolk, discloses three sets of arched braces with carved and traceried spandrels. The carvings, when the eye adjusts itself to the dim light of the room, are found to include winning, realistic representations of a tiny mouse running in and out of a bowl.

Apart from the elaboration of the roof, there were other changes in the furnishing and fitting of the hall, some conducive to greater comfort and all symptomatic of the gradual emancipation of the designer from basic needs. Floors, for instance, were now, in the houses of the great, often paved with stone, tiles or brick. The greater height of the walls in the new unaisled structures allowed space for large windows. Those at Woodlands Manor are tall, handsome openings, one at the dais end of the hall and a rather shorter example near the former screens passage. Both are square-headed with cinquefoils in the upper lights. Such windows obviously derive from ecclesiastical example, but window design of the fifteenth century nevertheless shows an inventive spirit in many of its details which is independent of church precedent. The window of the former hall at Market Deeping, just mentioned, is distinguished by windows which have no parallel in either church or manor house. The lights are shouldered, with tracery to match, a pattern of such captivating gaiety that it is difficult to believe it truly belongs to the Middle Ages and not to the early Gothic Revival. The resemblance is all the more sharply pointed by the presence of orange, emerald, scarlet and ultramarine Victorian glass in some of the tracery, an addition clearly made by one who understood the frame of mind in which these windows were conceived.

Again, the bay window which occurs in numbers of fifteenth-century halls and which is mentioned already in some fourteenth-century documents relating to London houses and published by Mr Salzman, was a peculiarly domestic feature. It was probably a development of the oriel, a projection from an upper storey which is thought to have originated in the porch at the head of an external staircase, the name for which in Cornwall still survives as 'orell'. Among the best preserved and the most impressive of all medieval bay windows is that of the house in the High Street at Chipping Campden built by the fifteenth-century wool merchant, William Grevel. The fine-grained limestone composition sweeps from the bottom to the top of the house, divided into two sides and four front panels by the long, unbroken lines of moulded mullions. Stone, instead of glass, fills the central part of the bay, and this is sparsely adorned with cusping which is repeated in reverse, as if mirrored, in the heads of the lights immediately below it. Monstrous, nervously carved gargoyles lean from the angles of the bay. Another fifteenth-century, two-storeyed bay at South Petherton Manor,

organized as a framework for glass, but the monotony of the transparent panels is subtly varied by the articulation of the framework. Between the buttresses dividing the bays rise smaller buttresses, and the severity of the design is softened by the trefoiled heads of the windows and by the carved masks which terminate the projecting spouts of the water drains.

Abbot Selwood built a house at Ashbury in Berkshire which was nearly contemporary with the Shropshire Priory lodging and almost as sophisticated in design. This manor house shows an arrangement not unlike that found in the abbot's palace at Meare, but here the double hall takes the form of an upper and a lower room, of which that on the first floor leads into a solar divided by a traceried screen from a small oratory over the porch. As at Meare and Much Wenlock, the bays of the house are marked by buttresses, and a strong sense of design is conveyed by the consistent spacing and uniformity of the windows, which are all straight-headed with twin cinque-foiled lights. The array of glass is modest beside that of Prior Shrewsbury's house, but the composition is none the less remarkable for its period. The porch is centrally placed with three bays on either side of it, and it is clear that the builder was consciously aiming at symmetry although he had to embody in his building a small dwelling already in existence. This accounts for the two different roof levels at Ashbury Manor.

The first floor at Ashbury is reached by a stone spiral staircase rather like the winding stairs of castle keeps and turrets, where each step forms at its inner end a circular section of the newel. The slightly more advanced but closely allied form of stair in which the newel was a stout circular post rising from floor to ceiling, with the solid timber steps framed to it, was the most commonly occurring means of ascent in the late medieval house and replaced the step ladders and straight steep flights, consisting of notched balks, which had led to the upper

Tower staircase, Sawston Hall,
Cambridgeshire

The spiral staircase of this Elizabethan
mansion is constructed of bog oak
from the near-by Fens. Each step is of
solid wood framed into the stout
newel post. Such wooden newel
staircases were deliberate copies in
Elizabethan times of the medieval
stone version of the form.

floor of each wing in the house with an open central hall. At Ashbury Manor
the staircase is enclosed in a projection near the upper end of the hall and the
builder extended this feature to include a small chamber on each floor and a
garderobe, now appropriately converted into a bathroom. The projection turns
the rectangular block of the house into an L-plan like that of the Manor House
at Meare and that of the Prior's Lodging at Castle Acre, though with quite a
different usage of the additional space.

Another of Abbot Selwood's houses was probably the very individual Old
Parsonage at Walton, Somerset, which is two-storeyed throughout and is
planned as a rectangular house with a parallel wing attached at the north-west
angle of the main block. A newel staircase in the common angle gave access from
the wing to the rooms above the ground-floor hall. Bishop Beckington built the
rectory at Stanton Drew in Somerset as well as an interesting small house at
Congresbury in the same county, now known as the Old Vicarage, both with a
rectangular plan. Although it is conspicuously furnished with a handsome two-
tiered porch with the figure of an angel in its gable and a traceried window
lighting a tiny oratory (as at Ashbury Manor), the fifteenth-century part of the
Congresbury Old Vicarage, which then constituted the whole house, contained
only four rooms: a low hall with a chamber above it and a solar over a service
apartment. The Old Rectory at Winford a few miles away, dating from the
same time, is even smaller. Here the rectangular, two-storeyed block is reduced
to its simplest form with only one room on each floor. The hall, on the ground
floor, is dignified by a hood-moulded window with arched, cusped trefoil
lights. A lean-to, opening from the screens passage, houses the buttery and relates

this little house to hundreds of later cottage dwellings with their inclining 'outshuts'.

An even earlier example of the small oblong house, the plan of which was adopted for the standardized dwellings of yeomen and tenant farmers, now regarded as cottages, is the enchanting little Priest's House at Muchelney, again in Somerset. According to the evidence of the mouldings of the doorways at either end of the former screens passage, the building must date from the fourteenth century, although the windows belong to the end of the fifteenth century. This is a traditional hall house in miniature, but the solar and service wings, instead of projecting at right-angles to the central hall, have been brought into line with it to make a rectangular composition. The thatched roof, with its hipped gable-end, is continuous and high pitched. The four-centred door, placed asymmetrically, as in the early hall house, leads into the screens passage; to the right lies the hall, and opening from it is the parlour with the solar above it, while on the left of the passage are the buttery and kitchen. The growing importance of the parlour in the later Middle Ages is reflected here in the size of its window. It is as wide as that of the hall, and surmounted similarly by a dripstone, or label, dropped down a few inches at either end and neatly turned, though its four arched lights are plain, while those of the hall window are cusped ogees. And the hall window rises to the full height of the wall.

Small oblong structures of this kind, and still more the even simpler plans exemplified by Winford Old Rectory and the Old Vicarage at Congresbury, could be readily adapted to a row of cottages with a uniform roof-line; and although the terrace house proper only played a major part in the development of domestic architecture after the Great Fire, rows of identical houses did make

The Priest's House, Muchelney, Somerset

An early example of the small rectangular house combining a central hall open to the rafters with a two-storeyed block. It may date from the fourteenth century, but the cinquefoiled, ogee-headed lights of the hall window show a popular fifteenth-century motif and the parlour window to the right is of even later date. The small dormer lights the solar, which is reached by a screw staircase in a projection at the rear of the house entered through a door in the parlour.

MUCHELNEY, PRIEST'S HOUSE
1. Buttery or kitchen   2. Screens passage   3. Hall—open to roof
4. Parlour, solar above   5. Roof truss above

Cottages at Melbourn, Cambridge-shire

The compact rectangular plan is here adapted to a row of chalk marl cottages with a continuous thatched roof. Each contains four rooms: hall-kitchen and parlour below, with two chambers above. An interesting feature of these cottages is the shutters (since removed): they are hinged to the sill and, when pushed up at night, are kept in position by a wooden prop.

their appearance during the Middle Ages. Abbot Selwood was the author of a scheme for rebuilding the Somerset town of Mells with four straight streets radiating from a focal point in the Roman fashion; and New Street still stands to bear witness to the partial realization of his plan. Leland described Mells as 'a praty townlet of clothing', and the abbot's houses were intended for clothiers. Each consists of a screens passage between a larger and smaller room with two rooms above reached by a spiral staircase enclosed in a polygonal projection placed by the back door. At Wells, Bishop Beckington built rows of houses for forty-two vicars in two parallel ranges, each with two rooms, one on each floor, and a minute yard or garden in front. These little dwellings have been much altered, but the original arrangement is known from drawings made by Pugin: the ground-floor chamber was entered through a four-centred arch and the screw staircase to the upper room was encased in a square projection at the back of the house. Both rooms were furnished with fireplaces and square-headed windows with trefoiled lights. The plan of the Mells terraces is repeated almost identically in a late sixteenth or even early seventeenth century row of clunch, thatched cottages at Melbourn, Cambridgeshire. The only difference is that the Melbourn staircases are steep and straight and lead up from an angle in the principal room beside the fireplace.

Several important secular houses built at the close of the Middle Ages in the county of Somerset show the direct influence of the advanced two-storeyed and rectangular plans realized by ecclesiastical designers. Gothelney Manor, near Bridgwater, for instance, is an oblong house with two floors throughout. But the ground-floor hall rises almost to the height of an open hall, and with the room above it, an impressive chamber crowned by an arch-braced timber roof, this part of the house assumes tower-like proportions to the left of the porch. Beside the porch, projecting alongside it, is a garderobe, an unusual position for this convenience in a medieval house, though the modern cloakroom (the word exactly translates 'garderobe') is often found close to the front door. This projection at Gothelney is balanced, with a nice sense of composition, by another to the right of the back entrance to the screens passage, and this contains a spiral staircase leading to a tiny chapel opening from the solar.

Blackmoor Manor, near Cannington, has features in common with both Adam de Sodbury's residence at Meare and Ashbury Manor, Berkshire, as well as incorporating characteristics of the traditional hall house. It was the home of Sir Thomas Tremaill, whose will is dated 1508. It is two-storeyed throughout and shows a double hall arrangement with one hall above the other, as at Ashbury; and as at Meare, it takes the form of a rectangular block with a wing turning it into an L-shape. But here the wing juts forward at right-angles to the façade like the cross-block of the old hall house, to the plan of which the gable at the opposite end of the building also alludes. The projecting arm of the L contains the chapel with a large three-light window and a solar above it. The lower of the two halls was perhaps, here as well as at Ashbury, used for the transaction of the official business of the estate.

Sir Thomas Tremaill's manor, like Adam de Sodbury's summer palace, has become a farm and shows similar signs of decline in status in its dilapidated fabric. But if little has been done to counteract the wear and tear of centuries, later owners have nobly refrained from modernizing the house. Externally, the scabrous building which confronts the visitor behind a permanently open, unhinged gate, rusting, unworthy iron railings and a patch of weeds, is the same in its essential details as the proud manor which gladdened the eyes of Sir Thomas.

Gothelney and Blackmoor are not, however, really typical of the very large number of new small houses in which the two-storeyed, oblong design materialized at the end of the fifteenth century. These houses sprang into being in response to the needs of an emerging class of yeomen and tenant farmers whose welfare had become a particular concern of Tudor policy as one of the principal means of counteracting the results of two centuries of agricultural depression and unrest. The rise of such a class was symptomatic of the disintegration of the feudal system, heralded more than a hundred years earlier by the revolutionary utterances of the 'mad priest of Kent', John Ball; and the unprecedented demand for houses which followed marked the gathering of a great wave of inspired domestic building which was to reach its height in the Elizabethan period, the visual counterpart of that glorious outburst of poetry which then transfigured our national drama. The newly created yeomen were not usually able to employ masons to build for them, for they were working chiefly for the Church and the nobility, and so it fell to the carpenter to emulate the advances in domestic planning which had already been achieved in stone. While ecclesiastical builders, perhaps encouraged by recollections of the Norman house, seem to have reduced the hall house plan of a central block with cross-wings to a rectangular composition without any intermediate stages, the timber worker only arrived at the two-storeyed and rectangular design by a gradual metamorphosis of the three original units of the traditional hall house. The first stage in the conversion took place when the lower storey of the cross-wings was brought into line with the hall, while the upper storey still projected at one or both ends. A cottage showing this arrangement can be seen at Pembridge, Herefordshire. Brick House, once a yeoman's dwelling, has been much altered in the course of several centuries. Brick has taken the place of the original wattle and daub filling of the timber framework of the hall and one of the cross-blocks, while the other cross-block, now converted into a separate cottage, has been encased in rough-cast. But none of these modifications obscures the original design.

The projections of the upper storey of this house constitute a feature known as 'jettying', which became extremely popular during the fifteenth century. The source of the jetty has been variously explained, but the simplest and most obvious reason for its existence is that the device occurred naturally to builders when they were laying the joists to support the floorboards of the upper storey of one of the cross-wings. The advantages of the oversail were probably the consequences rather than the cause of the innovation. It shielded the ground floor from the weather, and in towns, where the high value of land necessitated economy in its use, it was a means of increasing the size of the upper rooms. This very considerable convenience, specially appreciated when the lower part of the house was a shop of the kind preserved in Lady Street, Lavenham, and King Street, Saffron Walden, gave rise to a tendency to increase the height of of the house, and as its size increased too with each storey, the narrow streets of late medieval towns were darkened by top-heavy timber 'skyscrapers' such as can still be seen at Shrewsbury and Chester.

At Brick House, Pembridge, the eaves of the hall, which was open to the roof when the house was built, are much lower than those of the cross-wings. A considerable advance in design was made when, in the two-storeyed house, the eaves were made level throughout, as at Dixie's Farm, Ashwell, Hertfordshire, though the three units of the hall house are still perfectly distinct here, owing to the higher level of the roof of the main block necessitated by its greater span. At Place Farm, Ashdon, also in Essex, a continuous jetty along the entire front of the house harmonizes the structure yet further, and here the separate origins of the main block and cross-wings are discernable only in the different level of the roof of one of the wings. The other wing has been successfully merged into the unified structure as a gable. The ultimate development along these lines of the early hall house with cross-wings appears in dwellings such as Ufford Hall, Fressingfield, where the two storeys are framed together in one wall, braced by cross-girders, or summers, and the three units are smoothed into a long low design without a jetty, with a gable at either end and a roof of gentle and consistent pitch.

The plan of the little Priest's House at Muchelney, where the components of the hall house were contained in a rectangular structure covered by a single roof, had its counterpart in timber in the form of house called 'wealden'. Jettied end storeys still, as in the Herefordshire house at Pembridge, mark the position of the cross-wings, while the deeper projection of the eaves over the central hall, supported by curved braces from the wings, secures a continuous roof-line. This form of house is popularly associated with Kent, but is by no means limited to that county. There is a 'wealden'-type house dating from the fifteenth century at Stratford on Avon, and examples are fairly common in the north-west corner of Essex and in the adjoining counties of Suffolk and Cambridgeshire. Bridge Street and Castle Street, Saffron Walden, boast several houses of this kind, some of them now divided into two or more cottages; and a large farmhouse conspicuously illustrates the style at Swaffham Prior. Rectangular houses of this pattern, which oversail at each end but not in the middle, were almost certainly built with an open hall originally. When, with the decline in the importance of the hall, two-storeyed houses became common, the 'wealden' design evolved into a rectangular block with a single roof and a continuous façade, characterized at first, like that of the evolving house with gables, by an unbroken line of jettying along the front, as at Baldwin's Manor, Swaffham Bulbeck, Cambridgeshire, or the famous Paycocke's, Coggeshall, and in countless village houses of Suffolk and Essex. The final form of this single-roofed, oblong, half-timber house is among the most familiar sights in south-west England, striped with dark struts or tiled and clapboarded in Kent and east Sussex and plastered in East Anglia, where, startlingly white or coloured ochre, peach and sometimes crimson, it stands out dramatically against the uneventful landscape (p. 143).

In some jettied houses the upper storey oversails the lower at the sides as well as along the front, and even, when the walls are not interrupted by external chimney-stacks, on every side. This highly self-conscious effect could only be accomplished by a sophisticated method of construction far removed from the basic processes of the early timber workers. The projection of two adjacent sides

Stages in the evolution of the two-storeyed, rectangular, timber-framed house

At Brick House, Pembridge, Herefordshire (left), the lower storey of the cross-blocks of a fifteenth-century hall house with cross-wings has been brought into line with the wall of the one-storeyed hall, while the upper storey is jettied. The early sixteenth-century Dixie's Farm, Ashwell, Hertfordshire (opposite), shows the same form of construction, and the three components of the hall house are still distinct and separately roofed, but the eaves-line is continuous, and although the roof ridge of the hall block rises above those of the cross-wings, this is because it is two-storeyed, the house having been conceived on two floors from the beginning.

PLACE FARM HOUSE

The continuous line of the jetty along the front of Place Farm, Ashdon, Essex (left, below), another two-storeyed sixteenth-century house, unifies the central and cross-blocks still further. It is only the variation in the level of the roofs of the hall block and one of the wings which reveals the ancestry of the plan. At Ufford Hall, Framlingham, Suffolk (right, below), dating from the early seventeenth century, the gables at either end of the low façade give no hint of crossblocks. The roof is of consistent and gentle pitch, the door is centrally placed without reference to a screens passage, and the jetty has yielded to smooth walls reaching from foundation to roof.

of an upper storey necessitated two sets of joists set at right-angles to each other. To allow of this, a large diagonal beam, called the 'dragon beam', was fixed across the floor, and it was into this that the joists were framed. The outer edge of the dragon beam, protruding from the angle of the house, rested upon a heavy corner-post, a tree, shaped and inverted, such as can be seen at Pattenden Manor, Goudhurst, Kent, and in a house near the church at Clavering, Essex, among innumerable other examples.

The corner-posts of both these houses are elegantly moulded, and this feature of the fully developed half-timber house is indeed often prominently ornamented. An eye-catching example at the corner of Bridge Street and Myddleton Place, Saffron Walden, is expressively carved with a motif like folded, embroidered cloth, a free and pleasing variation on the theme which inspired linenfold panelling.

The oak of which the framework of these late medieval timber-framed houses was fashioned, was so eminently suitable for the carver's art that it naturally became a medium for rich and intricate decoration. Bargeboards, which were fixed to the ends of a gable a short distance from the face of the wall, with the object of protecting the ends of the roof timbers from the effects of weather, might be cusped and pierced or carved with quatrefoils or trefoils, like a number which have triumphantly survived at Weobley in Herefordshire. Fascia boards, which very often shielded the ends of the timbers of the jetty, displayed a great variety of sculptured devices and mouldings: commonly a running ornament deriving from the vine, the oak, the rose or the pomegranate; sometimes embracing Gothic motifs such as the quatrefoil; almost always conceived with the same enchanting fantasy as that which delights us on the screens, benches and wall-plates of churches of this great period of the wood carver's art. Accurately observed birds perch among twisted leaf ornaments, antlered stags bound through intertwining branches, foliated dragons peer from behind huge rosettes; kings, queens, angels and monsters spring like leaves from an undulating stem. Engaged

The 'Wealden' House

This manor house at Goudhurst, Kent, built *c.* 1470 by the Pattendens, after whom it was named, shows another device by which the three units of the hall house, the central block with cross-wings, could be transformed into a rectangular plan. The upper floors of the cross-wings are jettied, but a single roof covers the whole structure, the deeper projection of the eaves over the hall being supported by curved braces springing from the corner-posts of the wings. The upper floor of the hall block was not inserted until the sixteenth century (probably not later than 1553, when Henry VIII divorced Catharine of Aragon, for the badges of the king and queen appear in the quarries of the hall window).

72

shafts, like delicate silvery little buttresses, sometimes embellish the lower storey of oversailing houses. Such a slender-fluted column adorns rather than strengthens the wall of The Close, Saffron Walden, and pilasters of even greater fragility, with sensitively moulded capitals, stand in the shadow of the projecting upper floors of Monk's Barn, Newport, Essex, an outstanding example of the 'wealden' house. The corbelled base of the oriel window of the solar of this building, wrought out of a solid balk, provides the setting for a carving of the coronated Virgin holding the Child and brandishing a sceptre between two musicians, an organist and a harpist, all informed with a zestful immediacy which shines through five centuries of decay. The spandrels of the four-centred door-ways of late fifteenth-century houses frequently show leaf and rosette motifs or emblems relating to the builder. Above the fabulous doorway of the de Vere house in Lavenham, flanked by male figures set on high pedestals in niches with crocketted canopies, carved shields bearing the devices of the family, the star and the boar, are accompanied by the unusual and exquisitely formalized representa-

Fifteenth-century jettying at Clavering, Essex

The corner-post in the foreground of the picture, with its finely carved capital, supports the diagonal beam, known as the 'dragon beam', the end of which can just be seen coming through the plastered wall, and into which the floor joists are set at an angle to each other. This structural device was necessitated by the projection of the upper storey of the house on two adjacent sides. The ends of the joists are concealed behind well-moulded fascia boards. In houses of later date, such as Place Farm, Ashdon (shown on page 70), the ends of the joists are left visible below the bressumers of the jettied upper storey.

tion of a squid. Figures of a cruder character than those at Lavenham, but bursting
with vitality, stand on the capitals of the stout shafts rising on either side of the
cartway at Paycocke's, a woman clasping a distaff and a smiling man bearing a
shield with a head upon it that might be intended for the Medusa.

Contrary to popular belief, the timber-framed house at the height of its
development in the late Middle Ages is not a flimsy structure, but, apart from
the risk of fire, the most durable of habitations. The oak timbers, all morticed
and pegged into one another, have grown ever harder and stronger with time,
and form a unit far better able to resist the effects of heavy traffic than stone or
brick, and so complete that it could, if necessary, be moved as a whole. The first
buildings of St Catharine's College, Cambridge, consisted of two 'framed'
houses bought at Coton in 1473 and transported to Cambridge. Mr Salzman
gives several instances of such removals: timber-framed houses bought at
Northall were taken to Sutton and set up there as part of the royal manor, and a
hall was moved from the manor of Thundersley and re-erected in Rayleigh Park,
Essex. In our own century, Lutyens transferred a house at Benenden in Kent to
Northiam in Sussex, where it became part of Great Dixter. And workmen
putting a damp course into a late fifteenth-century house at Radwinter, Essex, in
1966, were able to raise the whole edifice bodily from the plinth without
damaging it.

Regional distinctions in the arrangement of the studs of timber-framed houses
were becoming apparent in the Tudor period. They will be discussed in a later
chapter. It was probably at this time, when centuries of work on familiar
materials by familiar methods had culminated in such a florescence of fine craftsmanship, and when individual specialization was coming to the fore, that the
wattle and daub filling of the spaces between the partitions of a half-timber
house acquired the intriguing names by which it is still known in different parts

Moulded ceiling beams, Pattenden Manor, Goudhurst, Kent

This ceiling was inserted in the former open hall of Pattenden Manor in the early sixteenth century and is divided into compartments by heavy beams upon which rest the joists of the upper floor. Whitened plaster between the timbers emphasizes the magnificent moulding of the immense beams, all executed with the limited tools then available: the chisel and the gouge. The long lines of the moulding are effectively repeated on the lintel of the fireplace, which was inserted with its back to the screens passage at the same time as the ceiling.

of the country, although only to a generation which is fast disappearing. In Leicestershire it was called 'stud and mud'; in Cheshire it went by the name of 'rad and dab' or 'raddle and daub'; in parts of Lancashire it was termed 'clam, staff and daub'; in Kent it was referred to as 'loaming'; in the west country it was known as 'freeth' or 'vreath'; and in the north as 'rice and stower'. In some of the larger late medieval houses, brick nogging was used instead of wattle and daub as an infilling of the timber frame, very often replacing an earlier filling of wattle and daub. The conjunction of timber and brick seems strangely incongruous, for the timber frame becomes unnecessary in a brick house. But tradition encouraged the persistent use of the familiar framework, while the glamour attaching to a fashionable new material prompted the predeliction for brick. The bricks were generally laid diagonally, as at Monk's Barn, both for effect and maximum strength.

The medieval two-storeyed houses built for prelates and nobles in the fifteenth century were provided in most cases with outside chimney-stacks and wall fireplaces on both floors. It was the widespread adoption of the chimney-stack, usually constructed of brick, and the consequent substitution of a wall fireplace for the central hearth, which enabled builders to carry the first floor across the whole of the house in much humbler dwellings and to insert one or more floors in the house originally open to the roof. Pattenden Manor, for instance, which was built in about 1470 with an open central hall, was altered in the early sixteenth

75

century by Sir Maurice Berkeley, who introduced a large chimney-stack with its back to the screens passage. The passage became what we should now call the hall, while the hall was divided horizontally into three rooms. The room on the first floor is graced by a stone fireplace and the walls and ceiling are lined with oaken boards reeded with mouldings of the linenfold pattern, though not divided into panels. Above this room a long attic abruptly presents the visitor with the giant timbers, the tie-beam, moulded crown-posts and collar-beam and the blackened rafters of the former hall with its central hearth.

It was not unusual for a chimney-stack inserted into a house with an open hall to be set against the screens passage; this is the position it occupies in the Priest's House at Muchelney, at Monk's Barn and also at Abbas Hall, Suffolk. The central stack allowed for back-to-back fireplaces on the upper floor, and could thus serve both hall and parlour blocks. The types of fireplace common towards the end of the Middle Ages have already been briefly mentioned. Brick fireplaces were generally spanned by an oak lintel, which might be richly moulded, as at Pattenden, where it matches the magnificently moulded joists of the new floor. Extremely ample fireplaces, like that at Abbas Hall, may have been used at first for hearth cooking. Sometimes, when there is an outside chimney-stack, a bake-oven is found built on to its base under a pyramidal or lean-to roof.

In districts where stone was available, fireplaces and chimneys of this material had appeared very early, but where timber was the principal building medium, the central hearth persisted until brick became fashionable. It is not surprising that in such regions the advent of the brick fireplace assumed special importance and that it was marked by an extraordinary development of the brickworker's art. It is largely to the Tudor craftsman's fantasies in brick that the following chapter will be devoted.

5

Tudor Renaissance

Modern historians, among them E. M. W. Tillyard, have rejected the idea, once common, that with the dawn of the sixteenth century all the medieval forms of art and literature, economics and politics, philosophy and religion, came to an end and emerged in an utterly new guise under the influence of the Renaissance. It is true that medieval modes of thought still carried weight in the Tudor period, and it is true that in the visual arts change did not come as abruptly as at a casual glance it might appear to do. The huge windows and fan vaults of the last great age of church building, which coincided with the reign of the first Tudor, embody a spirit which combines clarity of design with picturesque detail: the soaring vault and richly romantic heraldic ornament of King's College Chapel, Cambridge, are part of an insistently rectangular and rhythmic composition, and the actual structure of Bath Abbey is as rigidly controlled and unified as any classical building, despite its fretted pinnacles, pierced parapet, elaborate tracery and ornate mouldings. But the forms used are essentially medieval, and the fan vault, the most spectacular invention of the age, is the logical development of the intricate stellar vaulting of the late fourteenth century. The style associated with Henry VIII's reign obviously follows upon that exhibited at King's, differing from it chiefly in that it embraces certain details which not only suggest classical architecture but actually derive from it. Several outstanding houses of the fifteenth century, Oxburgh Hall and Tattershall Castle, to name but two, fore-shadow the striking developments of the sixteenth century; and the continuing part played by tradition in the evolution of the smaller house is shown by the illustrations in the previous chapter, which include examples from the late Gothic and Tudor periods.

But it is always possible to find basic, underlying, enduring attitudes linking apparently diverse phases in the social and cultural history of a country. Just as classical forms and ideas can be shown to have persisted in Italy throughout the Early Christian and medieval centuries, to burgeon with fresh vigour during the Renaissance, so the whole notion of a 'Gothic Revival' in England can be replaced by the concept of a 'Gothic Survival', of Gothic modes sustained through a time of intense classical enthusiasm by an inherent propensity. Yet the general tendency cannot but be modified by such divagations in an opposite direction; and a modification of this kind was taking place in Tudor England. The implications and the drama of it were so great, producing such profound sociological and political changes and an architecture so idiosyncratic, that they cannot be contemplated without an instinctive reference to some such term as Renaissance, even if it is used only in its strictest sense. Firstly, even though the habit of mind which is most typical of the sixteenth century can be seen as the culmination of a process rooted in the Middle Ages, it is utterly averse to the attitude encouraged by the formal, abstracted dialectics of medieval philosophy. The vision of man's destiny emanating from Renaissance Italy embraced horizons far beyond the narrow confines of the medieval world. Every reader of the literature of the Middle Ages realizes that knowledge of ancient history, philosophy and mythology was far from extinguished during the Gothic period. There are hundreds of classical allusions in the works of Chaucer alone. And anyone who has studied the imagery of medieval churches is aware of pagan elements. But just as extensive contacts with far-off lands made only the most superficial impression and aesthetic influences were absorbed into a native style which, vertical and dynamic, was the tangible expression of an aspiring but circumscribed ideology, so these remembrances of antiquity were unrecognizably transformed by a view of life totally opposed to that of the civilization in which they had originated.

But now the study of Greek, introduced into England by William Grocyn (1446?-1519) and Thomas Lineacre (1460?-1524), and the change in ideals of education from the training of priests and scholars to the training of accomplished gentlemen versed in the classics, engendered a fresh approach to antiquity, so that it became a source of imaginative enrichment instead a depository of whimsical embroideries in word or stone. This procreant intellectual and educational activity was supported by the development of printing. William Caxton (1422?-91) began printing in England in 1476 and was followed by his apprentice Wynkyn de Worde and by a succession of king's printers, of whom Thomas Berthelet and Richard Grafton are the best known. Streams of books and pamphlets poured from the presses, immensely facilitating mental contacts. At the same time, the exploration of strange continents fanned the breath of a fantasy newly released from a constricting metaphysics and opened fresh paths of bold endeavour to the artist as well as to the scientist and adventurer.

Ecclesiastical dominion was fast declining. The one great medieval profession, the clerical, was now rivalled by those of the lawyer, the doctor and above all the merchant. The end of the absolute supremacy of the Church in secular matters was dramatically symbolized by the Dissolution of the Monasteries (1536-40). One result of this was that the importance of the Monarchy was enhanced, especially through the creation of the Privy Council, while the House of Commons gained strength by representatives from new boroughs. The wealthy merchants who had supplanted the former feudal lords, decimated by the Wars of the Roses (1455-85), had acquired land, often from monastic establishments, and were demanding houses in keeping with their state; new houses also were needed, as we have seen, by yeomen and tenant farmers, and a sudden population explosion, similar, though on a less frightening scale, to that which we are experiencing today, gave yet further impetus to domestic architecture. Church building almost came to an end, and for the first time house rather than church design expressed the most advanced ideas of the period.

The Dissolution had other effects which bear on our story. Apart from the economic consequences of the redistribution of the vast estates of the medieval church, enormous numbers of skilled men, formerly occupied in the never-ending task of repairing and maintaining the monasteries, were freed for employment by the rising class of traders. A large proportion of the abandoned abbeys and priories became quarries for building materials such as had hitherto been rarely used for housing the laity other than the greatest lords. These materials, in conjunction with the growing fashion for brick, were an inspiration in themselves. And in addition to this, knowledge of planning and building construction was fostered by the detailed surveys of the convents and their estates which had to be undertaken before they could be re-allocated. The work turned those engaged in it into embryonic architects, the first of yet another nascent class of professional men, who were more consciously concerned with design than with the traditions within which the medieval master craftsmen had achieved their most splendid triumphs. Sometimes the owner of a house might be his own master of works, collaborating with his chief mason in a plan to which both contributed. A recently discovered indenture of 1547 for the building of Mount Edgcumbe in Cornwall, shows that Sir Richard Edgcumbe provided the design, or 'platt', and that the company of workmen, who came from North Buckland,

Lacock Abbey, Wiltshire

An example of the conversion of an abbey into a house, a common procedure in the years following the Dissolution. Sir William Sharington purchased the former Augustinian abbey in 1540 and himself planned the conversion. The long south front (shown here) is strikingly classical in feeling. The proportions of the design and the prominent balustraded parapet masking the roof-line create an impression of horizontality which outweighs the effect of the medieval buttresses, of the lack of symmetry, of the fact that the tower, despite its severity, is polygonal and un-Italian, and of the presence of the battlemented oriels. The latter are not medieval and were not part of the Tudor conversion: they were the work of Fox Talbot, the pioneer photographer, in *c.* 1828. Sir William's niece married a Talbot and the house remained in the possession of the Talbots until 1958.

near Bideford, nearly forty miles distant, with Roger Palmer as their head mason, agreed to follow 'alwayes in their seyd work the devise, advyse and platt of the seyd Sir Richard Eggecumbe and his assignes'. Similarly Sir John Thynne of Longleat is known to have controlled the design and building of his own house. The day was to come when the division of the creative act of building between the man of ideas and the workman was to have disastrous results, but that day was still far off and for a long time the disadvantages of the separation were offset by the force of a tradition of craftsmanship built up over five hundred years. That same force also counteracted the threat to quality implicit in the high-pressure work with much overtime which, as Professor Knoop and Dr G. P. Jones have shown, now became common for the first time, owing to Henry VIII's insistence on speed and the tremendous demand for houses. The number of great country houses alone which were built in the early part of the sixteenth century is staggering by comparison with the output of the fifteenth century. They include Hampton Court, Fawsley Manor, with its dower house of about the same date (*c.* 1537), Thornbury Castle, Hengrave Hall, St James's Palace, the legendary Nonsuch, Layer Marney Hall, Sutton Place, Barrington Court and Brymton D'Everecy, Forde Abbey, Athelhampton Hall, Bramhall Hall, Speke Hall and Compton Wynyates, to name but a few.

This spate of domestic building, encouraged by a heightened sense of personality, an awareness of the past and a love of ostentation, and sustained by the burst of creative energy liberated by a changed outlook and by the current emphasis on secular rather than ecclesiastical matters, was carried out by men trained in the Gothic tradition but often working under foreign artists schooled in the classical idiom, many of them brought from Italy by Henry VIII. The result was an architecture which curiously prefigured that of the early Gothic Revival.

Just as in the mid eighteenth century Gothic imagery, perceived poetically rather than historically, was grafted on to a classical mould, so in the first half of the sixteenth century classical motifs, imperfectly but imaginatively grasped, were fused with medieval forms. The architecture of both periods exhibits a strong predilection for the picturesque (although this word was unknown in Tudor England) and a romantic attitude to the past. The same continuing excellence of craftsmanship underlay both phases.

While the Tudor mansion still embraced the hall-house plan, often as part of the quadrangular pattern introduced during the Middle Ages, it revealed many novel features, the products of a mounting appreciation of the house as a work of art, modified by individual taste and fancy rather than by utilitarian needs. One indication of an altered view of the house is that now, for the first time, the garden was deliberately created as a setting for the building. While there is no evidence that the fruit and vegetables cultivated by some noblemen and the regular clergy during the Middle Ages were part of designed layouts, Tudor gardens were highly stylized geometrical arrangements of topiary, statues and masonry, and were enlivened by new species of plants brought to England from all over the known world. The most famous of these gardens was the one at Hampton Court, planned by Cardinal Wolsey and familiar from contemporary descriptions and from the painting by Leonard Knyff. Such formal gardens were of a piece with the style of houses which were becoming ever more elaborate. Both were alike informed with a keen eye for composition and an inclination for extravagant detail. When Sir William Sharington converted the conventual buildings of the Augustinian Abbey of Lacock into a residence in about 1540, he was obviously inspired by a feeling for classical architecture, although he did not attempt to impose a forced symmetry on the medieval structure. But his interest is revealed in the markedly horizontal character of the south front, where the irregular roof-lines are hidden by a balustraded parapet and by the plainness of the tower, which is yet the one romantic feature of the façade. It was used as a belvedere and Sir William was his own architect. Barrington Court, Somerset, built soon after 1514, is a still more eloquent and much earlier expression of the Tudor preoccupation with symmetry. Though the plan is based on that of the hall house, it is completely logical and balanced, principally because the three-tiered porch, the traditional position of which was determined by the screens passage and was thus never central, has been made the focal point of the main elevation. Thus, with its wings, the building, receding and advancing, already makes the E-shape popularly associated with the Elizabethan period. The walls are plain, except for the hood moulds above the rectangular, mullioned windows, and might even be considered stern, were it not for the warmth of its yellow, lichen-encrusted stone walls. But this severity is counteracted by exotic, spiralling chimneys and by twisting finials, which extend and accentuate each vertical line of the house and crown the gables of dormers and wings, each capped by star tops or by the miniature pepper-pot domes which are such a hall-mark of Tudor architecture.

By comparison with a simple manor house of the previous century, such as Cothay in the same district, Barrington Court contains a bewildering variety of rooms, including a 'small' dining-room and one of the earliest long galleries, the apartment which, like the E-plan, is usually considered to be peculiar to Elizabethan houses. Inventories of other mansions of the early sixteenth century now, for the first time, mention such rooms as summer and winter parlours, studies and private dining-rooms, while the number of bedrooms, even if they were only 'thoroughfare' rooms, multiplied. At Hengrave Hall, Suffolk, there were forty bedrooms, and the former buttery and pantry of the hall house had been enlarged to embrace still-rooms, a pastry room, laundry and linen rooms. This great house illustrates most of the characteristics of the residences erected by the new and wealthy trading families and by the favourites of Henry VIII. It was

Detail of the oriel above the entrance, Hengrave Hall, Suffolk

This florid ornament was carved by John Sparke in fine limestone brought from King's Cliffe in Northamptonshire and bears the date 1538. The photograph shows the curious lobed or scalloped design of the oriel, which resembles that of one of the oriels on the garden side of the Duke of Buckingham's great house of Thornbury Castle (1511–22). This may have been the house of which John Eastawe, the designer of Hengrave, saw a model at Comby (*see* adjacent text). Italian Renaissance influence is seen in the mouldings of the corbels and the treatment of the cherubs holding coats of arms beneath them.

built in 1523–38 for Sir Thomas Kytson, a London merchant and a typical representative of the upstart nobility, after a 'frame', or model, by John Eastawe, based on one which, so runs the contract, 'the said John has seen at Comby' (a house belonging to the Duke of Buckingham). Eastawe, of whom little is known, was the mason and bricklayer, the freestone work was done by John Sparke, Thomas Dyricke was the joiner and Davey the carver. The building is quadrangular in plan, but its character is no longer even as playfully defensive as that of Oxburgh Hall (p. 43). The entrance is purely domestic and decorative, tremendous windows articulate the long façade, which was wholly symmetrical until the bay to the right of the central gateway was removed and the three gables, which once matched those to the left, were changed to battlements in the eighteenth century. A comparison of the two sides of the elevation shows the affinities and disparities of the two periods more graphically than any description could do. Without its gables and bay, the altered side is an excessively horizontal composition and could be taken for a work of the early Gothic Revival. The pepper-pot domes heighten the resemblance. The original gables and jutting bay on the other side of the entrance, however, impart a vertical element to the design which, like the chimneys, gables and finials of Barrington Court, belongs to the Gothic tradition.

But the flamboyant central feature of the Hengrave façade, the oriel over the portal – the work of John Sparke, dated 1538 – follows no tradition. It is an early and zestful instance of classical influence, shown not only in the meticulous rendering of Renaissance motifs but in the mingling of the familiar and rousingly unfamiliar in an exuberantly individual work. It assumes the shape, on plan, of a gigantic, swelling trefoil, a form known in the later Gothic ages, corbelled out from the face of the wall on tiers of multiform mouldings of classical design;

and in the shelter of these ornate curves, pairs of cherubs, either nude or dressed in Roman armour, support heraldic shields, the middle one displaying the Fish-mongers' arms. Capricious, scaly, crocketted half-domes surmount each of the three billowing windows of the oriel and complete an extravaganza which comes close in spirit to the Gothic folly.

This picturesque invention springs from the same impulses, romantic and at the same time ebullient, which led Sir Thomas Kytson and other magnates of the time to indulge in conscious archaisms. The hall at Hengrave is not entered directly from the courtyard in the customary manner, but from a corridor running round three sides of the quadrangle, an individual and progressive arrangement. But the hall itself is open to the roof, rises to the full height of the two storeys of the other ranges and was once furnished with all the components of the great medieval hall, the dais, the screen, the timber roof and the long dais window, thus reviving the traditions of the vanished feudal order. Again, at Adlington Hall, Cheshire, the medieval trappings are prominent and elaborate. The dais is emphasized by an ornamental panelled canopy with a crenellated bressumer and lavish carvings of heraldic devices. The roof is supported by massive columns said to be the trunks of trees standing where they grew. At Rufford Old Hall, Lancashire, not only is the hammer-beam roof conspicuously ponderous, but the movable screen is adorned by extraordinary pinnacles which, though based on Gothic example, would not look out of place on a Baroque altarpiece. At Fawsley Hall, Northamptonshire, the splendid mansion of Sir Edmund Knightley, a three-tiered oriel, more like some grandiose Gothic Revival conceit than a genuinely medieval work, stresses the importance of the old-fashioned hall; it has much in common indeed with the bow windows at Arbury, Warwickshire. It resembles a tower, made half of glass, vaulted within and flinging down a pattern of glowing colour from its brilliant heraldic lights. At Horeham Hall, Essex, the home of Sir John Cuttle, Treasurer of the House-hold of Henry VIII, the hall is distinguished by a truly colossal dais window with arched and cusped lights, running the whole height of the great apartment, from the ground sill to the battlements and parapet. And the builder even went so far in his aping of medieval usage as to provide the hall with a louvre for a central hearth.

Externally, Horeham Hall is intentionally irregular, with its stepped gables, asymmetrical façade and picture-book battlements outlined in stone, and it must have been so even before the addition of the tower in the reign of Elizabeth I. Such irregularity shows another aspect of the deliberate attempt, at a time when the theme of the balanced design had already been established, to perpetuate the Middle Ages. One of the most famous of such rambling houses, Compton Wynyates, the great hall of which, with its curiously carved, linenfold screen, was mentioned earlier, owes its present appearance to William Compton, Squire of the Body to Henry VIII, who rebuilt the manor which had belonged to his ancestors since the twelfth century. Like many Tudor buildings, it lies low, its brick walls smouldering against a dark, wooded slope. In the sixteenth century the russet glow stained the water of a moat which completed and magnified the picturesque character of the crowded quadrangle. Familiarity never diminishes the pleasure or quite removes the surprise of the sight of Compton Wynyates from the rising ground opposite the entrance front. The queer, fat, bottle-shaped porch is not in the middle of the façade; the windows, though all square-headed, vary in size and treatment; erratically disposed diaper-work interrupts the plain brick of the walls and the fabric is further diversified by two timber-framed gables. Each gable rises above two windows, one above the other, placed off-centre. The herring-bone pattern of the timbers is the same in each gable, and each is lit by a strongly defined window, the head of which is the width of the gable. But though the gables match as designs, they differ in size, so that from the distance at which the house is first glimpsed, the larger gable seems to start forward while the smaller recedes; the effect on the eye is as if the façade, with roofs, tall, ornate chimneys and battlemented towers of all heights and sizes clustering behind it, were viewed in a distorting mirror. When the moat existed to double the image, the impression must have been intensified almost to the point of hallucination.

Another unforgettable creation of Tudor romanticism, little known beyond its own district, is the former home of the Uffords and Willoughbys, Moat Hall, near Parham in Suffolk. It was once approached by a magnificent gateway, bearing the six shields of the two families, but that was sold and moved to the United States in 1926. A second gateway, more in keeping with the shrunken state of the house, breaks the decaying, ivied wall on the south side. Battlements and stone carvings in flanking niches of wode-houses, or wild men, skin-clad, hairy creatures brandishing clubs, whose pagan but distinctly Gothic images are to be found in wood and stone all over Suffolk, impart a legendary air to the simple brick arch which anticipates the atmosphere of the hall. T-shaped and part brick, part timber-framed, it is still encircled by an ancient weed-grown moat, which was never more than ornamental. From it, ghostly and faded, rises the tall north façade. Two decrepit gabled bays project into the water, half the arched lights of their upper windows blocked with wattle and daub or pieces of sacking. One of these gables is almost central, the second soars up adjacent to it, and on its other side, even closer to it, the pitted wall is buttressed by a chimney-stack adorned with arcading and, like the bays themselves, with diaper-work grown dim with age and neglect.

Diaper-work of this kind, like the actual use of bricks, was based on French practice. Bricks which were more deeply burnt in the kiln than the rest became a deep purple or even turned black, and were then employed to make patterns in the prevailing red or yellow material. Other designs were invented by Tudor builders, whose preference for brick established it as the successor to half-timber in all those parts of the country where stone was not available. The sudden prominence of domestic architecture in the early sixteenth century and the eclipse of ecclesiastical building were underlined by the fashion for the new material and the way in which it was treated. Tudor brick was generally red in colour, but by no means uniform, for the red varied with the quantity of iron in the clay from palest rust to burning crimson and deep mulberry. But bricks of other colours were occasionally made. Hengrave Hall is distinguished by its walls of blanched, silvery brick, exquisitely harmonizing with John Sparke's freestone work. Even though these bricks were the kind most easily procurable from the local calcareous clay (for it was the custom for a brickworks to be set up near the site of building operations), the fact that they were deliberately selected rather than bricks of some shade of the universally popular red testifies to the serious aesthetic concern which now informed domestic design. Early bricks vary in size, and although they tend to be thinner than the $2\frac{1}{2}$ inches which became common in the seventeenth century, it is not possible to date buildings more than approximately by brick dimensions. During the second half of the eighteenth century the general thickness was $2\frac{3}{4}$ inches, but there were always exceptions, and surprisingly, it was not until 1936 that the size of the common brick was standardized, the thickness being $2\frac{5}{8}$ inches. Thorough baking caused shrinkage and distortion in early brickwork, which necessitated wide mortar joints. This mortar, laid flush with the bricks, was at first the colour of the clay, and only later, when more lime was added, did it assume the greenish-white hue now associated with brickwork. If the joints were exceptionally wide, they were often strengthened by small stones or fragments of flint, a practice known as 'garretting' or 'galletting' (*see* p. 160).

The method of laying bricks varied considerably in the sixteenth century. Although what is now called 'English Bond', in which the bricks are laid in alternate rows of headers and stretchers, as in the stepped gable of Horeham Hall

Picturesque irregularity

Horham Hall, Essex (left), Compton Wynyates, Warwickshire (below) and Great Cressingham Manor, Norfolk (right) all date from the first half of the sixteenth century. The first two houses are expressive of Tudor delight in deliberately irregular composition. They also illustrate the popularity and social importance of brick, which encouraged its use even in the limestone district where Compton Wynyates lies. The roof of this house, significantly, is not of tile but of local stone. Great Cressingham Manor is one of the most exciting examples in the country of that exotic combination of brick and terracotta which, under the influence of Italian workmen brought to England by Henry VIII, was fashionable for the first fifty years of the sixteenth century. The Manor is believed to have been built by John Jenny in about 1545.

and in the beautiful gatehouse at Charlecote, had been almost universally adopted by the mid sixteenth century, irregularities very often pattern the brickwork of this period. At Little Leez Priory, for instance, the rhythmic sequence of a row of stretchers followed by a row of headers is suddenly interrupted by rows of stretchers sandwiched between courses of alternating headers and stretchers. It was not until the eighteenth century that 'English Bond' was superseded by 'Flemish Bond', in which each course consisted of alternating headers and stretchers.

Whatever their colour, and whatever the method used in the laying of them, bricks formed the medium of some of the most startling inventions of Tudor builders. Gatehouses, towers, manor houses and chimney-stacks all assumed fantastic shapes in brick. Towers, ostensibly used as look-outs, like the one at Lacock, but which at the same time paraded the importance of the owner, were as popular as the folly tower of the Gothic Revival. The free-standing tower at Freston, Suffolk, only measures 10 by 12 feet on plan, but rises to a height of six storeys, and with its openwork parapet of arches and attenuated pinnacled angle buttresses, looks still taller. It is placed with as acute a perception of the picturesque as that of any eighteenth-century landscape gardener and adds a dramatic accent to the quietly shelving, wooded banks of the Orwell estuary. The brickwork is red with diaper patterning of dark, shiny blue, and some of the windows are already pedimented. The arrangement inside is unlike that of any earlier tower house, for the principal room is on the topmost floor.

Gatehouses, even more than towers, were the showpieces of the age. No longer needed for defence, they became splendid vehicles for the display of pomp and pageantry. The gatehouse known as Kirtling Tower in Cambridgeshire was once part of a moated, quadrangular mansion, and the fragment is perhaps more powerfully moving in isolation than when the house was entire, though its effect also depends on the remarkably unchanged character of the landscape in which it stands. Not a single reminder of our own age ruffles the mood of these twin octagonal turrets and the great swelling two-storeyed oriel between them. The huge, six-light, curving windows, so grandly domestic and ornamental, endorse the playful intent of the battlements, and the very texture of the structure – diapered brickwork striped by irregular quoins of the same warm-hued stone as the oriel, the base of the parapet and the tops of the crenellations – suggests woven material rather than solid walls: Kirtling might be a castle in a tapestry, set about with winter trees, venerable yews clipped to represent gigantic birds or, shaggy and spreading, invading the wide, deep moat, long since dry and overgrown with brambles. Traditional and classical details mingle, as at Hengrave, in the treatment of the oriel, but in so harmonious, so delicate an assemblage that it is only in the light of acquired knowledge that the motifs are seen to be drawn from disparate and incompatible origins. Tiny battlements and a frieze of quatrefoils and shields rise like a diadem banded with a classical leaf ornament above the arched lights of the upper window. The same leaf motif adorns the sills and forms one of the classical devices that enliven the mouldings of the corbelled-out underside of the oriel.

The fine gatehouses of Leez Priory reveal a different aspect of the Tudor instinct for the picturesque. After the Dissolution, the Augustinian priory became the property of Lord Rich, who pulled down the monastic buildings and erected a fashionable mansion in their place, a mansion, however, which, unlike Lacock, was inspired and haunted by the character of the priory it had dislodged. Lord Rich built a courtyard on the site of the cloister, his principal living-rooms replaced the refectory, dorter and frater of the monks, with the hall on the south side in the position once occupied by the nave of the priory church. Just as in the claustral plan, there was an outer court entered by a monumental gatehouse. Like the rest of Lord Rich's residence, and unlike the former monastery, this is of red brick. The design, a broad, flat arch in a square head, with moulded shields

Kirtling Tower, Cambridgeshire

Kirtling Tower is the gatehouse of a quadrangular mansion built *c.* 1530 by Edward North, a lawyer. It is all that survives after wholesale demolition in 1801 following upon the removal of one wing in 1752. A drawing of about 1735, now in the British Museum, shows the house as it was before 1752. The texture of the brickwork, varied by quoins, copings and string courses of warm stone, is enriched, like that of Moat Hall, Parham (page 85), with diaper work, the pattern being formed of flared headers of dark colour, partially vitrified, a fashion which originated in France. The prominent oriel is a clear indication, if any were needed, that this gatehouse was designed from the outset as a picturesque introduction to the mansion and not for defence.

Leez Priory, Essex

The photograph shows the Inner Gatehouse seen from the Outer Gatehouse, the principal survivals of the great house built by Lord Rich from 1536 on the site of a dissolved Augustinian priory. The patterning on this structure includes not only the popular diaper (on the left-hand turret), but also a chequer design (on the right-hand turret). The inconsistency of the decoration enhances the romantic aspect of the gatehouse. The open half of the double door in the foreground of the photograph shows the inner side of a battened door. Here the horizontal, spaced timbers are strengthened by vertical supports. A separate opening has been constructed in the lower part of the door for the use of pedestrians. The wooden latch of this secondary door represents a development from the wooden bar which for centuries was placed across the domestic door at night to serve as a lock. The latch is secured at one end to the door and the unfixed end slides up and down in the staple on the door and drops into the catch on the jamb. It was worked from outside by the piece of string tied to the latch and passed through the tiny square opening which can be seen in the top of the door. The latch could be made secure by the insertion of a piece of wood in the staple.

in the spandrels set between sturdy polygonal turrets, is markedly severe. A single, straight-headed window breaks the great expanse of wall framed by the turrets. Battlements decorated with banded or moulded brick, angle pilaster strips and two corbelled friezes on each turret provide the only enrichment apart from a terracotta coat of arms. The trefoiled friezes add a distinctly ecclesiastical touch to the composition. The beautiful door of this structure is designedly Gothic in style: the heads of the panels are filled with cusped tracery of a type commonly found on the screens and doorways of Perpendicular churches in East Anglia. The inner gateway, taller, narrower and more ornate, also exhibits trefoiled corbel friezes, but here they are combined with diaper and chequerwork patterns in the brick, with lavishly moulded chimney-stacks and with a pediment over the upper of the two large windows between the flanking turrets. As at Kirtling, these two noble gatehouses are almost all that remain of the Tudor building. Lord Rich's mansion was razed to the ground in 1753.

These compositions are dominated by the medieval past: a freer fantasy can be seen at work in the charming gatehouse of West Stow Hall in Breckland. It is a long, narrow structure and a touch of unreality is imparted to the already bizarre aspect of the tall, confined entrance by the juxtaposition of a very small plain arch to the right of the gatehouse. A strong oriental flavour pervades the design of this portal. Squeezed between battlemented, octagonal turrets, adorned with crocketted pepper-pot domes and terminal terracotta figures, it is crowned at either end by a stepped gable surmounted by a third figure raised on a niched, octagonal drum. Above the entrance arch stretches a broad rich band of lozenge-shaped panels, each containing a quatrefoil. The upper storey of the long side-elevations, overlooking a slight depression that was once a moat, shows close-set timber studding filled with brick nogging. Nothing could be more unclassical than the shape and details of this gatehouse, and it is with something of a surprise that the eye comes to rest on the regular openings of what was once a brick colonnade joining the detached structure to the mansion and which later became the lower storey of a prolongation of the gatehouse. The arches of the colonnade continue inside the passageway, calm and clear after the riotous gallimaufry of the exterior.

The upper room of the gatehouse at West Stow contains a crude wall painting, added in the Elizabethan period but at one with the building in its expression of the profoundly altered attitude which divided the sixteenth century from the Middle Ages. The subject is one which was dear to medieval artists: the Wheel of Life, which is interpreted with such memorable conviction at Longthorpe Tower. This West Stow version of the theme no longer contrasts the worldly with the spiritual life: instead of linking the brief span of man's earthly days with the eternal mysteries of the Nativity and the Passion, the painter combines the Four Ages with a hunting scene. The pivot of his sequence is a representation of a man and woman embracing; love is celebrated as the highest joy in life, and middle age is to be regretted because those youthful pleasures can no longer be experienced. Woman has no place in the Longthorpe Wheel; there the vigour of manhood is symbolized by a huntsman with hawk and lure. Whereas the medieval master never for a moment forgets the didactic significance of his subject, the sixteenth-century painter has followed the matter but not the meaning of the traditional cycle. Another singular gatehouse can be seen at Erwarton, where the building takes the form of a vaulted tunnel entered at each end by a round arch and surmounted on each of its four sides by semicircular pediments. Fat round buttresses suport the walls in the centre and at the angles, each topped by circular pinnacles with beehive caps. Similar pinnacles burst through the pediments over the openings, creating forms that anticipate the broken pediments of Baroque architecture. No ornament is needed to elaborate the strange, even grotesque aspect of this structure, and the brickwork is plain except for a band of projections, like widely spaced modillions running all round the

building, following the curves of the pediments and the swelling shapes of the buttresses.

This gatehouse, which was probably completed before 1549, must rank as one of the most eccentric and yet prophetic of Tudor fantasies in brick. But for sheer ostentation no conceit of the period can rival the towered entrance of Layer Marney. It is carried out in brick and terracotta, that finer counterpart of brick introduced into England by Italian craftsmen, unknown in the Middle Ages and hardly ever found after the first half of the sixteenth century until the Lombard Early Renaissance style made its appearance in Victorian London. The stupendous gatehouse was to have introduced a mansion which was scarcely begun and is itself a mansion with four towers, loftier than any which had preceded them. The towers and the house behind them were intended to form part of a grand pictorial, irregular group in which the church to the west of the gatehouse was included, for it was rebuilt by Lord Marney in diapered brick as an essential component in his design and is itself a romantic work with a priest's chamber and an unexpected chimney at the end of the north aisle. Within the church, on tomb chests, lie the lean-faced Henry Lord Marney, who died in 1523, and John, his son, who followed him two years later, both effigies shaded by amazing balustered terracotta canopies, that of Lord Henry adorned along the top with huge semicircular battlements, reminiscent of those forming part of the frieze of the Church of San Pietro at Modena, but much bigger and supporting dolphin-flanked urns. Kindred motifs embellish the gatehouse, where the same Italian-inspired craftsman was no doubt at work. The towers are decorated with Gothic trefoiled friezes and crowned with prodigous shell-shaped battlements and dolphins. Eight tiers of arched windows light the towers confronting the flight of steps leading up to the entrance, seven tiers of glass glitter in the towers pro-

Layer Marney Towers, Essex

Layer Marney, planned as a courtyard house and probably begun *c.* 1520, was never completed, for Henry, Lord Marney, Treasurer to Henry VIII, and his son John, with whom the line became extinct, were both dead by 1525. The stupendous gatehouse is an indication of the scale on which Lord Marney intended to build. It is a conspicuously original and individual building. There is no pretence here of the gatehouse theme serving any purpose but that of display. Layer Marney differs from other gatehouses of the period in the size and number of its windows, the absolute symmetry of the design in every detail, and the sophistication of the composition, the exaggerated character of which is emphasized by the difference in height between the toppling inner and outer turrets. The decoration of the building is as arresting as its design. The brickwork is patterned not only by diapers but by huge zigzags (seen in the outer turrets), and the terracotta work, in which Gothic features such as battlements assume classical forms and in which Gothic shapes such as ogee-headed lights are fashioned from classical motifs, is unique. The Layer Marney terracotta work is a pale biscuit colour and counterfeits stone. The unusual shapes of the leaded lights in the window from the west wing (left) foreshadow the variety of design which became common later in the century. These leaded lights, protected by a grille, like the windows of Grevel's house (page 52), were fixed with wire to iron bars: the window could not be opened.

jecting to the left and right behind these. The difference in height in conjunction with the steps imparts an unnerving sense of movement to the pile, as if those toppling façade turrets were leaning slightly backwards. But of all the oddities of this extraordinary composition, it is a single detail, in addition to its immense height, which imprints itself most clearly on the memory: the unique character of the large windows between the entrance towers and some of those in the partly built west range. They are square-headed, mullioned and transomed, but the mullions and transoms are all of terracotta, covered with classical ornament. The heads of the lights, which from a distance might be taken for the Gothic ogee shapes they were intended to simulate, are in fact composed of classical scroll, urn and leaf motifs. The result is typical of the whole spirit of the gatehouse, which is neither Gothic nor classic but as peculiarly English and as proudly individual as Fonthill.

This terracotta work at Layer Marney is ascribed to one of the Italians who came to England in the king's service and who was appointed Court Architect, Girolamo da Trevisi, or Trevisano, but there is no evidence for this, and it seems unlikely, for the same name is associated with the decoration at Sutton Place, Surrey, which is entirely different. It is more conspicuous than at Layer Marney and transfigures the strict logic of the plan with enchanting fantasy. The symmetrical house was quadrangular, but the fourth side was destroyed in the eighteenth century, and the builder's concern for form is strikingly shown in the composition of the south range, where the bay of the hall to the right of the

East Barsham Manor, Norfolk

The terracotta work of this Norfolk house, the horizontal friezes and panelled battlements, is of the same red colour as the brick and is almost indistinguishable from carved and moulded brick itself. The decorative panel over the gatehouse showing the royal arms is a superb example of this craft. It was carved on the spot.

entrance is precisely matched by another bay to the left which serves no practical purpose but is introduced solely for the sake of design. The terracotta ornament, mostly of a creamy hue varied by rose and yellow, is arrestingly pale against the dusky red brick of the house. Groups of panels embellished with crudely modelled yet wonderfully robust *amorini* and rows of quatrefoil lozenge and cusped-arch patterns, stretch between the thin polygonal turrets flanking the entrance bay and along the parapet, creating an effect like that of gay embroidery, while the quoins are enlivened with panels containing the initials of Sir Richard Weston, the builder, assistant to Cardinal Wolsey and Thomas Cromwell, and a tun.

Sutton Place has no parallel, but the kind of imagination which gave it birth can also be seen at work in a celebrated Norfolk house, East Barsham Manor, built at the same time, the early 1520s, for Sir Henry Fermor. East Barsham is a less ordered composition and its decoration includes no classical details, but the long, embattled façade with its large, regularly spaced windows wears the same look of tightly spread embroidered fabric, kept in place by absurdly slender polygonal buttresses and turrets; and the outlandish character of the ornament is exaggerated by a group of ten gigantic chimney-shafts dominating the roof-line. Each of these shafts is encrusted with decoration carried out in carved and moulded brick: fleurs-de-lis, diapers and net patterns. It is these bedizened objects and the elaborate crenellations and the little domed caps and fretted finials of the buttresses and turrets which first rivet the eye as East Barsham comes into view from the road running above the hollow in which it lies. The friezes of terracotta panels beneath the parapet show coats of arms, Gothic tracery and heads, making a display similar to that at Sutton Place, but without a hint of foreign influence in the motifs. The porch is adorned over the entrance with the royal arms, the griffin and the greyhound, while a panel over the gatehouse parades the griffin and the lion. The change in the royal device took place in 1527 and thus the mansion itself must have been built before then. All this enrichment is of the same rose-red as the house, and it is impossible always to distinguish between terracotta and moulded or carved brick. The ornament already exhibits the remarkable ingenuity which was soon to inform the brickwork of even minor houses.

Carved and moulded brick mostly superseded terracotta as the medium for decorative work on brick houses after the Dissolution. Among the latest instances of terracotta ornament, probably like that at East Barsham, executed by a native craftsman who adapted the skill he had learned from foreigners to express a personal and thoroughly English conceit, is that which distinguishes Great Cressingham Manor, also in Norfolk, as one of the most unforgettable of small houses. Still partly moated, it stands in a hollow amid tussocky fields. For many years a farm, it was derelict when the writer first saw it. The eccentric façade invites comparison with the more extreme fancies of the Picturesque movement, but the poetry of this relic is of a higher order. A rich mantle of ornament expands rhythmically across a structure which is notably simple in line. Only half the south façade, alas, survives. This half, beyond a castellated, square-headed gateway, is flat except for turret-like angle buttresses and an identical central buttress, from which rises a brick chimney-stack with octagonal shafts and moulded bases. Between the buttresses the wall is interrupted by severely rectilinear windows which still retain their leaded lights. The upper and lower storeys are divided by a moulded frieze combining a broad, intersecting arch motif, used in reverse, with a Gothic trefoil and a Renaissance curving leaf ornament. Above this frieze the whole wall is covered with traceried panels in rust-coloured terracotta, the vertical lines of the panels contrasting with the bold curving forms of the tracery and the horizontal character of the building itself. Each of the panels contains a device, either a monogram composed of two crossed J's and a capital E joined by an intricate knot, or a hand clasping a falcon. The initials are those of John Jenny, who is believed to have built the house some time after 1542, and his wife

Elizabeth, daughter of Robert Spring. The hand with the falcon was the Jenny crest. In some instances the roundels bearing the initials have been set upside down, and there are two distinct versions of the hand and falcon. The ground floor of the house is crudely rendered with cement replacing an original covering of plaster to imitate stone. Such treatment was often applied to the cut and moulded parts of the brickwork of Tudor houses.

The tall, narrow panels with pointed, trefoiled heads adorning the central buttress of the Great Cressingham façade have their counterparts on the central, polygonal chimney of the gable-end of a house at Methwold, also in Norfolk and also fast falling into decay, though except for the trefoils in the heads of the panels there is no tracery at Methwold. This is the only part of the magnificent chimney decoration to be carried out in terracotta: all the rest, delicate lattice work and a vertical motif echoing the shape of the stepped gable, as well as the rope-like hoods above the windows and the mouldings outlining the gable, has been contrived in brick. The more usual method of finishing off such stepped gables was to furnish each step with a little gable, as at Horeham Hall. The Methwold gable-end is an extraordinary object in the village street; even the uncommonly tall, slender spire of the church on the other side of the road attracts the eye no more than the rich invention, the varied texture and fiery colour of this composition, all the more conspicuous in its humbled state as part of three abandoned cottages.

Though it is rare to find the whole chimney-stack as finely ornamented as it is here, the brick chimneys of the early sixteenth century are among the most astonishing productions of the age. It has already been remarked that the intro-

Brick fireplace, Abbas Hall, Suffolk

The fireplace dates from the Elizabethan period, when the former open hall was altered (*see* page 27), and is set with its back to the former screens passage. Such a fireplace would at first have been used for hearth cooking. The oak lintel spanning the huge opening was a customary feature. Its back was canted to encourage a draught up the chimney. The arched recess on the right is an ingle-nook, and a person sitting in it would use the small niche near it to hold a glass or cup.

Former Vicarage, Methwold, Norfolk

Apart from its rich ornamental brick-work, described on the opposite page, this sixteenth-century gable-end is an expressive example of 'English Bond', the method of laying bricks which came into general use in the late fifteenth century and persisted until the third quarter of the seventeenth century. The pattern consists of alternating rows of headers and stretchers with an occasional irregularity due to differences in the sizes of the bricks. It is the absence of mechanical uniformity which imparts such life to the wall texture.

duction of fireplaces, and especially of brick fireplaces, was an event to be celebrated; externally it was advertised by a dazzling display of the brickworker's skill. The proportions, shape and decoration of the chimney were intended to draw the eye, and on the many houses where they survive they still dominate the elevation. Very often dramatically placed in the centre of the roof, they tower above great mansion, farmhouse, cottage and small town house alike, and although the most outrageous examples occur, as I have said, in stoneless districts, they are found in most regions, even crowning stone-built houses, as at Thornbury Castle in Gloucestershire, the great palace in the form of a feudal fortress built for Edward, 3rd Duke of Buckingham. Built at first with only a single shaft to serve the one fireplace in the hall, the Tudor chimney-stack soon began to boast four, five, six and occasionally, as at East Barsham Manor, even ten shafts. A description of but one or two of these remarkable constructions, in addition to those that have been mentioned in passing, must suffice to show their diversity and liveliness. A cluster of four shafts, two circular and two octagonal, cannot fail to attract the eye of anyone walking or driving along Nethergate

95

Street, Clare. They belong to a house known as The Cliftons, rise from broad, octagonal bases set on a square, moulded plinth and terminate in scalloped, corbelled, octagonal capitals, the tip of each scallop projecting in a thin spur. The shafts are entirely sheathed in prominent patterns in relief, bold, intersecting zigzags, chain meshes and a design based on Gothic dog-tooth moulding. A similar group of four shafts with spurred and scalloped tops looms above a half-timbered house in Newport, Essex. Here, however, the shafts are all circular and much shorter and fatter, and it is as if the patterns on them had been compressed by the reduction in height, they are so intricate and so closely knit. One is over-spread with a design recalling the geometrical yet flower-like shapes of snow crystals, another is netted with minute lacy reticulations resembling and perhaps inspired by Saracenic design; another is animated by repeated hexagons enclosing rectangles. At Broadoaks, a moated brick house at Wimbish, assemblages of two or three slender octagonal shafts rest on high gabled plinths and are topped by heavily corbelled octagonal capitals with triple rows of projecting spurs. Four shafts rising from a house at Preston, Suffolk, are surmounted by star tops and stand on a plinth decorated with four rows of square panels, each filled with dog-tooth ornament. The freedom and originality with which themes from diverse sources have been blended and reinterpreted on the bases, shafts and capitals of such chimneys place these aerial pillars among the most inventive variations of the column motif in the whole history of architecture.

Chimney, Newport, Essex

The popularity of the brick chimney in the sixteenth century was such that it is found on many stone-built houses of the period. The clustered brick shafts at Thornbury Castle, Gloucestershire, are well known. The reasons for this popularity were two: first it was found that brick was more resistant to fire than was stone, and secondly, the material itself represented the height of fashionable taste. The prominent chimney advertised the important fact that the house had fireplaces. As a status symbol, therefore, in an age given to ostentation, the chimney became an object of elaborate display. Very often, as here at Newport, the magnificence of the exuberant shafts on their high base is out of all proportion to the modesty of the house upon which it is set. Like so much in English domestic design, the extravagant and highly individual Tudor chimney has no parallel outside this country.

6

Elizabethan Baroque

Screen ornament and plaster ceiling, The Hall, Knole, Kent

The flourish and movement of the heraldic Sackville leopards, the romantic presence of the screen so long after the great hall had become an anachronism in domestic design (1603) and the geometric angularity of the ribbed, pendentive plaster ceiling all epitomize the spirit of the Elizabethan house.

The tendencies which marked the domestic architecture of the early Tudor period were intensified during the reigns of Elizabeth I and James I, especially during the last quarter of the sixteenth century. The self-awareness and ostentation, the passionate and romantic interest in the past, coupled with a predilection for the picturesque, the preoccupation with design, the fusing of foreign and native influences and the secular emphasis all deepened to inspire an art as vital, as superbly organized and as free from rusticity as the poetry of Shakespeare, Ben Jonson or Donne. The age was prosperous and the demand for houses, already under way, increased fantastically in momentum. So extraordinary is the wealth of houses left by this period that, despite the losses occasioned by the Industrial Revolution and the greater vandalism of our own day, many hundreds of Elizabethan dwellings, all over the country – great mansions, manors, farm-houses and cottages – still testify to the dynamic, restless, often aggressive spirit, allied with but a few exceptions to a surpassing sense of beauty, which sets this age apart from all others. They still seem to echo with the sound of the throbbing, vibrant life which once filled them. There is a peculiar poignancy at the present time about the murmurs sent forth from the domestic shells of our Elizabethan

97

Windporch, Montacute, Somerset

Internal porches such as this were introduced in response to a growing demand for comfort. They were particularly fashionable in the south-west, the earliest dating from the second quarter of the sixteenth century, and they remained popular for about a hundred years. As a design this aspiring porch, with its flicker of obelisks and combination of contrasted refined and correct and bold, idiosyncratic rendering of the Renaissance idiom, is peculiarly expressive of its period. The motifs of the cornice and the panelled pilasters, varied by an inlay of wood of another colour, derive from French example, but the extraordinary 'strapwork' volutes flanking the pediment are wholly individual. (Flat, interlacing strapwork is itself employed in all materials in Elizabethan architecture and perhaps originated in Eastern damascene work.) The curious form of the niche decoration on the bases of the pilasters is an instance of the craftsman's misreading of one of the few available pattern books of the day, perhaps Delorme's *Architecture* (1567); he has used console forms instead of pilasters to support the arch. The geometric panelling shows a design often found during the period: it occurs at Broughton Castle and at Crewe Hall and resembles the formal layout of Elizabethan gardens.

forebears: they speak to us of activities, of discoveries, of adventures which have made us what we are; they stress the gulf which divides a people flushed with the excitement of a newly achieved maturity and a people in decline. A continuous line of development links the sad remnants of Beaupré Hall, Outwell, with the hideous prefabricated bungalows lining the drive that once led up to the gatehouse. For the whole basis of our modern industrial pattern of living goes back to Elizabeth's reign. It was then that coal-mining first made significant advances; it was then that the stocking-knitting frame was invented; it was then that the foundations of modern science were laid in the intense activity described by Wolf in *A History of Science, Technology and Philosophy in the 16th and 17th Centuries*. Mathematicians, such as the celebrated Napier, the inventor of logarithms, geographers like Hakluyt, naturalists, of whom William Turner was one, astronomers like John Blagrave and Thomas Digges, cartographers including Norden, Saxton and Speed, and physicists such as William Gilbert of Colchester were preparing the way for men like Newton. Their work was decisive for the character of our lives today: and even greater was the impact of the English expansion overseas and the emergence, as one result of it, of a North America peopled by English-speaking stock.

Domestically these reasoned, practical enterprises were paralleled by the invention of devices for greater comfort and convenience. Some of them have been mentioned in a previous chapter. Internal wind porches, such as can be seen at Montacute, kept out draughts. And it was at the close of the sixteenth century that Sir John Harington invented the water closet which he described in his *Metamorphosis of Ajax; a Cloacinean Satire* (1596). He installed his device in his own house at Kelston near Bath, and it was afterwards copied for the Queen's

Palace at Richmond. The illustration accompanying Sir John's description shows a low flush cistern with fish swimming in it, an overflow pipe, a flushing pipe and a waste together with a large rectangular seat and a pan. 'If water be plenty,' says the inventor, 'the oftener it is used and opened the sweeter; but if it be scant, once a day is enough, for a need, though twenty persons should use it.'

But just as the inevitable results of the experiments, the enthusiasm and perseverance of the Elizabethan scientists and explorers have only become fully apparent centuries later, so Sir John's contrivance had to wait until the nineteenth century before it came into general use, and it was not until our own age that comfort and convenience outweighed and finally ousted aesthetic considerations in house design. Despite developments in comfort in the sixteenth century, the house was first and foremost a vehicle for the expression of personality and fantasy. To a greater extent than ever before it became part of architecture instead of the product of a largely unselfconscious tradition.

I have purposely used the word 'Baroque' in the heading of this chapter because it suggests both the explosive, exotic character of Elizabethan inventiveness and the remarkable synthesis achieved in the more ambitious houses of the period. In its brilliant creativity, sense of rhythm and exploitation of unexpected combinations, this architecture has a great deal in common with the Baroque art of Europe of the following century. The divergences between the two manifestations are as fascinating as the resemblances. The vertical Gothic and the horizontal classical modes conspire together in both to create an original image. Both are spectacular, even theatrical. But whereas the sweeping diagonals, the ascending spirals and billowing curves of the Baroque correspond to a revival of religious fervour and make use of classical forms for a purpose once served by Gothic art, the stately, angular movement of great houses such as Hardwick, Burghley or Wollaton is secular in inspiration, but finds expression in forms largely derived from Gothic tradition.

The concept of synthesis, the reconciliation of vividly contrasting opposites from which the special character of Elizabethan house design derives, dominates every aspect of this complex age. It would be beyond the scope of this book to embark on more than a fleeting reference to the general phenomenon, but one or two examples must be mentioned. First of all, this age, which was so ardently forward-looking, which may be said to have laid the foundations of our modern world, was also passionately attracted by the past. The Elizabethans were the first English topographers, antiquarians and historians in the modern sense, and Leland was followed by Carew, Lambarde and Camden. Shakespeare's history plays were written in response to an urgent popular demand. Drayton devoted himself almost entirely to historical poetry, and in his finest work, *Polyolbion*, attempted to survey the whole country and to put Camden's *Britannia* into verse; and even Spenser, dreamer and visionary though he was, conjured up his country's legendary past in one of the cantos of the *Faerie Queene*. This past, which in the Elizabethan imagination was peopled by King Lud, founder of London, Brutus, Lear, Cymbeline, Boadicea, Constantine and Uther Pendragon, was united to a future of expanding trade by an ardent feeling of patriotism, movingly expressed by Spenser in the words of Prince Arthur:

> Dear country, O how dearly dear
> Ought thy remembrance and perpetual bond
> Be to thy foster child, that from thy hand
> Did common breath and nouriture receive?
> How brutish is it not to understand
> How much to her we owe, that all us gave,
> That gave unto us all, whatever good we have.

The domestic architecture of the age bears many signs of this preoccupation with the past. For the moment it suffices to call attention to the way in which the

Elizabethans clung to the Gothic great hall, investing it with even more picturesque reminders of medieval usage than did their immediate predecessors. Perhaps the most spectacular of all is that of Hatfield House built by Robert Lyminge. The screen is barbaric in the profusion of its carved ornament. It is crowned by a projecting gallery, and facing it at the other end of the vast room is a second gallery corbelled out from the wall on monstrous brackets. Whereas the architect of Hatfield combined some original features, such as the loggia between the wings of the traditional E-shape of the design, with deliberate archaisms, the author of Burton Agnes, perhaps John Smythson, produced one of the most wholly original plans of the period and in the rich decoration of the interior made use of Renaissance flower, figure and geometric motifs without a backward glance at Gothic imagery. Yet he could not forego the medieval hall, even while embellishing it with forms unknown in the Middle Ages. This romantic and nostalgic vein in the Elizabethan temperament is confirmed by the attitude to older houses which were altered or enlarged at this time. Horeham Hall, which was described earlier (p. 82), was furnished with a battlemented tower in *c.* 1580, which emphasizes the irregularity of the façade. The rambling character of Haddon Hall, the silvery-grey house which, set on a grassy slope above a stream, comes nearer than any medieval manor to realizing the dream castle of the age of chivalry, was encouraged by the addition of oriels, a long gallery and castelled bays. Sir John Bellingham of Levens Hall, Westmorland, was moved by an existing medieval tower to make it part of a picturesque composition of gables, tall chimneys and battlements. A sixteenth-century gatehouse, stone on the ground floor but vigorously patterned above with lozenges and stripes in half-timber and adorned with carved brackets, underlines the romantic mood of Stokesay Castle (pp. 36–7).

Medieval strongholds were modified to accord with a glamorous view of the Middle Ages. Wardour and Carew were among them, and it was at this time that Kenilworth was ornamented with its picturesque gatehouse, ostentatiously 'medieval' in spirit if not in detail, and that Leicester's new wing was built to harmonize with the Gothic ranges. And Naworth, in the border country, also assumed its present spectacular aspect in Elizabeth's reign. The new rich, who were building magnificent palaces and manors of stone and brick as memorials to themselves and their age, were often self-made men, ruthless, ambitious and dangerous, but the upper ranks of English society in the sixteenth century included men of noble birth and it was the Elizabethans who created the ideal of the gentleman which was to exert so powerfully civilizing an influence for the next three hundred years, an ideal first realized in the person of the knight, poet and humanist, Sir Philip Sidney, and again a synthesis, for it joined classical learning with medieval chivalry.

Again, the Church which resulted from the Act of Supremacy of 1559, the complete break with Rome and the establishment of the Queen as supreme governor of things temporal and spiritual, was as much a synthesis of opposing forces as the architecture of the period. If it was Protestant in doctrine, it was Catholic in order, and the majestic, consoling and poetic language of the Prayer Book celebrates their union. This book also symbolizes the severance of England from the direct current of Renaissance influence, an event which did much to encourage the striking individuality of Elizabethan house design. For many decades the Englishman's experience of the classical idiom was limited to transmogrifications from France and the Netherlands. They were sufficient to leaven the forces of tradition, sufficient to stimulate without possessing an imagination fired by the excitement of national tension and national triumph. Removal from the fountain-head of classical inspiration postponed the day when the classical Orders were to impose their extraordinary and exclusive tyranny in this northern land. The Elizabethans were familiar with the Orders, and when they wished they could apply the principles and disciplines they incorporated perfectly correctly. The hall screen and the fireplaces in the long gallery at Hardwick are instances of this. But the foreign ideas were not upheld as the only means of achieving a noble architecture: they were merely recognized as useful ingredients in the fabrication of some of the most exotic, daring house designs which have ever taken shape.

The French and Netherlandish versions of classical proportions and ornament were known from handbooks which were in circulation at the time and which were the forerunners of the pattern books of the Georgian and Victorian periods. Among them were the books of the Fleming, Vredeman de Vries, especially his *Variae Architecturae Formae* of 1563. And copies of Serlio's *Architecture*, of which Books III and V were published in Venice in 1537 and 1540 and Books I, II and IV in France in 1545 and 1547, provided details for chimney-pieces and ornament, although Serlio's influence on English designers only became important after his work was published in translation by Robert Peake in 1611. To these foreign books must be added the one English publication on architecture to appear during Elizabeth's reign, *The Firste and Chief Groundes of Architecture used in all the auncient and famous monyments: with a farther and more ample discourse upon the same, than hath been set out by any other. Published by Jhon Shute, Paynter and Archytecte. Imprinted at London at the Flete-strete near to Sainct Dunstans Churche by Thomas Marshe, 1563*

Shute's title contains the first use of the word 'architect' as applied to a specific person. It occurs again in the next century in the church register of deaths at Blickling, Norfolk, where Robert Lyminge, dying in 1628, is described as 'the architect and builder of Blickling Hall'; and Robert Smythson, in 1614, was called 'Architector' on his tombstone. These instances show that the conception of the architect as distinct from the master craftsman was beginning to emerge more clearly. At the same time the men who designed the distinguished houses of the late sixteenth and early seventeenth centuries were still closely connected with the crafts. Robert Lyminge was by trade a carpenter, Robert Smythson, author of Wollaton and probably at least partly responsible for Hardwick, Longleat, Fountains Hall and Barlborough as well as – according to his biographer, Dr Girouard – of the enchanting Wootton Lodge, Staffordshire, was trained as a mason, as was his son John. Two of these craftsmen-architects, Robert Smythson and John Thorpe, have left behind them large collections of plans which would bear eloquent testimony to the astonishing power of invention which characterized the age, even if no actual buildings survived. Thorpe's book of drawings, now preserved in the Soane Museum, contains plans of many famous Elizabethan and Jacobean mansions, including Wollaton and Kirby, but Sir John Summerson has shown that many of these plans are for houses built before Thorpe was born and that they are in the nature of surveys rather than original creations. But included among them are a Thorpe extravaganza, a design based on the architect's own initials, and an eccentric plan for a circular house containing three rectangular compartments. Smythson's drawings now belong to the Royal Institute of British Architects and again many of them are surveys of known houses, but among them are numbers of brilliantly original plans and elevations as well as ingenious designs for screens, tombs and fountains. Some of Smythson's more exotic plans look like the strapwork compartments of Elizabethan and Jacobean plaster ceilings.

It is in the prodigy houses, as Sir John Summerson calls them, built by these and other genial designers, many of them nameless, that domestic architecture first became an art comparable in importance with the ecclesiastical building of the Middle Ages. And it is in these houses that all the varied and conflicting characteristics of the age are most perfectly synthesized.

Kirby Hall, Northamptonshire, is traditionally quadrangular in plan, and in the principal range, in accordance with medieval custom, the porch leads into a screens passage, with the kitchen, buttery and pantry on one side and the hall

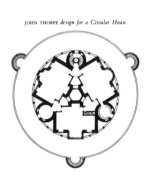

JOHN THORPE *design for a Circular House*

and living-quarters on the other. The hall, again following established practice, rises to the full height of the building and is roofed with a barrel vault divided into rectangular compartments with wavy diagonals passing through them and with flowery bosses at the intersections. The design is carried out in timber and the diagonals recall the windbraces of medieval halls, but the roof curves above a Renaissance cornice and the timbers are all most delicately carved with classically derived foliage and mouldings. The exterior of this range is governed by the same refined and imaginative interpretation of Renaissance motifs applied to a traditional theme. Despite the internal arrangement, the projecting porch is in the centre of a symmetrical façade articulated by giant pilasters with fanciful Ionic capitals taking the place of the buttresses of a Perpendicular building and set between large mullioned windows. The porch itself makes as strange and as inventive a use of classical forms as Dr Caius's gateways at Cambridge. It rises high above the rest of the building, standing up like one of the elaborate frontispieces of the books of the period changed into stone. The third, attic storey of the structure has been added, like that of countless Baroque façades on the Continent, purely for its dramatic effect, for there is nothing behind it. The round-arched entrance is flanked by twin fluted Ionic pilasters with a strong entasis, and a third pilaster, set round the corner so that the angle of the porch juts out between the two pillars, imparts a lateral movement to the design. A frieze of elegantly carved foliage divides this stage of the porch from the superstructure. The balcony set on bold brackets immediately above the arch and the round-headed window crowned by a broken pediment bear the date 1638 and are thus more than sixty years later than the rest of the porch, though they entirely accord with the ascending mood of the composition. On either side of the window pairs of fluted Corinthian columns, again with a third column on the east and west walls, project most curiously on large, sculptural leaf-carved brackets and introduce a bold advancing and retreating motion to the frieze they support. The attic storey takes the form of a curving Dutch gable flanked by flaming ball ornaments surmounting a screen of Corinthian pilasters, again perched on brackets above a strapwork frieze. The fantasy of this structure, poised above the roof-line, where it consorts with tall, polygonal, coupled chimneys, is heightened by the exquisitely carved decoration – shell devices, cartouches, roundels and foliage – which wholly covers it. The felicitious contrast between this exciting, busy porch and the calm, restrained lines of the façade in which it is set makes an indelible impact. It is all the more poignant because of the ruinous state of the house and all the more potent because of its setting. This richly poetic conceit stands in an oddly menacing landscape of little hills, ravaged by the consequences of ironstone mining: slag heaps and livid pools.

In no other Elizabethan exterior are classical motifs used in such profusion as at Kirby. Classical influence makes itself felt for the most part in the conspicuous symmetry of the Elizabethan elevation and is otherwise confined to a few details. Longleat is generally regarded as the most classical looking of the great Elizabethan mansions, and it is an important house, for certain motifs which were to play a decisive part in the design of Hardwick, Wollaton, Burghley Fountains Hall and Barlborough, to name only these, appear here for the first time. Longleat rose on the site of a former house of Austin Friars and had been taking shape from 1547 onwards when it was severely damaged by fire in 1567. Rebuilding began in the following year, but the final remodelling, which left the exterior much as we now see it, only started in 1572, which makes this house the contemporary of the Elizabethan part of Kirby. The plan is completely balanced and all the façades are to the eye of the same height and design, though Dr Pevsner points to irregularities in the proportions of window to wall. The significant features of the design and those which reappear in later houses are the great height of the house, the uniformity of the ranges of enormous windows, taking up more wall space than the stonework, the high basement containing the offices and

Kirby Hall, Northamptonshire

The house, now a ruin, was built for Sir Humphrey Stafford of Blatherwick between 1572 and 1575. The designer is unknown, but the mason is thought to have been Thomas Thorpe, one of a family of masons from King's Cliffe and the father of the famous John Thorpe, the surveyor (*see* page 101).

The hall, with its beautiful canted oak ceiling, combines traditional and Renaissance features, and while it takes its traditional place in the interior design of the house, externally it forms part of a symmetrical scheme of which the bizarre and prominent porch is the centrepiece. The large windows, with their regular, rectangular divisions, are the typical expression of the Elizabethan passion for glass. The giant pilasters, which give this façade its particular rhythm and emphasis, are a French motif rarely found in Elizabethan architecture.

kitchen – an entirely novel arrangement in England – and the articulation of the façades by three-storeyed jutting bays. The storeyed bay used as a repeating unit is one of the most spectacular inventions of the Elizabethans, for by its means their designs are informed with that stately advancing and retreating and aspiring movement which is their special distinction. The bay appears in this new form for the first time at Longleat. Thirteen bays control the powerful rhythm of Sir John Thynne's great house; with their array of glass they are like giant lanterns, although their square shape is reminiscent of that of the medieval tower. They are set at a little distance from the corners of the house, so that the angle of the building juts out sharply between them creating a colossally magnified version of the effect achieved by the pilasters and angles of the porch at Kirby.

Although it incorporates so many original and distinguished features of

The east front, Montacute, Somerset

This garden side of the house was originally the main entrance and has remained unaltered. The house was probably begun *c.* 1590, and, according to Mr Arthur Oswald in *Country Houses of Dorset* (1959), the designer may have been William Arnold, the architect of Cranborne Manor, Dorset.

Elizabethan architecture, Longleat lacks the note of high romance, the tingling excitement and ebullience which are as typical of the period. Seen from a distant height across the landscape garden designed by Capability Brown and Repton, the long house basks in an almost classical serenity.

Traditional and foreign elements conspire together to produce a composition which is more truly expressive of the temper of the age and infinitely more poetic at Montacute. Though transformed by symmetry, this Somerset house is as firmly based on native usage as Kirby. It is in fact a highly elaborated version of the medieval hall house with cross-wings. Built of mellow Ham Hill stone, its height emphasized by obelisks, by semicircular and curving gables with a wavy Baroque silhouette and by tall cylindrical chimneys, it has a three-tiered porch in the centre of its main front with a round-headed rusticated door; the façade is more than half glass, so large are its windows, and it is adorned on each of its floors by niches, shell-headed along the plinth and circular above the first-floor sills. This façade looks towards a forecourt which is all fantasy. It is enclosed by a balustrade ornamented with regularly spaced obelisks and interrupted midway along the left- and right-hand walls by open rotundas, outlines in stone, which might be taken for playful little classical temples, except that they are surmounted by ogee cupolas crowned with finials composed of two intersecting stone rings, suggesting, as they may have done to the device-loving Elizabethans, the universe. In each corner of this courtyard is a pavilion, square, with obelisks at its corners and with an ogee dome rising from a parapet of shell-shaped battlements, the tapering crown of the dome again topped by an open sphere. Two-storeyed oriels swell each façade. House and forecourt are entirely individual and extraordinarily expressive of their period. The size and splendour of the building

Rotunda and garden pavilion, Montacute, Somerset

Elizabethan delight in pattern is shown in the combinations of shapes: square and quatrefoil, circle, ogee and obelisk, in this garden forecourt. The fusion of Gothic and classical forms in magical harmony, the ogee cupolas, tapering closed and open against the sky, the battlements, the Doric columns and obelisks, anticipates the early Gothic Revival.

proclaim the importance of its owner, Edward Phelips, a lawyer, later knighted, Speaker in the House of Commons and Master of the Rolls; the design goes back to the past, but the obelisks recall the Rome of Sixtus V, the roundels and the rusticated door are Florentine in feeling, and the gesticulating statues of Roman soldiers in the niches along the top storey allude picturesquely to antiquity. All these elements are welded together in a harmony transcending every allusion and dominated by the mood of the strangely proportioned, strangely symbolic rotundas and pavilions.

Fountains Hall, Yorkshire, is, again like Montacute, based on the old hall-house plan, and it again reconciles seeming incongruities in a balanced design, but it is more dramatic, more exuberant. Despite the strong horizontal lines of its cornices and the screen between its wings, Fountains is animated by a surging upward movement, which is quickened by the position of the house, pressed against the side of a wooded declivity, and by the flight of worn steps ascending first to a gateway embellished with fragments of medieval columns set on classical plinths and then to the main doorway which is adorned with coupled Ionic columns entrancingly associated with medieval knights. More knights look out from niches above the entrance and yet more stand on the balustrade of the screen. The advancing and retreating movement is far more complex and sophisticated than that which enlivens Montacute. For square, embattled angle towers jut forward beyond the gabled wings, themselves furnished with projecting bays, and the angularity of the design is checked and softened by the curve of the tall castellated oriel above the screen which lights the great chamber. The hall, with a traditionally placed and asymmetrical screens passage, runs below the great chamber with its entrance concealed by the external screen, which has its own pillared doorway in the centre of the whole façade.

At Barlborough Hall, the traditional quadrangular design is transformed into a compact mansion with a tiny inner courtyard surmounted by a cupola. The main elevation, set up on a basement, is one of the lightest and most enchanting of Elizabethan compositions. It is animated by hexagonal bays, which, almost completely fashioned of glass, shoot up above the roof-line like proud coronets, augmenting the vertical emphasis of the house and contrasting with the square, two-storeyed projection of the porch, where the round-arched entrance is flanked by exaggerated twin columns rising, with a theatrical and truly Baroque touch, to twice the height of the opening. The façade is adorned with medallions enclosing busts and with battlements assuming fanciful semicircular and tall rectangular shapes.

Barlborough anticipates the design of the monstrous Wollaton Hall, the most grandiose and showy of all Elizabethan houses, where the hall ingeniously occupies the centre of a quadrangular composition and rises higher than the rest of the building in a great tower-like mass surmounted by a parapet and corner turrets with saucer domes. Robert Smythson's plan for this house is remarkably original and the elevations are spectacularly symmetrical and brilliantly enlivened by projections and recessions, but the building is so overloaded with ornament, with strapwork, angular banding, busts and obelisks, that the magnificence of the conception is blurred in an effect of restlessness which perhaps reflects the personal unhappiness and unease and also the vulgarity of the builder, Sir Frances Willoughby, who had made his money in coal and iron, and something of whose mentality is revealed by the fact that he had some of his accounts bound up in the leaves of fine medieval manuscripts. At the same time this audacious disregard of 'taste' is a prominent attribute of the Baroque spirit and Wollaton is a product of the same flamboyance which prompted the hideous but overwhelmingly vital dolphin fountain at Caserta.

Another lesser house, which like Wollaton is overpowering instead of buoyant, is the Hall, Bradford on Avon, perched up on a high terrace with ornate balustrading. Here semicircular bays project grandiloquently from the fronts of

WOLLATON HALL *Ground floor*
1. *Hall* 2. *Gallery* 3. *Pantry* 4. *Buttery* 5. *Kitchen*

Barlborough Hall, Derbyshire, and (below) Fountains Hall, Yorkshire

Both Barlborough, dated 1583 on the porch and 1584 on an overmantel and built for a lawyer, Francis Rodes, and Fountains, built *c.* 1611 for Sir Stephen Proctor, Collector of Fines on Penal Statutes, have been attributed to Robert Smythson. There are obvious affinities in the façade designs and in the way both are set up on a high base to enhance the architect's fine sense of drama and romance. Both houses show great originality in their planning. The ingenious way in which the hall house arrangement has been adapted to a symmetrical façade at Fountains is mentioned on the opposite page. Barlborough is an early instance, one of the first in this country, of the basement kitchen plan. While its quadrangular layout relates it to Wollaton (1580–8), the unusual feature of a corridor running round the sides of the courtyard on each floor shows the possible influence of Hengrave, which is also conspicuous for such a corridor (*see* page 82). Dr Girouard shows that the Kytsons of Hengrave and the Shrewsburys, patrons of Francis Rodes, were connected for a short period, so the architect of Barlborough may have known Hengrave. The medallions with busts below the main first-floor windows of this house were perhaps inspired by those on the great gateway at Hampton Court, where this charming device was first used. It was a Northern Italian invention which was to catch the imagination of English builders and prompt them to some of their most delightful variations on the theme of classical antiquity.

square bays on either side of a two-storeyed, aggressive and florid porch, the forward movement of which is skilfully counteracted by the recession of pointed gables and tall chimneys set back diagonally behind a parapet, where at the same time they carry the design triumphantly upwards. The front is all glass, but the effect is pompous rather than airy, and the doorway, weighed down by gigantic scrolls curiously surmounted by finials, is only distinguishable from the bastard products of the Edwardian era by its superior confidence and vigour.

Bays and gables combine to create an utterly different atmosphere at Chastleton, illogically tall and designed for romantic effect. The advancing and retreating movement is particularly emphatic, for the central recession containing the entrance in the side of one of the bays, is almost as cavernous and mysterious as that at Borthwick (p. 46) and the rhythm is given a staccato momentum by the spiky, stepped gables which crown both the projections and the recessions. Square battlemented towers rise from each of the side elevations and contribute to the picturesque way in which the grouping of the angular forms shifts as one walks round the house.

But for unforgettably dramatic grouping, no house can rival Hardwick which is seen, now as three, now as four mighty towers in zigzag perspective as the building is viewed now from the west, now from the south, now from the south-east. In this glorious house all the high aesthetic and intellectual excitement, the freshness, the intensity of experience, the swagger and vitality of the age find their fullest expression. It seems to incorporate all the most dynamic and satisfying features of the houses so far described. The builder, Elizabeth, Dower Countess of Shrewsbury, or Bess of Hardwick, was as vivid an embodiment of her age as her great mansion, a parvenue, formidable, proud, scheming, immensely

Hardwick Hall, Derbyshire

The west front of this great house (built 1590–7) is remarkable for its severe angularity, relieved only by the ornamental parapets of the towers containing the initials of the proud builder: 'E.S.' for Elizabeth Shrewsbury; for the austerity and straight entablature of the classical colonnade now running between the towers, but originally designed to continue all round the house; and, above all, for the proportion of glass to wall.

Although the Elizabethans had a passion for light, their houses seldom face south. The south wind was traditionally the bearer of pestilence and therefore to be avoided. Caliban, cursing Prospero, cried: 'A south wind blow on ye and blister you all o'er.' The Elizabethan hygienist, Andrew Boorde, advised builders to 'order and edify' the house so that the main prospects might be east and west, preferably north-east, 'for the south wind doth corrupt and make evil vapours'.

Burghley House, Northamptonshire

References in his correspondence to French architectural books, including that of Delorme (1567), show that William Cecil (created Lord Burghley in 1571) was personally interested in architecture. Work was in progress at Burghley, the site of an older manor house belonging to Cecil's father, from 1556–*c.* 1587. The west front, shown here, is dated 1577, when John Symondes, who also made a 'platt' for Kyre Park, Worcestershire, may have been Cecil's mason. The eighteenth-century landscape setting by Capability Brown enhances the fantastic character of the huge quadrangular mansion. The pepper-pot domes and the gatehouse are in the earlier Tudor tradition, but the quivering skyline—the tall chimneys in the form of clustered columns; the turrets; the arched and obelisk-adorned parapet; the receding and advancing movement set up by bays, towers and oriels; the powerful horizontal moulding dividing each storey and emphasizing the unity of the composition; and the regularity of the fenestration—all speak the language first formulated at Longleat.

zestful and dominated by a passion for building which was prompted by an irresistible creative urge as much as by the desire to demonstrate her wealth and consequence. The powerful secular bias she shared with her age is sharply revealed by a detail in the furnishing of the house, by the remarkable needlework collages, perhaps the work of Bess herself and certainly conceived by her, made from copes which came into the possession of her second husband, Sir William Cavendish when he was acting as Commissioner for Monastic Estates in Derbyshire. Bess put the Virgin and Saints from the copes into Renaissance niches and labelled them Justice, Prudence, Labour and Charity. The daughter of a small country squire, she was married four times, multiplying her possessions and enhancing her social position with each untion until she was among the richest subjects in the kingdom. After years of bitter quarrelling with her last husband, George Talbot, 6th Earl of Shrewsbury, Bess left him and returned to Hardwick, the manor in which she had been born. She had already engaged in vast building enterprises at Chatsworth, Worksop, Bolsover and Oldcotes, and now at the age of sixty-seven, she began to reconstruct her old home on a grand scale. Three years later, while the work was still in progress, Lord Shrewsbury died, leaving his widow mistress of vast resources in addition to those she already had. Only a month after her husband's death she embarked on a new Hardwick a stone's throw from the original manor. The gaping windows and roofless walls of the earlier unfinished house now confront the glittering pile of the new building with a more forcefully romantic contrast than any eighteenth-century juxtaposition of porticoed villa and artificial ruin.

Hardwick stands high and the flicker of its fanciful openwork parapets, holding up the proud builder's initials, 'E.S.', to every corner of the sky, catches the eye

from afar. Yet the actual approach to the house is mysterious. Trees and hollows conceal the full aspect of the great building so that the impact of the fabulous west front is sudden and overwhelming. The westerly aspect has much to do with the profoundly romantic mood of Hardwick. It is impossible adequately to convey the stupendous effect of this façade seen at sunset at the end of a summer day or in the fading light of a wild autumn afternoon. The immense diamond-paned windows flash and vibrate with a hundred molten colours, setting up a brittle rhythm of their own within the large angular motion of the stone frame-work with its perfect symmetry and severity. The house is planned as a rectangle from which six great square bays advance and rise one storey above the already lofty elevations like towers, and with two broad, shallow bays projecting from the centre of each main front. The towers are set one on each side of these central features and one at each end of the rectangle. So the plan has something in common with both Chastleton and Barlborough; and the towers, like the bays at Longleat, are set away from the corners of the house, thus intensifying the drama and complexity of the movement. There is nothing classical about the exterior of Hardwick except its symmetry and the colonnade running between the east and west façade towers: it is as wholly English and individual as Shakespeare's plays.

The internal plan comprises all the rooms which were traditionally considered necessary for a great house, a great chamber, a withdrawing chamber, a long gallery, a staircase leading up to them from a vestibule off the hall, together with a chapel, a bedchamber and a dining-room. But the designer, again Robert Smythson, although Bess played a major part in the organization of her house, introduced a brilliant though simple innovation into the standard plan by altering the position of the hall, so that instead of running parallel to the façade, it was centrally placed and ran across the house from front to back. The buttery and kitchen open from one side of it and the pantry on the other. This position, which accorded with the decline in importance of the hall, was to become the normal arrangement for the hall in the classically designed houses of succeeding centuries.

In an age when the ideal of chivalry was kept alive by the colourful and romantic spectacle of the tournament, when knights wore devices which, more often than not, were relevant to the state of their hearts and when they appeared under such picturesque names as the Forsaken Knight or the Frozen Knight or impersonated characters from the Arthurian legends, such as Sir Lancelot, Sir Gawain or the Green Knight, it was natural that castle architecture should hold special attractions. It has already been mentioned that the Elizabethans refurbished medieval castles as grand, romantic houses, and it has been shown that towers and battlements played a prominent part in their original designs. Occasionally they built in direct emulation of the castle form as their descendants, equally obsessed by the Middle Ages, were to do two hundred years later. Fantasies such as East Lulworth and Bolsover embody the same roseate, enchanted view of medieval knighthood as Spenser's poetry. In its ruined state, set above the sea in a countryside which more than any other part of England is still haunted by the Elizabethan sense of it as a place of magic, peopled by elves and fairies, the Dorset Castle vividly evokes that wholly and delightfully artificial conception of chivalry; it strikes the eye at once as a product of the same burning sensibility, the same love of intricate allegory and archaisms which make *The Faerie Queene* one of the most highly charged of all English poems. Lulworth is a battlemented, rectangular block with big circular angle towers soaring above the main elevation and banded by broad string courses to counteract the upward impulse of the building. This latter is encouraged by the high, curving basement and terrace on which it stands, approached by a rush of shallow balustraded steps. The windows are not the large square-headed openings usually favoured by the Elizabethans, but consist of paired, arched lights with lion masks beneath them, reminiscent of

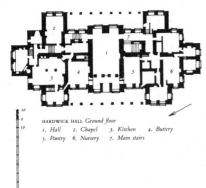

HARDWICK HALL *Ground floor*
1. Hall   2. Chapel   3. Kitchen   4. Buttery
5. Pantry   6. Nursery   7. Main stairs

East Lulworth Castle, Dorset

The house was perhaps begun by Henry Howard, 2nd Viscount Bindon, in 1588, and finished in 1609 by Thomas, 3rd Viscount Bindon and younger brother of Henry. The high-set rectangular block, with its angle towers is a typical example of the Elizabethan castle style, consciously evoking the age of chivalry and at the same time mingling classical with medieval motifs in an original synthesis. Lulworth remained in the possession of the Howards until 1641, when it was sold to the Weld family. The house was gutted by fire in 1929.

Gothic design. These and arched niches, filled with statues of knights and ladies, together with the conspicuous string courses, relieve the simplicity of the façades. The plain, round-arched entrance, between cartouches and shell-headed niches flanked by Ionic columns, is surmounted by a wheel window, filled by five tangent circles which seem strangely significant; and on either side of this window, large figures, bare-headed and in the dress of Roman soldiers, raise their arms in salutation of whomever climbs the weed-encumbered steps towards this castle of high romance. Before the house was burnt out in 1929, the central space, where sycamores have taken root among nettles and brambles and grown to maturity, was roofed, like that at Wollaton, with a square tower contrasting with the circular corner turrets.

Bolsover is a more theatrical interpretation of the medieval stronghold and one of the most memorable buildings of any period. It is as superbly placed as Cashel, on a lofty promontory of the same ridge from which Hardwick rises, looking across a far-flung, undulating territory in which fields and farm houses, industrial housing, scarred hillsides and slagheaps are veiled in the smoke of collieries. The contrast between this scene and the withdrawn, make-believe and utterly overpowering atmosphere of the castle gives the great building a potency stronger even than that of its own masonry. The person chiefly responsible for the unique character of Bolsover was Bess of Hardwick's third son, Sir Charles Cavendish, who shared his mother's passion for architecture but who was especially addicted to castles. He was concerned with the planning not only of Bolsover but also of Slimsby, Blackwell-in-the-Peak and Ogle. The castle consists primarily of a massive keep, deliberately recalling those of Norman castles, a high, almost square block with three angle turrets and a staircase tower rising above the

Bolsover Castle, Derbyshire

John Smythson, son of Robert, who may have planned Bolsover, but who died in 1614, was sent to London by his patron William Cavendish in 1618. While there he made drawings of architectural details, particularly of rustication. But the notion of applying rustication to the panels of a wooden door is peculiarly his own, and the vermiculated design covering the door leading from the keep on to the garden wall is one of the strangest sights at Bolsover. (Smythson's sketch for it is in the Royal Institute of British Architects.) The hooded fireplace of local marbles, probably also designed by John Smythson, is as remarkable an improvisation on traditional forms and Renaissance motifs. In the spectacular terrace and gallery façade (right), dating from *c.* 1629, rustication of a highly individual character again plays a conspicuous part.

formidable, castellated walls; but this keep is also crowned by a pretty cupola and lantern filled with mock-Gothic tracery, and it is further adorned with a projecting bay and balconied windows between rusticated columns. In front of it, adding to its impressive height, is a small raised forecourt of stony, angular character, entered between sturdy, square, battlemented pavilions and enclosed by battlemented walls. The interior is arranged much like a tower house, with kitchen and offices and a large cellar for storage in a vaulted basement, the hall and parlour, known as the Pillar Parlour, on the ground floor, and the Great or Star Chamber and withdrawing room, the Marble Closet (together with a bed chamber and two inner chambers, the Heaven Room and the Elysium Room) on the first floor and a group of small rooms leading off an octagonal lobby under the cupola on the top storey. The mysteriously gloomy interior translates the visitor to a world of strange devices suggesting the Middle Ages in the manner of an inspired stage set rather than by the reproduction of actual details; for although the principal rooms are vaulted, the intricate decoration and the truly remarkable chimney-pieces are works of pure fantasy prompted by memories of the past mingled with imagery from some of the Renaissance source-books available at the time.

If this keep is an outstanding instance of the Elizabethan brand of Baroque, the outer façade of the ruined range added by Sir Charles's son William rivals the most daring and extravagant of Baroque achievements on the Continent. It is 170 feet long and in front of it runs a broad terrace on the edge of a precipice commanding the view I have just described. The windows of this immense façade are surmounted by pediments oddly and feverishly broken into three instead of the usual two parts; and the main entrance, approached by a double stair, is heavily rusticated and crowned by a broken pediment with a detached segmental pediment hovering above it. The mighty wall is further articulated between the windows by astonishing rounded projections which are without parallel in any other building. These massive shafts, which are entirely covered with vermiculations and flamboyantly banded, serve no functional purpose, for they support nothing, but they do control the rhythm of the long composition like the bar lines in a sheet of music and they refer boldly and picturesquely to the military inspiration of Bolsover, for their shape is that of upright canon with the bolt at the lower end. Pedestals on ogee-shaped corbels set at regular intervals along the embattled parapet and huge, vigorous waterspouts increase the variety of the design. The end nearest the keep turns diagonally instead of at right-angles and is crowned by a curved and pedimented gable. The breadth and grandeur of the conception are such that the eccentricity of the detail in no way disturbs the soul-stirring harmony of the whole; this ravaged façade in its dramatic setting must rank as the climax of the Elizabethan architecture of fantasy.

All this display of vitality, pomp and wild invention, this affirmation of the triumphant secular world, also conjured up its counterpart, the keen sense of the brief transitoriness of life which informs so much Elizabethan poetry.

> Since brass, nor stone, nor earth, nor boundless sea,
> But sad mortality o'ersways their power,
> How with this rage shall beauty hold a plea,
> Whose action is no stronger than a flower?
>
> O how shall summer's honey breath hold out
> Against the wreckful siege of battering days,
> When rocks impregnable are not so stout
> Nor gates of steel so strong, but time decays?

Yet it is not often that this consciousness of the vanity of earthly achievement is expressed directly in stone other than the tomb, and even the tombs of the

The Triangular Lodge, Rushton, Northamptonshire

Built for Sir Thomas Tresham as an allegory of the Trinity, the Triangular Lodge dates from between 1593 and 1595, the date on the chimney-shaft. Every detail of the building is dictated by the number three, and it was a fortunate coincidence for Sir Thomas that the Tresham emblem was a trefoil. The banded ironstone and pale limestone underline the exotic character of the lodge. The Elizabethan predilection for polychrome effects was shared by the Victorians.

Elizabethans celebrate the secular bias of the age in their magnificence and continue to assert the consequence of the deceased after death has claimed him. It is only necessary to recall the huge and splendid four-poster monument to Fulke Greville at Warwick or the arresting composition at Braybrooke, Northamptonshire, commemorating the Griffin family, to realize how large wordly importance loomed in the very face of the grave. But at least one sixteenth-century builder called attention to our mortal state and impressed upon all who set eyes on his work the fervour of his belief. Sir Thomas Tresham, like Byrd, whose music so affectingly echoes the disquieting undercurrent to all the extravert activities of the age, was an adherent of the old faith. He had been brought up as a Protestant and was knighted by the Queen in 1575, but was converted to Catholicism by Campion. Like many converts, he was fanatical in his zeal and he combined this ardour with a pronounced Elizabethan characteristic, the love of the device. The house he built to replace a property of his ancestors at Lyveden, Northamptonshire, was planned as a religious conceit to a design for which Sir Thomas must have been responsible, although it was worked out by Robert Stickells, Clerk of the Works at Richmond. New Build, as it was called, was never finished and stands, an empty frame without glass or roof, at the end of a lane amid the mournful remains of a terraced garden which once announced its maker's piety as vehemently as the house. This latter takes the form of a Greek cross with three

115

rooms, symbolic of the Trinity, on each of the three floors, a basement and two upper storeys. Each limb of the cross ends in a two-storeyed bay, one of which contains the entrance. Emblems of the Passion and the Sacred Monogram adorn a metope frieze above the first floor, the basement is adorned with shields which were to have borne sacred imagery, and on the surviving portions of the frieze crowning the upper floor, fragments of inscriptions can be made out which once ran all round the house: 'JESUS MUNDI SALUS – GAUDE MATER VIRGO MARIA'.

Before embarking on New Build, Sir Thomas Tresham had erected another and more emphatic monument to his faith, the famous Triangular Lodge at his Rushton home. The lodge is a miniature and perfect product of Elizabethan Baroque, horizontally banded with ironstone and with the lines of frieze and stringcourse and yet shooting upwards with flame-like urgency, and for all that it moves with so darting a rhythm, animated by the same religious frenzy as the sinuous façade of S. Maria Zobenigo in Venice. The plan, elevations and ornament of this exotic little structure are all expressive of the Trinity. It is three storeys high and shaped like an equilateral triangle, and each of its three walls is pierced by three windows on each floor, the windows taking the form of trefoils, triangles and crosses. Three crocketted gables, crowned with triangular-topped obelisks, surmount each wall above a frieze containing an inscription of thirty-three letters on each façade: '*Aperiatur terra germinet salvatorum*'; '*Quis separabit nos a charitate Christi*'; and '*Consideravi opera tua domine et expavi*'. The gables are decorated with central panels carved with holy emblems, including the Chalice, the seven eyes of God, the seven-branched candlestick and the Pelican, and with dates and further inscriptions. The dates are 1580, the year of Sir Thomas's conversion, 1626 and 1641, which fell after his death, and two utterly mysterious far future dates, 3509 and 3898, which must be prophetic. The tall triangular chimney-shaft is pierced by smoke holes arranged in threes and is adorned with the Sacred Monogram, the Lamb and Cross and the Chalice. The principal rooms within are hexagonal with smaller triangular rooms in two of the corners of the building and a newel staircase in the third. Visually Sir Thomas Tresham's lodge is as much a picturesque folly and as little concerned with function and utility as that at Rendlesham (p. 257), but whereas the Gothic Revival lodge was conceived as no more than a romantic landscape garden ornament, that at Rushton, however spectacular, was an intensely felt, a subtle and considered symbol erected to the glory of God.

The Elizabethan houses so far discussed stand apart from the vernacular and more modest dwellings of the period in the extraordinary brilliance and originality of their composition, but the unmistakable stamp of the age distinguishes these lesser buildings too. They also were usually designed with an eye to display, and in many a town and village all over the country it is the surviving houses of this period which most rivet attention and linger in the memory. Morley Old Hall, Norfolk, red brick, moated and with arrogant stepped gables and a huge chimneybreast, dominates its surroundings; Bourne Mill, Colchester (p. 160), positively startles the passer-by at a first encounter; the village of Somersal Herbert, in every other respect insignificant, can never be forgotten by those who have glimpsed the amazingly patterned façade of its hall. The whole bewitching impact of Long Melford is decided by the way in which the elongated pepper-pot domes and shell-shaped battlements of the hall turrets shimmer above the wide expanse of the village green. An awareness of tradition and the past, a lively appreciation of design and power of invention, stimulated by a superficial acquaintance with foreign motifs and sustained by a thorough knowledge of native crafts, governed the character of these houses as well as of the great masterpieces of the age. Not unexpectedly, at a time when imaginations were stirred by the historical past, the builders of these houses followed established practices, and as the following chapter will show, made the most of the variety afforded by environment and available materials. Old-fashioned features and forms were often retained, as they were in the houses of the great, in response to the romantic attitude to the Middle Ages. Thus North Lees Hall Farm, Hathersage, was built as a tower house, admirably suited to its position, high above the village on the edge of savage moorland, approached by a steep, stony track. The general shape of the house is much like that of Little Wenham Hall (p. 34), for it consists of a tall, three-storeyed rectangular block, almost like a tower itself, consisting of three large rooms, with the actual tower containing the projecting staircase turret and four storeys rising only a little above it. The whole building is crenellated with semicircular, niched battlements. It is not only visually romantic, but romantic in its associations. It was known to Charlotte

North Lees Hall, Hathersage, Derbyshire

The theatrical and chivalric architecture of the Bolsover Keep and of East Lulworth Castle consciously refer to medieval castle design, but North Lees, a much smaller and more modest building, is more directly related to the medieval tower house and the vertical domestic design. The romantic character of the conception is revealed immediately by the large windows and decorative battlements. The remains of plasterwork in the large ground-floor room above the storage basement bear the date 1596.

Brontë, who often stayed at Hathersage with her friend Miss Nussey, and it seems likely that it played a considerable part in the creation of *Jane Eyre*. It may well have been the origin of Thornfield Hall, despite the fact that the name Thornfield was probably suggested by that of a neighbouring estate called Thornhill. The view from the leads, reached by a door in the staircase turret, is remarkably like that seen by Jane from the leads of Thornfield Hall. Furthermore, the property belonged until after the Second World War to the Eyre family, who built the house, and during the seventeenth century a woman, said to have been insane, was kept in the first-floor room of the tower and lost her life in a fire.

Another house connected with Charlotte Brontë, Oakwell Hall, Birstall, the original of Fieldhead in *Shirley*, follows the plan of the traditional hall house with cross-wings, but although it is conceived as a unified composition with continuous eaves, it is not two-storeyed throughout but contains a hall open to the roof. The arrangement differs from that of the medieval house only in so far as the screens passage, instead of shutting off the kitchen and offices, divides the hall from the parlour and solar, while a gallery runs all round the hall to give access to the upper chambers – which would otherwise be cut off from each other – and to obviate the need for more than one staircase.

At Snitterton Hall, Derbyshire, the basic plan of the central hall with cross-wings is combined with modest classical details. The builder stressed the link with the past by crenellating the façade between the wings and preserving the asymmetrical position of the entrance. These medieval features are associated with ball-topped finials on the broad gable-ends and a picturesque doorway flanked by tapering columns set on high bases and crowned with Ionic capitals, the volutes of which are almost tangential, and a frieze carved with naturalistic floral motifs. The wide, rather low windows accentuate the horizontal lines of the house, and at the same time, with their mullions and lattices, they evoke an atmosphere which is neither classic nor Gothic, but movingly individual and poetic.

An even freer juxtaposition of disparate motifs is resolved in a yet more personal and more fantastic harmony in the humble Dorset manor of Hammoon. Here a roof of velvety reed-thatch is combined with bow windows filled with the arched lights of the early Tudor period and a porch defying classification, the whole steeped in a delicious magic like that which translated the prosaic weaver in *A Midsummer Night's Dream*. The round, Renaissance arch is set between swelling, banded columns on high bases like those on either side of the keep windows at Bolsover. In the spandrels are garlands of spiky leaves. The little room over the porch is lit by three arched latticed lights in a square frame, to match the centre part of the bays, and the dripstone above it ends in an Ionic volute. The scrolled and semicircular gable was once adorned on both sides by a heraldic beast and an obelisk, but only one obelisk remains.

Another equally romantic and satisfying union of the vernacular style and foreign details can be seen at Fleming's Hall, Bedingfield, a house built for a branch of the Bedingfield family of Oxburgh Hall (p. 43). This is a long rectangular building, typical of the final stage in the evolution of the hall house and different only in the perfection and greater elaboration of its detail from the hundreds of Elizabethan and seventeenth-century houses of the same shape to be seen in many parts of the country, more especially in East Anglia. Fleming's Hall does not hark back to the past in its actual style, yet it is consciously picturesque. It is moated and richly coloured, for while the ground floor, the striking porch and the tall, conspicuous polygonal chimneys in their clusters of four are of red brick, the upper floor shows the vertical stripes of half-timber. Classical pediments surmount the four-centred entrance arch and the mullioned windows, and obelisk-like finials flank and crown the stepped gable of the porch and rise from the curly end-gables.

None of these four houses is exactly symmetrical, but there are numbers of

Long Melford Hall, Suffolk

Long Melford, a house of soft red brick, seen here on a snowy February day, shows little of the drama and none of the more startling innovations of the daring compositions reproduced on some of the previous pages. But the design boasts some unexpected features and is already informed with the sense of movement which became so striking a characteristic of houses built during the last quarter of the century. Long Melford was built at the beginning of Queen Elizabeth's reign for Sir William Cordell, lawyer, Solicitor-General, Speaker of the House of Commons and later Master of the Rolls. The wings project to embrace a courtyard and the composition combines a classical porch with tall chimney-shafts and pepper-pot domes, two of them crowning turrets placed excitingly against the inner sides of the courtyard wings, giving a twist like the final steps in a pavan to the gentle recessions and projections of the design.

The Hall, Somersal Herbert,
Derbyshire
Fleming's Hall, Bedingfield, Suffolk

These two houses, and the two on the
opposite page, give some idea of the
picturesque individuality of the
smaller Elizabethan manor. At
Somersal Herbert (left) the arresting
pattern of the half-timber work is
informed by a conscious striving for
dramatic effect. At Fleming's Hall
widely disparate features, stepped and
curving gables, obelisk finials, classical pediments, brick and timber have
been synthesized in a deeply satisfying
harmony. The present house, on the
site of an earlier building, dates from
c. 1586. The incorporation of the
ornate chimney-stack in the gable-end
is an unusually progressive feature.

Hammoon Manor, Dorset
Benthall Hall, Shropshire

It is the porch of Hammoon Manor
(right), named after William de
Moion, who 'brought 47 knights to
the battle of hastings', which gives
this traditional thatched house its
romantic distinction. The fabric of the
wall shows that this porch replaced an
earlier gabled structure. The juxtaposition of round-arched, leaded
lights and a classical opening with
ringed baroque columns like those
of Rubens's house at Antwerp could
occur in no other country.
Benthall Hall, c. 1583, is a rustic but
forceful version of the favourite
Elizabethan theme of alternating
gables and projecting bays (see also
pages 118, 123–4).

Elizabethan houses deriving from the hall-house plan in which the design is as balanced as that of Montacute or Fountains. Some of these follow the E-shape which had already appeared at Barrington Court, and the only fundamental difference between such houses and Snitterton or Oakwell Hall is that the entrance is centrally placed. Long Melford Hall is a noble example of this plan, where the wings project to embrace a courtyard and the design combines a classical porch with superimposed Doric and Ionic columns and a semicircular shell top, a pedimented upper window and turrets unexpectedly placed against the inner sides of the wings. Another favourite Elizabethan plan stems from the compact rectangular house, heightened and animated by rows of gables and groups of aspiring chimney-shafts and sometimes furnished, like the grander houses already described, with jutting bays to impart an advancing and receding movement to the façades. A sensational example of this arrangement electrifies the landscape at Amesbury, Wiltshire, where the upward surge of the immensely tall Lake House culminates in three groups of chimneys and five ball-topped gables, while three castellated square bays carry the design forward. A subtle touch is added to the whole composition by the placing of the chimneys. Two of the groups are parallel and the third is placed at right-angles to them, and it is this change in direction which sets the whole symmetrical arrangement in motion. A sparkling accompaniment to the principal stately theme is provided by the compelling chequerwork of flint and stone which decorates the entire building. This house, like Barlborough and The Hall, Bradford-on-Avon, is set up on a podium, forming a semi-basement in which the offices are placed.

A variation on the combination of gable and bay, yielding a more involved movement, occurs at Moyns Park, Essex, where four gables alternate with three bays. The sense of height gains impetus from the narrowness of the gables on either side of the central bay, and from the slenderness of the extremely tall chimney-shafts grouped in threes immediately behind three of the gables. In the sixteenth century there were four of these groups, but one has unfortunately been replaced by a low modern stack, thus breaking the dignified rhythm of this noble house. This rhythm is skilfully elaborated by minor themes which only gradually announce themselves. The three fat bays are polygonal and so are the attenuated chimney-shafts, and the parallel in shape draws the eye diagonally along the slopes of the gables from one to the other; the lower storey of the centre bay is occupied by a square porch with a square-headed door, providing a welcome break in the regularity of the articulation; and the enormous windows of the bays, so large that these projecting structures are nearly all glass, contrast with the exceptionally short, broad openings and big areas of blank wall on the first floor. Like Lake House, Moyns Park is rich in texture and colour, prominent stone dressings of chalky pallor outlining the main features of the design against fiery brick.

Gables and bays again govern the composition of Benthall Hall, Shropshire. The design is based on that of the hall house with one cross-wing and an asymmetrically placed entrance. But from this unlikely material the builder has created a rough rhythm and a shifting movement, which, loosely controlled and unsophisticated though they seem beside the subtle articulation of Moyns Park, yet make an impact of astounding vigour. The gable of the wing, cut short on its inner side by a square, flat-roofed corner turret, is matched by one of the same breadth and again with a longer outer than inner side, where it joins a high parapet at the end of the main block. The similarity in shape underlines the forward movement of the wing. Between these two gables, three others, steep and narrow, quicken the vertical tendency of the house. A big polygonal bay, placed neither in between nor exactly beneath the first and second of these gables, corresponds to another bay set half under and half to the right of the broad end-gable. The contrastingly square two-storeyed entrance projection, a squat version of the angle turret, rises close to the outer bay. The effect of the arrangement is that the two bays and the entrance seem to be not only advancing but sliding to the right, while a counter-motion is set up by the gables and wing, and the whole design is stabilized by an external chimney-stack at either end of the house supporting coupled brick shafts with flamboyantly moulded tops, dark red shapes soaring above stone warmed by tints of brown and pink.

The picturesque irregularity of Benthall Hall, as consciously sought as that of Compton Wynyates (p. 84) and more ingeniously contrived, is more commonly characteristic of Elizabethan half-timbered houses than those of brick or stone. Their frequently voiced concern over the diminuation of woodland occasioned by the heavy demands of the time for timber for domestic purposes, ship building and industry perhaps heightened the sensibility of the Elizabethans towards that most traditional of all forms of building, for some of their most exuberantly eccentric conceits are carried out in this medium. Parsonage Farm, Stebbing, stands three storeys high and is for much of its length only one room thick, lit by large glinting lattices, like a gigantic airy cage, to which the gentle over-sailing of the first floor imparts a slight but perceptible swaying motion. The vertical accents of the studding are abruptly checked by the horizontal lines of the bressumer, the eaves and the straight-headed attic, which is so broad that it embraces the three big main windows of the third floor. But this unsteady balance between vertical and horizontal yields on the narrow west front of the house to an impetuous upward movement. Here the ground falls steeply away, exaggerating the drama of a white-plastered, cliff-like, sharply gabled wall bisected by a long-necked, shouldered chimney-stack. Irregular gables along the rear of the house reinforce the insistent verticals of the composition.

A different mood, secret and withdrawn despite the dazzling richness of its timber patterning, informs Somersal Hall, Derbyshire. Like Benthall Hall, this building is a modified form of the hall house with one wing. The inventiveness of Elizabethan craftsmen could hardly be more vividly demonstrated than by the contrast between these two houses. The entrance of Somersal Hall is centrally placed, but the eye discounts this fact in a design which is apparently devoid of symmetry. This façade nevertheless moves to a rhythm which gradually makes itself felt. It is dominated by four gables of varying height. To the left, slightly projecting, is the broad, low gable of the wing. Next comes the taller, narrower gable of the entrance bay, and to the right of that, small twin gables, overhanging the rest of the house, rise above the roof-line. These twin gables are together of the same breadth as that of the wing, and they are decorated with the same ornament of quatrefoils in small square panels. This not only strikes a balance with the centrally placed door, but calls attention to the forward movement of both structures. The middle gable is distinguished by wavy diagonals. Very closely set vertical struts, banded by widely set horizontal timbers, stripe the wall beneath the two attics, giving a recessive effect. All this woodwork is poetically ashen in hue, while the roof and the tall chimney-stacks are of softest red. Unlike those of most Elizabethan houses, the windows of Somersal Hall are exceptionally small and oddly placed. The patterned front arrests the eye, as its designer intended it should; but it is a screen behind which the house remains mysterious and inward looking.

The timber work of the famous Little Moreton Hall is of the same character, but aggressively black and complicated against white plaster, creating a totally dissimilar effect. The entire structure is covered by the patterning of quatrefoils, trefoil-headed arcading, stripes, cusped lozenges and diagonals, most of it shaped in wood but some of it painted on the plaster. The windows of the bays are furnished with wavy external pelmets of wood painted black, outlined in white and inscribed in glittering white lettering with the name of the owner, William Moreton, and that of the carpenter, 'Richarde Dale', and the date, 1559. The Elizabethans seem to have been greatly taken with the Arabic numerals and Roman lettering which they had substituted for Gothic lettering and Roman

numerals, and from the middle of the sixteenth century onwards they lost no opportunity of exhibiting the year when they had founded or enlarged a house on the façade or perhaps on a gable-end. These windows at Little Moreton Hall belong to the grotesque, hexagonal bays of the hall which William Moreton added to his grandfather's house. Each of the bays is crowned with three steep gables and the upper storey of each oversails so that the top-heavy structures jostle one another and crowd the tiny courtyard. Not only is every inch of the timber-work embellished, but the leaded lights are of the most intricate geometric floral design. These and the windows of the gatehouse, where the glazing varies with nearly every opening, are the most remarkable of the many varieties of quarry shapes to be found in Elizabethan windows. Born of a similar enthusiasm for linear arabesques as the fanlight patterns of Georgian houses, they show even greater fertility of invention. By 1589 there were fifteen glass-works in England, and a book published in 1615 entitled *A Book of Sundry Draughtes, Principally serving for Glasiers* contains over one hundred designs for lead glazing.

William Moreton's ambitions were not satisfied when he had added these preposterous bays to his house: he intensified the already bizarre character of his long gatehouse by increasing its height by another storey, the side-walls of which consisted entirely of leaded lights. This storey is occupied by a single apartment, the Long Gallery, a peculiarly English and peculiarly Elizabethan feature. The room at Little Moreton Hall is narrow and homely with a Gothic collar-beam roof and decorative windbraces. The gable-ends are plastered and ornamented with coloured reliefs of naturalistic foliage and figures of a faintly classical air, associated with sententious mottoes. A woman in the dress of a Botticelli angel holds aloft a spear, while two lettered panels announce 'The Speare of Destinye whose Ruler is Knowledge'.

Long galleries are in general found only in the larger houses of the period, and apart from their length they vary considerably. The formal apartment at Chastleton, for instance, with its rich plaster barrel-vault and silvery panelling, is quite different from the timbered room at Little Moreton Hall, and neither of these rooms has anything in common with the sophisticated and amusing composition at Knole where, beneath a lozenge-patterned ceiling, the wall opposite the unusually small windows is closely hung with oval ancestral portraits all in identical frames. But the most spendid and atmospheric of surviving long galleries must be that at Hardwick, running along the entire east front of the second floor. Immensely high and lit on the garden side by lofty windows that almost fill three great bays and the wall between them, and made lighter still by

Windows, Little Moreton Hall, Cheshire

The photograph, like that on the opposite page, shows the elaborate quarry shapes with which the Elizabethans liked to fill their large windows, and which here compete for attention with the ornate black and white stripes and quatrefoils of timber and painted plaster of the bays themselves. These are the overhanging upper halves of windows added to the house by William Moreton in 1559. The inscriptions read: 'GOD IS AL IN AL THING THIS WINDOVS WHIRE MADE BY WILLIAM MORETON IN THE YEARE OF OURE LORDE MDLIX'; and, in the panel over the ground-floor bay: 'RYCHARDE DALE CARPEDER MADE THIES WINDOVS BY THE GRAC OF GOD.'

its plaster ceiling, this proud room is hung with the portraits of so many familiar figures of the age, including Bess of Hardwick herself, stern-featured and bright-eyed, three of her husbands and, confronting the visitor at the far distant end of the gallery, Queen Elizabeth I standing full length in a jewelled and embroidered pink dress against a darker pink background, that it retains more than a whisper of the departed. Their speech, broader, coarser and more vital than ours, lingers on the air, their vibrant energy is reflected in the crystal light falling in huge quivering rectangles across the rush matting and pulses in the shadows. The room was so designed to show off the thirteen Brussels tapestries illustrating the story of Gideon woven for Sir Christopher Hatton in 1578 and bought from his heir by Bess for £326. She then proceeded to cover the Hatton arms in the borders with cloth painted with her own device and to add antlers to the Hatton does to turn them into Cavendish stags. These tapestries are still the principal ornament of the apartment, although the compositions of blue and umber are partly hidden by the portraits hung on top of them. The effect, like that of Elizabethan dress and jewellery, is of extravagant richness.

Various suggestions have been put forward to explain the purpose of the Elizabethan long gallery. It is assumed that it was a necessary convenience in an age when a display of hospitality was required from all who wished to be of importance and when the Queen herself was in the habit of descending on her subjects with an enormous retinue. Two of the most fabulous palaces of the period, Holdenby and Theobald's, were built expressly by Hatton and Burghley as important feature, which is so eloquent of the romantic and spectacular character of Hardwick, was not part of the Elizabethan house, but was perhaps designed by the 6th Duke of Devonshire in the first half of the nineteenth century. But, as Dr Girouard points out, the staircase is mentioned as a striking curiosity of the house in the Torrington Diaries in a passage recording a visit to Hardwick in 1789.

residences for the Queen's entertainment. The Long Gallery is supposed also to have provided space for exercise on a rainy day and to have been used for music-making in an age of exceptional talent in this art. The room is usually furnished with two or more fireplaces, which suggest sedentary pursuits such as embroidery rather than games. It could certainly have been put to all these purposes, but these vast romantic rooms may have come into existence quite simply as a result of the designer's pleasure in varying the shapes and sizes of apartments to suit his creative impulse rather than to serve a practical end.

In addition to the long gallery, the feature which most attracts attention in the Elizabethan house is the staircase. The staircase had already gained in importance with the establishment of the two-storey plan. It now became a conspicuously ornamental structure. Even in a comparatively modest house like Parsonage

Farm, Stebbing, the imposing staircase draws the eye, leading up in short flights
to the upper floors from the one-storeyed hall which has already begun to assume
the function of the modern entrance hall. Here the solid timber steps of the
Middle Ages, still to be seen at Crows Hall, Suffolk (although this staircase,
ascending in flights at right-angles to each other and furnished with balusters,
cannot be much earlier than the late sixteenth century), have been replaced by
separate trends and risers constructed of boards. Carved newel-posts and moulded
handrails sometimes impart a monumental character to the staircases of relatively
small manor houses, such as Warren's Farm, Great Easton, where the newels are
surmounted by tall moulded vase-shaped finials and the balusters take the form
of Ionic pilasters. In larger houses, like Burton Agnes, the staircase could develop
into a composition of overwhelming intricacy. Here there are no less than eight
newels, joined in pairs by arches, every inch of the surface of which is covered
with carving. The staircase at Hardwick, on the other hand, is strikingly plain

Staircase, Crows Hall, Debenham, Suffolk

This simple staircase ascends in the same angular manner, in short, straight flights, as the grand example on the opposite page, but it represents a less developed stage in the evolution of the feature, for the steep steps are constructed of solid timbers instead of with separate treads and risers. The turned balusters were a seventeenth-century addition.

and yet unsurpassed for dignity, daring and romantic beauty by the most spectacular architectural staircases of Baroque Europe. It is of stone and very shallow, and climbs slowly through half the length of the great house, yielding mysterious vistas and recalling the night stair at Hexham.

The importance of the fireplace in the sixteenth century was pointed out in the previous chapter. In houses of more than minor consequence, Elizabethan chimney-piece designs show the same intriguing and imaginative fusion of motifs and moods as the houses they furnish. The overmantel, which had made a tentative appearance in the fireplace of the Abbot's Lodging at Mulchelney (p. 55), now played an essential part in the composition. The stone fireplace in the Elizabethan room beneath the chapel at Woodlands Manor is a superb interpretation of classical forms mingled with traditional details. The large rectangular opening is framed by egg and dart moulding and by Ionic columns rising from bases decorated with huge acanthus leaves to carry foliated urns. From two large brackets Corinthian columns, minutely carved with acanthus leaves, spring to support an entablature with a frieze of roses and to enclose a rich coat of arms surrounded by oak leaves. Big volutes flank the heraldic device and a volute motif combined with ears of corn runs along the lintel.

Magnificent architectural compositions form the fireplaces in the Long Gallery at Hardwick, and Dr Girouard has called attention to their affinities with chimney-piece designs in the seventh book of Serlio's *Architecture,* though it is the individual interpretation of the theme and the marriage of diverse motifs which gives these fireplaces their distinction. Square, fluted, banded and coupled pilasters of alabaster support overmantels set between pairs of smooth, black stone columns

and containing taut strapwork, immensely bold and Baroque, curiously adorned with little balls and forming the agitated background to oval medallions carved with figures of Justice and Misericord. At Hardwick, too, is one of the most poetic and inventive of overmantels, the unique alabaster relief of Apollo and the Muses in the State Bedroom by Thomas Accres. Almost as fine a composition, and one better suited to its purpose, is the alabaster panel of the Marriage of Tobit in the Blue Room, the classically draped figures set in front of architectural niches below a frieze combining modillions and fancy battlements, the whole supported by lionhead brackets and flanked, like the simple opening, by flat pilasters of banded alabaster and black stone. The fireplaces at Bolsover are as

The Elizabethan Room, Woodlands Manor, Mere, Wiltshire

The room is below the former chapel and the magnificent chimney-piece and plaster ceiling date from c. 1570. The conversion of this apartment and the chapel was the work of Christopher Doddington, descendant of the Thomas Doddington who built the manor house at the end of the fourteenth century.

130

The hall chimney-piece,
Burton Agnes, Yorkshire

This amazing late Elizabethan
composition, adorned in Baroque
profusion with plaster reliefs illustrating the parable of the Wise and
Foolish Virgins, shows, like the more
modest fireplace opposite, the
powerful development of the overmantel in Elizabethan fireplaces. The
broken pediment (a motif introduced
into this country through foreign
architectural source books), with the
lavish cartouche bursting through it,
accentuates the upward movement of
the design. Although it harmonizes
so well with the plaster reliefs above
the hall screen, this chimney-piece
was not made for Burton Agnes, but
was moved from Barmston Hall in
the mid eighteenth century.

remarkable and as picturesque as the whole extraordinary building. They are
like big sepulchral monuments projecting into the tiny rooms of the keep,
square or octagonal in shape with huge sloping hoods recalling the hooded
fireplaces of Norman castles. Made of local stone, they are studded with shiny,
fossil-patterned roundels and lozenges of Derbyshire marble and unite Gothic
ogee forms with classical scroll work and classical enrichments in a brilliantly
successful and strange synthesis.

The overmantels of Elizabethan fireplaces were frequently decorated with
plaster compositions, and although the plasterer's art underwent exquisite
refinements later on (pp. 238-9), it reached a pinnacle of freshness and vigour in
this first great period of secular creation which it never again equalled. Not only
the overmantel, but the newly introduced plaster ceiling, which was everywhere
taking the place of the ecclesiastical-style, open roof, offered wonderful scope
for the decorator, particularly as ornamental motifs could be repeated in plaster

without the labour which deadened the effect of a similar exercise in stone. The technique of casting repeating detail and of modelling individual figures and devices was brought to England by Italians engaged by Henry VIII to work on his palace of Nonsuch; but by the time of Elizabeth I, Italian influence had vanished in this as in other fields, and the names of plasterers of that period in the list compiled by the late Margaret Jourdain are all English.

So much of this work still exists, that the output during the last half of the sixteenth and the first quarter of the seventeenth centuries must have been

The Library, Langleys,
Little Waltham, Essex

Ceiling of the old dining-room, Langleys, Little Waltham, Essex

These fantastic ceilings are the most exuberant examples in the country of the broad flat bands of strapwork which replaced the finer ribbed designs of Elizabethan plasterwork after the beginning of the seventeenth century.

prodigious. The vitality and variety of it all could only be conveyed in a large volume dedicated to the subject. Something of its range can perhaps be gauged when it is realized that the wholly surprising frieze at Montacute, illustrating the story of a hen-pecked husband, and the overmantel at Court House, East Quantoxhead, where scenes from the life of Christ are placed between Red Indian caryatids, were exactly contemporary with the flowing, interlacing, all-over pattern of the long gallery ceiling at Chastleton, where ribbons of plaster adorned with charming bead and lozenge shapes loop, twist and burgeon into rosettes and fleurs-de-lis. Quite another impression is made by the crowded and unforgettable figure compositions at Burton Agnes. There the screen, traditionally placed but pierced by round-arched openings and adorned with coupled Ionic columns, is surmounted by tier upon tier of plaster reliefs of emblematic and biblical personages, including the four Evangelists, each shown in his appropriate landscape setting, the elements and the virtues. Some of these are based on Flemish engravings, but they are all endowed with such palpitating life in the new medium that the effect of the concentrated imagery is indeed memorable. Strange as is this conceit, it is surpassed by that of the amazing plaster overmantel of the hall fireplace, which looks like one of the wilder Baroque altarpieces. A relief representing the wise and foolish virgins is crammed with agitated figures of disturbingly disparate proportions, architecture, a writhing tree, an angel with a scroll relegating the wise virgins to the abodes of bliss and the foolish ones to the realms of woe, and grotesque corbel birds. Above this confused imagery three

133

This flowing design, with its wide, decorated, ribbon-like bands of plaster enclosing flower sprays, represents a type of ceiling which followed the more severely geometrical, ribbed arrangements seen in the hall of the same house (page 97) and at Woodlands Manor (page 130), and preceded the overwhelmingly rich strapwork style of the Langleys ceilings (pages 132 and 133). The main pattern of this ceiling, as at Langleys, was cast in plaster of Paris (sulphate of lime) from reverse moulds, while the sprays were modelled by hand.

panels, flanked by half-length armless caryatids, display heraldic devices, foliage, and cherub heads and soar up to a broken pediment filled with a large coat of arms.

This by no means completes the account of the exceptional plasterwork at Burton Agnes. The ceiling of the Oak Room is embellished with a scrolled and energetically modelled growth of honeysuckle, as peculiarly English as the pale coloured frieze by Abraham Smith in the High Great Chamber at Hardwick (p. 15), where forest and hunting scenes and representations of Diana presiding over her court and Orpheus working his magic determine the haunting and elegaic mood of this lofty and poignantly beautiful room. The ceiling of the long gallery at Hardwick, moulded by John Master, shows an exceptionally restrained, bold and rhythmic geometric design, a strong contrast to that at Chastleton and to most of the complicated patterns of the period. That in the Great Chamber at Gilling Castle, Yorkshire, crushes the room with as formidable an array of chalky white fans and pendants as those at Arbury or Castle Ward (pp. 244–5). The Elizabethan ceiling might display medallions of classical heroes, lozenge-shaped panels, semicircles and squares with leaves sprouting vigorously from their intersections as at Craigievar Castle, or thin-ribboned, square panels in deep relief with tangent circles breaking into them as in the room, of which the fireplace has just been described, made out of the former kitchen at Woodlands Manor, Mere, in about 1570, when the chapel above it was turned into a living-room (a significant sign of the times). Both circles and squares enclose bugles and acorns, elements from the armorial of the Doddingtons who came to Woodlands Manor in *c.* 1380 and remained in possession for more than three centuries. This geometric pattern is offset by a freely designed plaster frieze of a vine.

Another form of geometric patterning occurs at The Parsonage, Heytesbury, where bands of plaster form large rectilinear and curving shapes about rosettes and floral motifs and are themselves embellished with vines, while elaborately wrought pendants add another dimension, life and movement, to a rather flat composition. A dramatic development in this type of decoration with flat ornamental bands can be seen in the library and the old dining-room at Langleys, Little Waltham. The low waggon vault of the library exhibits bands of plaster so broad and so richly adorned with trailing foliage that they would seem oppressive were it not for the sweep and exuberance of the strapwork patterns they make. Scrolls and cartouches fill all the intervening spaces and set up a counter-rhythm to the emphatic measure of the strapwork curves and angularities. The movement is continued by the swirling draperies and undulating scrolls of the extraordinary overmantel in this ornate room, where a favourite symbolical theme of early seventeenth-century plasterers, the five Senses, is rendered with admirable spirit. The Senses take the form of women: Hearing with a guitar attended by a stag, Smelling clasping flowers and accompanied by a dog, Taste holding a basket of fruit with a monkey near by, Seeing gazing into a mirror with an eagle at her side and Touching holding a bird. These women are grouped about a cartouche adorned with a winged head and a skull, containing two *amorini* who are carefully extracting Jonah from the side of the whale; and the whole quivering composition is flanked by a staring, high-bosomed creature and a bearded divinity, whose arms terminate in Ionic volutes.

The character of this room, its splendour, animation, drama, symbolism and fusion of diverging themes and forms, sums up the substance of this chapter. Plaster was a particularly congenial medium to southern Baroque artists and there is a clear affinity between this Essex work and that of the stuccoists of the Counter-Reformation which overrides all differences of form and nationality. But the affinity was only a coincidence, and though a few architects continued to work in the Elizbethan spirit – preserving the power to synthesize and the feeling for movement and drama – increasing knowledge of the classical rules of order and proportion and the influence of Inigo Jones eventually destroyed the balance of the horizontal and vertical modes which appears to have been peculiarly in tune with the English temperament. It was never fully restored, and however enchantingly the belated classical Renaissance was at first transformed by native craftsmanship and imagination, it remained an alien discipline.

7

The Development of Regional Styles

The importance of regional materials in the construction of domestic architecture has become apparent in the preceding pages. With very few exceptions, among them Ashbury Manor, built partly of stone brought from Somerset and partly of the local, primitive-looking coral ragstone, all the houses which have been so far discussed are closely related to the soil on which they stand. Little Chesterford Manor incorporates the clunch and flint of the Essex-Cambridgeshire border; sandstones from two local quarries are the source of the contrast between the impressive greenish roof and the weathered red, pink, lilac and tawny walls of the Prior's Lodge, Much Wenlock, while Hardwick Hall displays sandstone of a very different aspect, the coarse, dusky-brown material of the Matlock quarries. Northborough Hall, Northamptonshire, is already finely expressive of the close-grained limestone which is most characteristic of the Cotswolds, but which runs down erratically into parts of Dorset, Somerset and Wiltshire and extends to Northamptonshire and Lincolnshire. Yet some of the most distinctive features of these houses, listed quite at random, only made their appearance with alterations carried out long after they were first built. The roof of Little Chesterford Manor, for instance, which so delightfully displays the variations in the composition of the clay of this district in its tweed-like mixture of yellow-brown, pink and muted red tiles, cannot be earlier in date than the sixteenth-century reconstruction of the building when the chimney-stack was inserted. It was indeed during this century, and the one which followed it, that vernacular building was most conspicuously marked by that vivid diversity of styles and texture and that brilliant exploitation of materials which still, after so much destruction, after so many later additions of a standardized, alien character, impress themselves upon the eye and imagination as elements of the changing landscape made into houses.

It is not necessary to cover a wide territory to experience this diversity. In a single county, Derbyshire, for example, carboniferous limestone, as pale as bleached bone, forms the material of the stone walls which everywhere emphasize the contours of the high bare land in the neighbourhood of the great prehistoric monument of Arbor Low. The same material imparts a sparkle to the façade of Old Hall, Youlgreave, and to the dry-laid enclosure of Snitterton Hall. But Snitterton lies on the dividing-line between limestone country and a band of rough sandstone, and the house itself is brownish-pink in colour. In both fabric and design there could be no greater contrast to Snitterton, as well as to Old Hall, Youlgreave, than Somersal Hall (p. 120), in the same county and of approximately the same date, mid sixteenth century. Somersal lies near the Staffordshire border where stone walls have given way to hedges, and rock has become clay. So the house is half-timbered with a tiled roof, the style resembling that of the west midlands, soon to be described, except that the timbers here are not black, but ashen. Such variety was yet another expression of the exuberant spirit of the period, but it was also a response to the growing scarcity of timber, of the steep rise in its price and of the urge to build in a more durable form.

Craigievar Castle, Aberdeenshire

There could be few more striking illustrations of the effect of locality on style than Craigievar. Built in 1610-24, it is a splendid example of the deeply-rooted preference for the tower house in a region where the need for defence had persisted long after the Middle Ages. The corbelled angle turrets which impart such a top-heavy air of fantasy to so many Scottish tower houses originated in the need for flanking features from which small arms could be fired. The fashion for conical roofs was introduced from France as a result of the close connection between the two countries. At the same time, Craigievar shows the pepper-pot domes which feature so conspicuously in English Elizabethan and Jacobean architecture. Scottish tower houses were traditionally coated with 'harl' or roughcast, both to protect the masonry and to give unity to the composition. At Craigievar the roughcast is made from local granite chips, so that the colour of this picturesque house is clearest pink.

The three materials which in the Middle Ages had been almost everywhere employed – the unbaked earths, timber and thatch – were now largely relegated to districts where there were no other resources to hand and where they thus acquired a regional significance which had not previously been associated with them. In the same way certain domestic plans, that of the long house in particular, which had formerly been common in many parts of Britain, were now retained only in areas remote from the centres of new development and so came to be regarded as peculiar to them alone. Long houses still exist in the south, particularly in Devonshire, but they are considered to belong especially to the Scottish Highlands, to Wales, Ireland and the Lake District, where the low, continuous roof-line of house and cattle-stall perfectly counterbalances the irregular, abruptly rising and falling contours of a mountainous setting. The Lake District is also remarkable for the long retention and distinctive development of the screens of the medieval hall. In numerous farm houses and cottages of this region, dating mostly from the early seventeenth century, the two principal ground-floor rooms are divided by a wooden partition, taking the form of highly polished, carved and fitted cupboards with a central door. The same part of the country also shows a conspicuously local characteristic owing to the type of work in which the women of cottage and farm house were once widely engaged: the 'spinning gallery', used not for spinning, but for drying wool. It runs the whole length of the house at second-floor level, supported on stout posts, and though such galleries are now becoming rare, they were still so common in the last century that De Quincey thought them the most striking peculiarity of the architectural style of west Lancashire, Cumberland and Westmorland.

Sometimes a local style became established through the chance impact of foreign influence. Thus Dutch fashions in brick building which affected the east and south-east coasts and penetrated into the east midlands were responsible for the curved gables so often encountered in East Anglia (p. 164). It is, too, in places which were engaged in trade with the Low Countries that the oldest pantiles are found, imparting a rhythmic wavy line to the roofs of sober brick, flint or, on the east coast of Scotland, stone houses and a richness of colour ranging from pink to tawny brown and deep red. But these tiles were imported when they made their first appearance and were probably not locally produced before the reign of Queen Anne; and the dark lustrous glaze which in Norfolk villages such as Morston and Blakeney reflects the sky and turns from black to blue was an even later innovation. The development of the fantastic castle style of Scotland, with its startling combination of traditional starkness and strength with corbelled angle turrets, extinguisher roofs and classical details, was a result of the close association of that country with France during the sixteenth and seventeenth centuries and the large numbers of French craftsmen employed. James V was married to Marie of Lorraine and Mary Queen of Scots was brought up entirely in France and encouraged a great influx of French talent into Scotland.

The once ubiquitous unbaked earths – cob, mud or clay or chalk lump – were still employed here and there almost until our own day. In William Pitt's *General View of the Agriculture of the County of Leicester* (1809), mud mixed with road scrapings is considered to make the best walls for cottages. And in a sophisticated period like the last quarter of the eighteenth century the Earl of Dorchester chose 'cob', the west of England word for mud, as the material for his planned village of Milton Abbas (p. 260), and the elegant cottage orné known as the Old Rectory at Winterborne Came is likewise built of cob. But the most striking manifestations of these materials belong to the sixteenth and seventeenth centuries and to districts where neither timber nor stone were easily procured, mainly the west country and East Anglia, especially Cambridgeshire, north Essex and parts of Norfolk. The long, symmetrical, sparsely fenestrated and strangely exciting expanse of the rear of Sawston Hall, Cambridgeshire, is, except for the rubble gables, of chalk lump, which unlike the rammed earth of other regions takes the

Features of the Lake District

The carved, fitted cupboards of highly polished oak forming a screen with a door in the centre and dividing the entrance passage or vestibule from the living-room of a farm house in Matterdale, Cumberland (above), are common in the Lake District and seem to have become an established local fashion in the early seventeenth century. They are usually carved with the date and the original owner's initials, and this example is dated 1631. The traditional name for the partition is the 'heck', and the passage from which it shuts off the living-room is known as the 'hallan'.
The so-called 'spinning gallery' (below), above the stable end of a long house near Coniston, Lancashire, is a rare survival of a feature common from the sixteenth century onwards in houses of the Lake District, where materials for the dalesmen's garments were woven in the home.

form of huge, brick-like blocks. Another remarkable feature of this house proclaiming its locality was shown in an earlier chapter (p. 65) – its screw staircase, dusky and polished with age, each of the steps of which is carved from a solid piece of bog oak from the near-by Fens. Chalk lump with clunch (or chalk stone) for the mullioned windows forms the material of a notable house at Burwell known as Parsonage Farm, while villages such as Blo' Norton, Norfolk, and Barrington, Cambridgeshire, are almost wholly composed of chalk lump, protected by a smooth coat of plaster, taking the shape at Barrington of modest single and paired cottages on the fringe of a large green dominated by a tall, lurching hall house with massive cross-wings and an elaborate chimney-stack. The unusual terrace at Melbourn has already been mentioned (p. 67). The better-known cob villages of the west country, such as Selworthy, Dunsford or Bryant's Puddle, assumed their present aspect largely during the seventeenth century; and Hayes Barton, Devon, the home of Sir Walter Raleigh, is an H-shaped manor house built of the earth on which it stands.

If they were not plastered, these earthen houses were covered with roughcast. There are many examples of whitened roughcast in Cambridgeshire, at Harston, Foxton, Haslingfield and Shepreth, for instance. At Cheadle, Staffordshire, the roughcast on older houses assumes the shape of fish-scale tiles, the rounded ends having been formed with the trowel. This purely local treatment of roughcast has been imitated with an unpleasant mechanical finish on some modern houses in Cheadle. In Scotland, where roughcast is known as 'harling', it became the custom during the late sixteenth and seventeenth centuries to cover the lower stages of tower houses with this protective surface, the plain texture of the harling providing a foil to the elaborate stonework of the corbelling, turrets and dormers.

From what has already been said, it is apparent that the composition of the unbaked earth varied with the character of the soil. In Buckinghamshire white clay known as 'witchit' was dug from a depth of about eighteen inches below the surface of the ground; in heathy districts loam, gravel and sand were mixed with the clay instead of the more usual straw; in Cornwall the clay was bound with tiny fragments of slate; in some chalk areas, three parts of chalk mixed with one of clay were kneaded together with straw and moulded into huge unbaked bricks, like those just mentioned in connection with Sawston Hall. This material is often called 'clunch' in the Cambridgeshire area, though technically clunch is the name for that harder, yet wonderfully tractable form of chalk, the startling whiteness of which gives such a distinctive air to so many East Anglian buildings, among them the Lady Chapel of Ely, the clerestory of Saffron Walden parish church, the great nave of Burwell and the exquisite Saxon chancel arch at Strethall.

Half-timber, like mud, might still occasionally be employed in stone districts for humble purposes in the sixteenth and seventeenth centuries, but it flourished noticeably in the west midlands, East Anglia and south-eastern England where wood was still comparatively abundant and where it was treated with astonishing and unprecedented ingenuity and variety. Owing to the very small number of timber-framed houses of medieval date which still stand, it is not easy to make a detailed comparison of the half-timber style of medieval and later houses. But judging from fifteenth-century examples, it seems clear that regional characteristics were far less in evidence at the time when wood was employed over the whole of the country. Buildings as far apart as the gatehouse of Little Brockhampton, Herefordshire (p. 42), Pattenden Manor, Goudhurst, Kent (p. 72), Porch House, Potterne, Wiltshire, and the De Vere House, Lavenham, Suffolk (p. 74), as well as many half-timber survivals at the backs of Cotswold houses which were given stone fronts in the seventeenth century, show obvious affinities in the proportions and spacing of the timbers. The square panelling associated with the west midlands, because it formed the basis of later developments, is seen not only in fifteenth-century houses at Weobley but also at Burwash and at

Cob at Bryant's Puddle, Dorset

The material of which these cottages and walls are built is literally identical with the soil on which they are standing. Wet mud was mixed with wheat straw, trodden either by oxen, horses, or sometimes by the workmen themselves, turned, trodden again, then forked in layers on to a solid plinth, here a mixture of stone, pebbles and brick. Each layer was left to dry before another was put on, so that it was a lengthy process. When completed, the walls were given a protective covering of plaster or lime-wash. The wall in the foreground of the photograph is without this covering and the composition of the cob with some of the ends of the straw projecting can be clearly seen.

Crowhurst, Sussex; it occurs on the courtyard wall of Southfields, Dedham, Essex, at Sutton Barrington, Nottinghamshire, at Cheam, Surrey, and at Chiddingfold, Kent. The close-set vertical studding, on the other hand, regarded as essentially East Anglian, can be found in medieval houses in widely disparate parts of the country. Kentish instances are numerous and a late fifteenth-century house at Aston sub Edge, the lower part of which was encased in stone in the seventeenth century, shows a range of tall, straight timbers, with the width of the plaster panel roughly equalling that of the timber, which gives no hint of locality.

It was, however, in the late Tudor period that this particular style of half-timber, of which the town of Lavenham is such a superb example, began to evolve the refinements which link it particularly to East Anglia. The contrast between Lavenham and Weobley, Herefordshire, where the 'black-and-white' walls are predominantly grid-patterned, is vivid but less intense, even so, than that between East Anglian houses of the sixteenth century such as Office Farm, Metfield, or the splendid house at Coggeshall known as the Woolpack Inn and a west midland house, such as the one at Clifton on Teme, shown here, or the celebrated Little Moreton Hall. And this contrast became yet more extreme during the second half of the sixteenth century. Unless the walls have been subjected to the stripping process prompted by the base fashion for exposed beams, the framework of these later half-timbered houses, both in East Anglia and in

Plaster and timber framing

The photographs on the left show the same houses at Lavenham, Suffolk, before and (below) after 'restoration'. It was customary in East Anglia by the late sixteenth or seventeenth centuries to give the half-timbered house a coat of plaster to protect the interior from draughts and damp. Growing taste for classical forms also prompted the substitution of smooth plain surfaces – and the horizontal emphasis they encouraged – for the insistent verticality of medieval East Anglian timber-work. The timbers revealed by the stripping process at Lavenham may have been exposed when the houses were erected, but the buildings have entirely lost the stamp of authenticity which marked them before the change was made. The alteration to the doors and windows and the addition of a carved corner-post cannot be justified. The unmasked timbers are furthermore pitted with holes left by the nails which secured the laths of the casing. Office Farm, Metfield, Suffolk (top right), displays the typical façade of the late sixteenth- or seventeenth-century East Anglian rectangular timber-framed house, with smooth unjettied walls, encased in plaster from the outset. The farm house near Clifton-on-Teme (bottom right) shows the wholly different and characteristic treatment of half-timber in the west midlands, where the timbers were arranged in a grid pattern instead of in close-set vertical stripes, and were never originally plaster-covered.

East Anglian pargework

Pargework, or pargetting (a word which once described any form of external plaster sheath, but which is now used only of external ornamental plasterwork), is a peculiarly English craft which developed in the sixteenth and seventeenth centuries, the finest examples of which are found in East Anglia. The lively calligraphic, floral decoration (top left) on the wall of Hubbard's Hall, a farmhouse at Bentley End, Suffolk, was incised in the wet plaster with a sharply pointed stick while the rows of small motifs (lozenge shapes, wavy lines and crosses) below the larger panels were made both with sticks and by pressing wooden moulds into the plaster. The flowing, looped ornament which distinguishes a house at Clare, Suffolk (top right) which is a sensitive renewal of the original seventeenth-century work, was executed with a small trowel together with a mould for the border roundels. The rich encrustation (centre) on the façade of Colneford House, Earls Colne, Essex, dated 1685, and arranged in symmetrical panels was first modelled then applied to the wall by means of wax or wooden moulds. This method was also used to produce the sumptuous almost three-dimensional frieze of cornucopias and flower heads running along the fascia board of a house at Saffron Walden, Essex (bottom). The strapwork border of the panel above it and the dolphin it encloses were created by pressing thin wooden templates into the plaster. The head of the fish was built up with the aid of a trowel and the scumbling was added last of all.

south-eastern England, is totally concealed by plaster or some other form of weatherproofing. These devices against the elements were not only necessary to protect the more widely spaced and less substantial timbers resulting from the scarcity of oak: they testified to a growing preoccupation with domestic comfort which was also reflected in the introduction at this time of glazed windows and, of course, in the increased number of fireplaces in all but the poorest houses. The wattle and daub filling of the framework inevitably shrank away from the wood as the building settled and must always have occasioned draughts and damp, but it was only now that these disadvantages were taken seriously. Not only were new houses of the late sixteenth and seventeenth centuries in East Anglia intended from the first to be plastered all over or protected in some other way, but older houses were very often given a plaster coating, so that the general appearance of villages such as Kersey (where a fifteenth-century hall house with cross-wings, now turned into two dwellings, presents the same plastered front to the street as its sixteenth- and seventeenth-century neighbours), Hartest, Fowlmere, Ickleton or Kettlebaston diverges even more acutely from that of Weobley than the vertical stripes of Lavenham.

The plaster sheath was composed of lime, sand, cow hair and dung, with the occasional addition of chopped straw and stable urine, blended together with a moderate amount of water. The mixture was both tough and thick, and it was in accordance with the spirit of the age that this hardwearing surface should not always be left plain but should be covered with the decoration it so clearly invited. And it is hardly surprising to find that external ornamented plasterwork, known as pargetting or pargework, reached the height of its development only in the seventeenth century, although a gild of pargeters had been formed in London as early as 1501. The art was not entirely confined to East Anglia. G. P. Banckart mentions a richly ornamented house in York, Bishop King's Palace, Oxford, is covered with incised geometrical designs and sporadic instances occur in isolated panels of Shropshire and Herefordshire houses. A sun head and a spray of thistles and oak leaves, for instance, adorn one of the gables of The Ley, Weobley. But owing to the fact that plaster was the form of weatherproofing most favoured for half-timbered houses in East Anglia and the adjacent county of Hertfordshire, the craft of pargetting is particularly associated with this region and it is only there that it can be studied in all its vigour and homely variety. The commonest designs were incised with a pointed stick, a fan of pointed sticks or a comb, making the zigzags, scallops, herring-bone patterns or interlacing wavy, flowing lines which so delight us on the walls of houses in such places as Stoke by Nayland, East Bergholt, Hadleigh or Coggeshall; or the decoration was contrived with the aid of a simple square wooden mould, perhaps showing a four-petalled flower, which was 'butter pressed' into the plaster, covering the whole wall. A mould frequently used in northern Essex was cut with three bars which, when pressed this way and that, produced a pattern resembling wattling. A house in Littlebury is conspicuously adorned all over in this manner and there are further examples near by at Saffron Walden and Ashdon. The Littlebury house was recently restored by a local plasterer who cut his own mould and exactly repeated the traditional procedure.

But these are simple forms of pargework. Very often the plaster wall would be divided into panels. The borders of these panels were either recessed, an effect achieved by placing templates of thin wood on the surface of the last but one coat of plaster, 'rough-casting' round them up to the level of the template boards, and then removing the templates; or the panels themselves were recessed, leaving the borders in relief. Both types can be seen at Ashwell, Hertfordshire. The most developed and expressive pargework takes the form of moulded ornament, either on the panels, as at Ashwell, or freely worked over the whole wall, as at Clare, Suffolk. Designs such as the scrolls on the house at Ashwell and the wonderfully free, bold leaf and flower pattern at Clare would be modelled by

Decorative tiles at Capel, Surrey (top far left), where the enormous slates of the roof are of sandstone quarried under the North Downs; plain tile-hanging at Cranbrook, Kent (top right), and at Brenchley, Kent (bottom right); a tile-hung gable-end at Biddenden, Kent (bottom centre), where the meagreness and wide spacing of the timbers shows the late date of the cottage (seventeenth century); alternating plain and fish-scale tiles at Brenchley, Kent (bottom far left); slate-hanging at Dunster, Somerset (top centre); and weatherboarding at Wortling, Sussex (above).

hand with a small trowel, the flowing line having first been described in rope on the last but one coat of plaster. Figure-work, incised like the dolphin in a strap-work frame on the façade of a house in Gold Street, Saffron Walden, the surface of which is wholly scumbled and pocked, or in high relief like the pretty, naturalistic finches and leaf scrolls on a house in the High Street of the same town, and the extraordinary fish-birds and crude representations of Thomas Hickathrift and the Wisbech giant in seventeenth-century dress on a house in Church Street, were also modelled by hand. The ambitious rosettes, leafy arabesques and cartouches in the panels of a house in Hertford and the striking decoration of strapwork, scrolls, fruit, rosettes, quatrefoils and shells which, arranged in leaf-bordered panels, completely covers the upper part of Colneford House, Earls Colne, dated 1685, were executed by means of wooden or wax moulds. Occasion-ally during this period, when more and more emphasis was being put upon durable materials, plaster was made to simulate masonry. There is a fine example of this in a late sixteenth-century house in Coggeshall, Essex. But such arts of imitation were not widely pursued until later.

Sometimes the borders of plaster panels were painted in bright colours: apple green, ochre or earthy red. A house at Newport, Essex, retains traces of such colouring. But generally the whole plastered surface was given either a white, ochre, peach pink or, less frequently, a deep terracotta wash, colours which are thrown into exciting relief by the dramatic skies and gently undulating pastoral landscape of East Anglia.

If the timber-framed house was not shielded from the ravages of the northern climate by plaster, then it was protected by clapboard or tiles. Clapboard, which is seen principally in Essex or Kent, the boards being pegged or nailed to the studding, was known in much earlier periods, and C. F. Innocent records an example thought to date from the Stone Age, discovered in 1833 in Drumkelin Bog, Donegal. And when a medieval house at Linton, Cambridgeshire, was being restored some ten years ago, it was found to be partially weatherboarded, the irregular boards following the line of the tree's growth. But it is unlikely that weatherboarding was commonly used before the eighteenth century when it became possible to cut the wood, generally elm, mechanically. The em-phatically horizontal aspect it imparts to a façade was peculiarly suited to the Georgian and Regency house, and it belongs essentially to the following section of this book rather than to this.

Tile-hanging appeared towards the end of the seventeenth century and was indigenous to Kent, Surrey and Sussex, and although it does occur sporadically also in Berkshire and Hampshire, it is especially Kent and east Sussex that glow with the lichen-stained russet red of this comfortable material. These wall tiles were flatter and thinner than those used on roofs and they were fastened to laths by means of pins of hazel, willow or elder and bedded solid in lime and hair mortar. It is often only the upper floor of a half-timbered house that is tile-hung, the ground floor, in many cases protected by the jetty, being plastered, as in the cottage overlooking the churchyard at Brenchley, Kent, and as at Burwash, Sussex; or the ground floor may have been covered with weatherboarding at a later period or brick-faced as in the case of houses at Goudhurst and Tenterden. But frequently the whole of the gable-end and occasionally the entire façade of a Kentish or Sussex house is tile-hung. The plain tile is commonly varied by patterning, fish-scale, flanged or semicircular tiles covering whole walls or taking their place with rectangular tiles in intricate designs which enrich the already robust texture of any tile-hung house.

In the west country, where the rare timber-framed house was not replaced by stone it was protected by slate, a material which Messrs Jope and Dunning have shown was quarried in Devon and Cornwall as early as the twelfth century and transported all over southern England for the roofing of ecclesiastical buildings. The important quarry at Delabole, the largest in England, was opened in the

Black-and-white work near
Pembridge, Herefordshire

This farm house at Clear Brook,
near Pembridge, shows the lively
elaboration of timber-work in the
west midlands common for about a
hundred years from the last quarter of
the sixteenth century. The startling
character of the pattern of plain and
ornamented square panelling is
strengthened by the tar or pitch with
which the woodwork in this region
was traditionally covered.

reign of Elizabeth I, and it was probably soon after this that slate was first used
as a wall covering. The two upper, jettied half-timbered storeys of the fifteenth-
century house known as the Nunnery, Dunster, Somerset, were slate-hung in
the seventeenth century, the regular lines of the slates being interrupted by
diamond patterns between the window of the top floor. Slate-hanging even
occurs, very rarely, in another basically stone district, the Lake District. The front
of the timber-framed overhang of the porch of Fellfoot Farm, Wrynose Pass,
Westmorland, a predominantly seventeenth-century house, is sheathed in the
thick, green-grey slates of this region. These forms of protecting half-timbered
dwellings thoroughly disguise the basic similarity in structure of the houses just
described and their contemporaries in the west midlands with their increasingly
elaborated and exposed framing. In earlier houses of this region, such as Lower
Brockhampton Manor, Brick House, Pembridge, and many of the cottages at
Weobley, the framing is simple, usually taking the form of a plain grid. But
houses built between *c.* 1575 and *c.* 1675 reveal an exuberant delight in rich
patterning for its own sake. Diagonal struts, bold zigzags, curved braces, pierced
quatrefoils (especially popular in the Ludlow area), fleurs-de-lis, trefoil-headed
arcading, concave-sided lozenges, semicircles and every variety of geometric
invention, cover walls and gables, the invariably black timber-work and dead-
white plaster starting up in the hilly, bosky landscape like giant examples of 'op'
art. Little Moreton Hall is the best known and certainly the most exotic of these
intricately decorated timber frames. But everywhere in the counties west of the
limestone belt and along the Welsh border, despite the destruction of countless
splendid half-timbered houses in the present century and the spread of subtopia,
the countryside is likely to be enlivened by some fantastic display of the
seventeenth-century carpenter's art and imagination. At Clear Brook near
Pembridge, for instance, three gables adorned with quatrefoils and cusped
braces above a stretch of small square-headed panels burst in a dazzle of black
and white from a rough, vividly green meadow, framed by ancient, knotted

Thatch at Glencolumbkille, Donegal, Ireland

The method of thatching shown here is found all along the north and west coasts of Ireland, but is particularly associated with Donegal. The ridge of the roof is rounded to offer the least resistance to gales and the thatch is held in place by a mesh of ropes (now of sisal, but formerly made of twisted bog fir) which are secured to the walls by means of rows of stone pegs below each eave and round the gable-end.

oaks. The village of Berriew in Montgomeryshire, whose black-and-white houses, shaded by huge oak and ash trees and watered by shallow, fast-running streams, are set against a mountain backcloth, owes its dream-like character almost wholly to the creative spirit of this great period of domestic building.

It is not only in the treatment of the framing that timber houses present such different aspects in different regions. The black-and-white houses of the west midlands stand on a stone or rubble base and are roofed with thick stone slates, while in eastern England the steeper roofs are thatched or tiled and flint or brick serve as a base. This contrast in roofing material, like that in the pattern of the walls, was not nearly so marked in the Middle Ages. At that time thatch was the commonest form of roofing and it continued to be used in all districts, except for the grandest houses, until the late Tudor period. In remote rural regions such as the west of Ireland and Scotland, thatch is still to this day the universal roofing material for cottages and small houses. Mr Salzman cites an instance, recorded in the accounts of St John's College, Cambridge, of a roof thatched in the last decade of the fifteenth century in the place which is outstandingly famous for its limestone roofing slates, Collyweston. A house in Winster, Derbyshire, is reported as still thatched in the eighteenth century, and even in the Cotswolds the humblest dwellings in a village such as Ebrington are thatched. With the gradual expansion of tile-making in the seventeenth century, tiles replaced thatch in districts where stone was not readily obtainable, while quarries opened up in limestone and sandstone regions under Elizabeth I and James I provided the stone slates which were generally preferred in those areas.

Thatched roofs require the steepest pitch; and it is the pitch of a tiled roof (when this was not subsequently rebuilt) which often reveals that it was once thatched. Old tiled roofs mildly undulating and sweeping almost to the ground are occasionally seen in Essex, Cambridgeshire and Huntingdonshire, but are most characteristic of Kent, where the sloping expanses, interrupted here and there by minute dormers, were probably all thatched originally. Sometimes they indicate the existence of a former aisled hall which assumed its present appearance during the great period of rebuilding, *c.* 1570–*c.* 1640. The chimney of one of the most spectacular of these roofs, at Biddenden, shows the projecting drip-courses under which the thick thatch of an earlier roof was tucked. The more widespread use of tiles was accompanied by the emphasis of a feature already prominent on the more important medieval house, the bargeboards, the purpose of which was to protect the ends of the roof timbers. They were fixed to the ends of a gabled roof a short distance from the face of the walls, and were invariably moulded and carved. Some of the few surviving medieval bargeboards have been mentioned in a previous chapter. Most of the bargeboards we see today are Elizabethan and Jacobean, if they do not belong to the eighteenth or nineteenth centuries. They are generally straight-sided in contrast to the medieval cusped boards, and are adorned with a running vine motif, as at Coote's Farm, Steeple Bumpstead, Essex; scroll-work, strapwork, the guilloche pattern, or a row of dentils, as at The Bangles, Elmdon; and sometimes exhibit the favourite period motif of a pendant at the apex, as in the gatehouse of Lower Brockhampton Manor, where the bargeboards and roof are certainly later additions.

Thatch itself was retained as the covering for many modest buildings and as the most suitable form of roofing where walls, such as those composed of mud, could not support a heavy weight or where no alternative and more permanent material could be easily procured. Despite regulations antagonistic to thatch, and despite much needless removal of thatch in favour of less attractive materials, this form of roofing is still surprisingly common in East Anglia, the southern midlands and the south-west, and, of course, in Ireland and Scotland; and it is not at all unusual for anyone travelling casually about the countryside to come upon a thatcher at his work. Like half-timber construction, thatching is one of the most ancient and characteristic branches of vernacular building in the British

Isles. Its great interest indeed is that it is a survival in a developed form of the most primitive type of roof covering, and thus, like the flint-knapping industry of Brandon, is part of a tradition which has continued unbroken for some 3,000 years at least. The materials used in thatching are the straw of the cultivated grasses, wheat, oats or rye; reed, the finest and most durable material, seen at its best in Norfolk and Suffolk and the fen country; and sometimes, in moorland regions where little corn is grown, heather. Thus the colour and texture of thatch, ochre, rich brown, near black, smooth and velvety as a mole's back, stiff as a hard brush, plump as a cushion, vary with local conditions. C. F. Innocent, who gives a most thorough account of the thatcher's methods, divides them into four types: the thatch can be sewn on to the rafters, pinned to them by means of rods and broaches, worked into a foundation of turves, or merely held in place by means of a rope mesh, the ends of which are weighted with large stones. This last is the most primitive method, confined today almost entirely to Ireland and the western Highlands. Sometimes, notably in Donegal, the ropes holding the thatch in place are fastened to pegs fixed in the walls. The second method is that most commonly followed in England, though the first also occurs and sometimes the two are combined. As straw thatch has to be renewed after twenty or thirty years, and even reed seldom lasts longer than eighty years, it is not possible to refer to actual examples dating from earlier than the last quarter of the last century. But there are indications that the fascinating varieties in the most developed types of thatching emerged during the sixteenth and seventeenth centuries. In the Middle Ages the law required that thatched roofs should be covered with a coat of limewash to retard burning in the event of fire (*see* in Bibliography, C. F. Innocent, op. cit., pp. 211-12), and during that period the ridge was often protected by clay or turves. So the traditions of ornamenting the

Thatch at Anstey Cross, Dorset, and (right) at Trumpington, Cambridgeshire

The Dorset cottage is thatched with 'wheat reed', which is long, specially grown and threshed wheat straw such as the combine harvester, which crushes the straw, cannot yield. It is used like true reed with the root-ends of the stalks forming the exposed surface. Bundles of the straw, known as 'bottles' or 'yelms', are trimmed, wetted, laid slightly diagonally, combed upwards and attached to the underlying layer of bundles by means of 'broaches' of hazel, which are pointed at either end with a twist in the middle. In the case of straw applied in the normal way, as at Trumpington, the bundles are combed downwards and are held in position by rows of hazel 'rods' or 'ledgers'. The thatchers of both these roofs, working from the eaves upwards, would have tapped and coaxed the straw into position with their 'ligget' or 'leggatt', a tool with a diagonal handle and a square, ridged face. When the thatch is new, the first layer of bundles is usually attached to

the rafters by means of a 12-inch steel needle and tar rope. The ornamental ridge of the Trumpington cottage is strengthened by rods and kept in place by broaches, which have become loose and project like hairpins in an untidy head. The way in which the thatch has been made to fit closely round the dormer window to form a pointed gable seems to be characteristic of East Anglia.

Tiled roof, Biddenden, Kent (above)

Irregularities in the sizes and shapes of these tiles and undulations due to sagging rafters, and also to the fact that the tiles were fixed on hand-riven timber, give delightful variety to the texture of this steep slope. The tiles were provided with holes for the reception of oak pegs by means of which they were fastened to oak laths. Each course overlaps the one below it, but adjacent tiles do not overlap, and in order to make the roof watertight, the whole structure, as Mr Alec Clifton Taylor has pointed out, must be covered with two thicknesses of tile. (*See also* page 150.)

ridge and the surface of the thatch which exhibit the thatcher's art at its most diverse and most accomplished could scarcely have taken root much before the sixteenth century; and the character of these ridge and surface patterns, generally formed of different combinations of scallops, V-shapes and half-hexagons, bears this out, for it is certainly related to the carved and moulded ornament of the Elizabethan and Jacobean periods. It is worth noting that the first mention of thatching as a craft occurs in the seventeenth century, in Henry Best's *Rural Economy in Yorkshire* or *Best's Farming Book* of 1641. It is significant also that two families of East Anglian thatchers trace back the practice of the skill by their forebears to the early seventeenth century. Moreover, the dormer window, which has given the thatcher yet more obvious opportunities for the cultivation of an individual style, did not exist until the small house had acquired a continuous upper floor, so the contrasts between the sharply cut semicircular dormer of the Ampthill district and the soft, wavy lines of Hampshire were unknown in the Middle Ages. But differences in the pitch of roofs, in the treatment of hips, between smooth rounded gable-ends and those where the thatch is drawn up in the form of a crude, pert finial, must be due to the idiosyncrasies of inherited styles, which, as Innocent pointed out, have never been thoroughly examined and which are possibly less prominent now than formerly owing to the fact that thatchers, who today are mobile as they never were in the past, now work in many areas remote from their home ground.

The contrast between roofs of thatch and tile and the lower pitched roofs of stone covering the timbered houses of the west midlands has already been remarked. The growing popularity during the Elizabethan and Jacobean periods of stone for both walls and roofs, wherever it was available, still further enriched the diverse patterns in texture and colour of domestic architecture. The Nunnery

seventeenth centuries and continued, in the case of cottages and smaller houses, right through the eighteenth and part of the nineteenth centuries.

The cottages which J. C. Loudon added to Great Tew when he planted the forest of evergreens which now embowers the whole irregularly-sited village, are almost indistinguishable from those built in the seventeenth century. The rich yellow of the masonry at Great Tew is the strongest of the colours assumed by Cotswold limestone, which is usually of a creamy, honied pallor, varying, however, in tone according to the quarry from which it was cut; and at the time when the Cotswold style was determined, nearly every village lay within reach of a quarry. This style is announced above all by the predilection for gables. In small cottages like those in the famous Arlington Row, Bibury, the gable takes the place of the normal dormer window, the wall being carried up to form a miniature gable into which the window is inserted. While in houses of greater pretentions, such as a conspicuous example at Finstock, the façade may boast a row of contiguous gables, adorned with carved finials in the shape of balls and sometimes with a cartouche or an oval or circular datestone. The date is not always an indication of the year when a house was built. It may refer to the rebuilding or alteration of an existing house, a common process in Elizabethan and Jacobean times when Arabic numerals first became fashionable and were used with pride and enthusiasm to record building activities (*see also* pp. 123–4).

In addition to their conspicuous use of the gable, the Cotswold masons were addicted to a counteracting, horizontal feature, the dripstone, dropped down a few inches on either side of an entrance or a delicately mullioned window, then returned, as at Burford (p. 156). In the same way the height of a Cotswold square chimney is counterbalanced by the pronounced horizontality of the fine mouldings. The clear, simple lines of these structures are as far removed from the intricate designs of the brick stacks of the sixteenth century as from the rough cylindrical or square shapes of the tall Lakeland and north Devon chimneys, where, in a sheltered position, a tall chimney facilitates the escape of smoke. In a few instances the decorative features of the reticent Cotswold style are varied by a sudden burst of fantasy: chimneys are set diagonally on their square plinths and twist like barleysugar sticks, and finials change from balls to obelisks and flaming onion-shaped urns as in the remains of Campden House, Chipping Campden, built by Sir Baptist Hicks in 1612.

The Arlington Row group of cottages owes much of its picturesque charm to its long, unbroken roof-line, a stone counterpart of the continuous roof of thatch which distinguishes the terrace at Melbourn, Cambridgeshire. And the stone roofs of the Cotswolds make a special contribution to the architectural style of the region. After northern or west midland roofs, this limestone covering looks unusually light and exactly matches and enhances the urbanity of the finely dressed stone of the walls. In fact the weight of a Cotswold stone roof is tremendous, for, as Mr Clifton Taylor remarks, every hundred square feet weighs almost a ton. Although these slates are remarkably regular, they are not all the same size and it is worth examining a roof at close quarters to see how they were laid. The larger slates were placed near the eaves and they diminished in size towards the ridge. It was when they were first widely used in the sixteenth and seventeenth centuries that the slates of different sizes were given whimsical names which changed with the district. Randle Holme, author of *The Academy of Armour*, writing in 1688, lists some of the names used in the north-west: 'Haghatees', 'Shorts save one or Short so won', 'Farwells', 'Wivetts', 'Warnetts', 'Batchlers', 'Short Twelves', 'Long Twelves', 'Jenny Why Gettest Thou', and 'Rogue Why Winkest Thou'. In the Cotswolds the slates bore names such as 'Cocks', 'Cuttings', 'Nobbities', 'Wibbuts' or 'Wivels', 'Becks', 'Movedays', 'Nines', 'Elevens to Sixteens', 'Follows' and 'Eaves'.

The texture of most stone roofs is enriched with random pads of rusty-brown velvety moss and in most areas moss was once grown purposely on stone-slated

Varieties in texture

Banded limestone (top left), creamy white and warm brown, due to oxide of iron staining, enlivens the walls of a house at Caldicott, Rutland; rough flints with brick door and window frames and brick quoins are seen at Castle Acre, Norfolk (top right); knapped flint and freestone (centre left) make a diverting chequerboard pattern at Wylie, Wiltshire; and a more unsophisticated and vigorous version of this design, carried out in brick and kidney cobbles (or oval pebbles of approximately the same size), comes from Mariners' Score, Lowestoft, Suffolk (bottom left). Walls constructed entirely of kidney cobbles are among the delights of East Anglian coastal districts and the example shown to the right of the Lowestoft wall is found at Cley, Norfolk. The stone-slated roof (centre right), enriched by moss and lichen, is characteristic of the refined masonry of the oolitic limestone belt. The example comes from Daneways, Sapperton, Gloucestershire. The slates are so placed that they diminish in size from the eaves to the ridge.

roofs to keep out draughts and snow. Periodically the so-called moss man would call to inspect the roof and, with the aid of a square-ended trowel known as a mossing-iron, he would poke in new moss wherever there was a suspicion of a gap.

To all the diverse textures and materials which make up the infinitely varied aspect of the traditional English house must be added flint, that mysterious silica found in nodules of strange, suggestive shape or in bands in the chalk districts of East Anglia, Sussex, Dorset and Wiltshire. Flints, gathered from the fields and

Patchwork at Colchester

This Elizabethan fishing lodge exhibits a patchwork of the building materials which lay to hand (*see* opposite page). An inscription on the freestone panel seen in this gable-end reads: 'THOMAS LUCAS ME FECIRE ANNE DOMINE 1591'.

used in their rough state or quarried and knapped, form the material of the majority of parish churches and monastic buildings in Norfolk and Suffolk, but I have found no house of earlier date than the eighteenth century built entirely of dressed flint, with the possible exception of South Flint House, Lowestoft, which bears the date 1586, but which has obviously been altered later. Rough flints, however, were widely used for domestic purposes before the end of the seventeenth century, especially in and around the district known as Breckland, where Norfolk and Suffolk meet, and where at Brandon the flint quarrying and knapping industry, now alas coming to an end, had been centred since prehistoric times. Castle Acre, in particular, shows a number of earlier houses built entirely of flint except for their quoins and door and window frames of narrow brick, and here the larger flints have usually been halved to expose the black hearts and enliven the walls with a jetty sparkle.

Flint is nowhere so dark or so lustrous as in Breckland. In the south the stones are smaller and browner and are generally much less closely set than in East Anglia. It is usual in the south, too, to find the flints laid in rough courses. Very often, as at Bingham's Melkham and Anstey Cross, Dorset, flint is banded with brick; and another wall pattern introduced in the seventeenth century and found in Dorset, Wiltshire and Sussex consists of chequerwork of stone and knapped flint, as at Martin, Dorset, and Wylye, Wiltshire.

A very different wall texture can be seen on the Norfolk coast near Cley and Blakeney, where cottages are constructed of carefully selected oval pebbles of approximately the same size, tightly and regularly set to make a design like that of plain knitting. Such pebbles play a part in an odd and vigorous version of the chequerboard theme which occurs on the walls of the Lowestoft Scores, where cobbles and bricks alternate in irregular rows. Brick, as we know, had made its appearance long before the sixteenth century, but it had by no means become universal, as it was later, and was at this stage of its development still to some extent an expression of place in the varieties of its colour and texture, which changed with the character of the soil. But these distinctions have already been described. The Lowestoft walls exhibit a delightfully fresh approach to the materials which lay immediately to hand, but for sheer invention in the use of whatever stuffs could be found near the building site, the prize must go to the house in Bourne Road, Colchester, which afterwards became a mill, but which was probably originally planned as a fishing lodge for Sir Thomas Lucas in 1591. The house stands beside a lake in what must once have been an enchanting wooded valley, but which is now a depressing, litter-strewn suburb. It is as exotic in form as in texture. Gigantic gable-ends disguise the basic simplicity of the rectangular shape; they are composed of thoroughly Baroque concave and convex curves festooned with obelisks, urns and balls, and this display of Italianate ornament is combined with angle buttresses in the Gothic manner. The compelling originality of this little structure owes as much, however, to its fabric as to its design. The builder has used those iron-stained nodules of clay which abound in east and north-east Essex and are known as septaria; lumps of dark-brown pudding-stone, which consists of coagulated flint pebbles; brick from the massive remains of Roman Colchester; and fragments of masonry from the near-by Benedictine Abbey. And each bit of this splendid patchwork is outlined in tiny, shining chips of flint, the galletting process, which can often be seen in flint districts, but which has seldom been used with more effect than here. This house, small though it is, is so wonderfully expressive of the ground on which it stands, makes such individual use of classical motifs and so brilliantly unites the horizontal and vertical modes that it could stand as a symbol of the whole attitude to domestic architecture in this extraordinarily creative age.

8

Form in Transition

As the classical idiom became more fashionable and knowledge of its forms more widespread, the synthesis between the vertical and horizontal modes, expressed in such endless variety during the sixteenth century, yielded first to an eccentric and often unbalanced combination of traditional and Renaissance motifs and then to a wholly horizontal manner. There is, in general, a manifest distinction between the uneasy juxtaposition of foreign and vernacular styles in many of the houses built or altered in the decades immediately preceding the full establishment of the classical ideal and that of the Elizabethan period. Sheer exuberance of individual fantasy and force of conviction had then achieved a marvellous unity unaffected by inaccuracies of detail or unorthodox renderings of alien practices. In a more rational age, a time in which all the ancient cathedrals of England and France could be dismissed as 'mountains of stone, vast and gigantic buildings indeed, but not worthy of the name of Architecture', a century which witnessed the founding of the Royal Society, the discoveries of Newton and the introduction by Pope and Dryden of disciplined systems of prosody, the power of invention which could merge disparate elements in a new harmony sometimes faltered. Foreign influences, moreover, were making themselves more directly and more disturbingly felt and could not at once be assimilated into the traditional stream of domestic architecture by craftsmen who relied on oral instruction and had as yet no pattern books to guide them. (The first of the technical guides for workers in the building trade which were to become so influential in the Georgian period was Moxon's *Mechanick Exercises*, published in 1677.)

Many regional builders, of course, as the illustrations to the previous chapter show, went on boldly disregardful or ignorant of fashionable trends, creating compositions which fused the horizontal and the vertical with perfect assurance. Houchin's, for instance, near Coggeshall, built at the very beginning of the seventeenth century, still soars, top-heavy and three-tiered, with jetties and prodigious angle ornaments to electrify a quiet, flat landscape, but its outrageous height is made part of a satisfying design by the heavy horizontal lines of dark bressumers against white, plastered walls. The effect is repeated, less flamboyantly and in brick, at Great Dunmow, where assertive string courses and broad, white-painted transoms check the upward tendency of a tall façade rendered yet taller by curly, ball-topped gables and a clock turret in the centre of the steep roof. Later on, as we shall see, certain architects, as distinct from local craftsmen, re-created this synthesis of the vertical and horizontal in a more classical form. But it was destined eventually to break down under the pressure of an instinctive preference for the horizontal, and its collapse was accompanied by the appearance of some extraordinary hybrids.

At Hall Farm, Kettleburgh, Suffolk, for example, classical details have been thrust upon a traditional pink, plastered East Anglian building without any unifying inspiration. The farm looks like a much altered hall house with one cross-wing. The star-topped chimney-stack of an earlier age looms high above the irregular roof-line, but what seems to have been the gable-end of the cross-block is in-

Ashdown House, Berkshire

Perhaps designed by John Webb *c.* 1650 for the 1st Earl of Craven, this house already exhibits some of the features which were to determine the Georgian style: it is conceived as a square block; the symmetrical façade is articulated by rows of identical windows and the pavilions flanking it foreshadow the wings which were to become an important component of English eighteenth-century country house design. The tremendous height of Ashdown House is, however, in key with the Elizabethan rather than the classical spirit and is typical of this period of transition. The principal influence behind the building, with its balustraded roof parapet and cupola surmounted by a gilded ball, is Dutch. The house is built of chalk, with quoins and dressings of darker limestone, and the luminosity and extreme pallor of the material add to the startling appearance of the tall block in a wide landscape.

New and traditional forms

The three houses on these two pages
show how seventeenth-century local
builders combined ideas going back
to the Middle Ages with new trends.
Houchin's, Coggeshall, Essex (bottom
right), is the earliest and most
traditional of the three. It dates from
the beginning of the seventeenth
century and is still constructed with
jetties, but the roof-line is not broken
by the gabled attics common in the
Jacobean period and one gable-end is
already half-hipped. The façade is
controlled by a rough idea of symmetry and its lines are emphatically
horizontal. The L-shaped Old House,
Blandford, Dorset, c. 1660 (top right)
unites Dutch influences with fantastic
traditional chimney-stacks of finely
moulded brick. At Brick House,
Wicken Bonhunt, Essex (left), the
roof-line is concealed by a parapet in
the classical manner, which is also
reflected in the headless statue
standing upon it and the bust of the
Roman emperor in a roundel over the
door, but there are precedents for all
these features in Elizabethan houses
(see pages 107 and 110), and the gables
and four-light, transomed windows
are traditional. The attempt at symmetry is, however, notable in a house
as modest as this.

Interior and (opposite) south gable-end, Haunt Hill House, Weldon, Northamptonshire

The house was built by Humphrey Frisbey, whose initials, 'H.F.', and the date 1643 appear in the apex of the south gable. Frisbey came of a family of masons related by marriage to the Thorpes of King's Cliffe (*see* page 103) and to the Grumbolds, another celebrated family of masons, the most distinguished of whom, Robert Grumbold, figured prominently in the architectural history of Cambridge during the second half of the seventeenth century. This small Weldon house is interesting on two counts: for its plan and for the extravagant character of its decoration. The plan derives from the hall house and resembles that of many East Anglian timber-framed houses of the period (*see* Office Farm, Metfield, p. 143), except that it is perfectly symmetrical, with two rooms on each floor on either side of the huge, central chimney-stack. In order that the entrance should be strictly central, it leads not into the principal room (the hall) but into a narrow vestibule between the stack and the front door. The niches (left) face the front door and are contrived in the stack. Within the farther one is a low opening into the main room, intended for a cat or dog. The significance of the date, 1636, and the initials 'IR' and 'TE' between the arches is not known. The extraordinary juxtaposition of traditional and individually interpreted classical motifs on the south gable-end of the house is a memorable instance of the eccentricity so often encountered in English house design.

congruously adorned with huge bays, one above the other, the central windows of which are flanked with fat, Tuscan pillars. A yet stranger, more unbalanced image confronts the visitor to Blandford, where one of the few houses to escape the great fire of 1731 shows what uncouth forms could result from an attempt to blend the classical and the traditional which was neither controlled by acknowledged rules nor sustained by creative vision. The air of exaggeration, the lack of proportion of Old House, are almost nightmarish. The builder clearly intended to impart a horizontal emphasis to the tall brick façade by the weight of the roof and the deep shadow cast by the grotesquely wide eaves, but the roof is abnormally steep and its height is dramatically increased by fantastic chimney-stacks. These remarkable structures dominate the elevation, an anachronistic and striking display of the brickmaker's art in the Tudor and Elizabethan tradition. It is only the design which reveals their later date. They are octagonal, rising from square plinths with moulded corbelling, and surrounded by detached angle shafts, all of brick, crowned, like classical columns, with annulets, and branching out in corbelled and intricately moulded capitals.

The chimney of Haunt Hill House, Weldon (so called because it is reputed to be haunted by the ghost of a man done to death there), though utterly different in its impeccably classical dress from those at Blandford, is as visually disturbing, for it is conceived on a different scale from the rest of the house, dwarfing the façade and at the same time calling attention to the contrast between its own elegant, classical proportions and the ungainly porch with its ogee arch flanked by the mullioned windows common to traditional houses in the limestone belt. The south gable of this small house displays an even more oddly assorted collection of classical and regional motifs: a stepped window, the arms of the Masons' Company and giant, idiosyncratic volutes and shields on either side of a mullioned opening. This composition, artless though it is, is conspicuously symmetrical and has something of the fire and abandon of Elizabethan fancy, although the mason,

Humphrey Frisbey, was probably only reassembling motifs he had seen in his neighbourhood at Kirby Hall and in the memorable works of Sir Thomas Tresham. An altogether confused, disjointed feeling, on the other hand, informs the façade of Old Hall, North Wheatley, Nottinghamshire, where decorative brickwork, executed with astonishing skill, takes the shape of classically derived motifs applied with neither understanding nor imagination. The pilasters on either side of the door end abruptly before they reach the entablature they should support, and the series of modillioned lunettes, curving heavily and meaninglessly along the cornice above the ground floor, is suddenly cut short by the angles of the house. At Eyam Hall, Derbyshire, a traditional plan, a half-H with projecting wings, has been forced into a semblance of the classical style with considerable grasp of its implications but with little fantasy. The composition needs height, but it has been rendered massively horizontal by bold string courses, by the transformation of the gable-ends of the wings into tiny pediments and by the concealment of most of the roof behind a parapet.

Very occasionally, a design of this period of transition does succeed in achieving a harmony which is classical in atmosphere if not in actual form or detail. The long pale symmetrical front of Ufford Hall, Suffolk, magically conveys the sense of order and proportion we associate with the classical style, although apart from the treatment of its chimney-stacks and its arrestingly horizontal line it shows no trace of Renaissance influence. Again, the modest front of Brick House, Wicken Bonhunt, exhibits no obviously classical features other than its symmetry and well-marked string courses, for the segmental pediment above the door was added later. Yet despite its gables, which are not only northern but dissimilar, and its steep roof, it is as instinct with poetic feeling for antiquity as the Temple of Venus at Stowe. The robed and headless statue standing on the parapet and the stone bust of a Roman emperor in the roundel between the two first-floor windows invest this little house with a Virgilian and heroic quality like that found in the epic poetry which enjoyed such special prestige in the seventeenth century.

But the likes of Brick House and Ufford Hall were never seen in any classical land. And it is extraordinary to think that before ever these houses were built the Italianate terraces of the great Covent Garden Piazza were in course of construction and that a mansion in the purest Renaissance style had risen beside the Thames to confront the robust individuality of vernacular architecture and the groping attempts of native craftsmen to understand the rudiments of the horizontal mode with a perfected vision of classical order. Inigo Jones's Queen's House at Greenwich, and his Banqueting House, Whitehall, both completed by 1635, must have looked as strange to the eyes of those who first saw them as the stone houses of the Normans appeared to the startled gaze of the Anglo-Saxon inhabitants of mud hovels and barn-like halls. Unlike the builders of the houses just described, Inigo Jones designed according to rule and with a complete grasp of the varying proportions of column and entablature, known as the Orders, which formed the basis of the architecture of antiquity. He had not only spent long periods in Italy, but had absorbed the spirit of Roman art and that of its most assiduous and scholarly admirer, Andrea Palladio. Without the inspiration of the great Vicentine, the whole development of English building in the eighteenth century would have taken a different course, yet the chance which attracted Inigo Jones to his work rather than to that of Bramante or Michelangelo was as unaccountable as that which led Palladio himself to base his art on the precepts of the pedantic and aesthetically insignificant Vitruvius. Jones saw Palladio's masterpieces at Vicenza and conversed with the aged Scamozzo, who had completed the marvellous Teatro Olimpico after the designer's death, a building which must have fascinated the inventor of masques. He was never afterwards without Palladio's book *I Quattro Libri dell' Architettura* and later published an annotated edition of it.

The Banqueting House, with its rusticated lower storey, alternating triangular and segmental pediments, frieze of masks and festoons, was finished by the early date of 1622 and is as amazingly beautiful in its present surroundings as when it made its surprising appearance among the half-timbered, jettied and gabled houses of Jacobean Westminster. It uses all the motifs found in Palladio's Palazzo Valmarana and Casa del Diavolo in Vicenza, though they are variously combined. The chief divergence is that the English architect replaced Palladio's giant columns by two Orders, thus imparting a much greater feeling of horizontality to the composition than is ever seen in a building by the Italian. The square, simple Queen's House is yet more static and much more severe. Both these buildings, though so exquisitely ordered, make an alien impression, and it is not astonishing that more than half a century was to pass before the full effect of Inigo Jones's influence was felt in the domestic architecture of Britain. Even when architects who had been close to Inigo Jones attempted to follow his example, either tradition was too strong for them or they were attracted by the French ideas encouraged by Charles II, or, later, they were swayed by Dutch fashions and the taste for red brick brought over to England by William of Orange.

Lodge Park, Northleach, is a delightful example of how country masons responded to the inspiration of Inigo Jones. The builder was Valentine Strong of Taynton, who was acquainted with the work of both Jones and his pupil and nephew by marriage, John Webb. At first sight, the house that stands so luminously against its backcloth of beeches looks like one of those villas of the Veneto glimpsed between the noble piers that now and then break the monotony of a high wall on minor roads in the neighbourhood of Vicenza and Verona. The façade is a plain rectangle, the windows are tall oblongs, of quite a different shape from the broad openings of traditional houses, such as Eyam Hall, and a central loggia instantly recalls a favourite Italian Renaissance feature. But the windows are mullioned and transomed; and the curious and continuous row of pediments along the cornice is related to the Elizabethan gabled façade, while the height of

Lodge Park, North Leach, Gloucestershire

The house was built *c.* 1655 as a hunting lodge for John Dutton of Sherborne House by a local mason, probably Valentine Strong, who was the architect of Sherborne House. Traditional motifs such as mullioned and transomed windows have here been absorbed into a classical mould, the total effect of which is stronger than that of disparate features such as the tall, asymmetrically placed chimney-shafts.

the balustraded parapet and of the clustered chimneys, diagonally set and noticeably asymmetrical, is disastrous, if judged by Palladian rules.

Even Webb did not adhere to Jones's formula. The most interesting house attributed to him, Ashdown, in Berkshire, built in 1650, incorporates both Dutch and French elements, and although it is extraordinarily sophisticated when compared with vernacular buildings of the period, such as Eyam Hall and Brick House, which it preceded by at least a decade, its height is so irrational, its contours so picturesque that it seems closer in spirit to Chastleton than to the Queen's House. The contrast between the incredibly tall central structure crowned with a cupola above its steep, dormered and balustraded roof, and the pair of low pavilions flanking it in the French style, is staggering, and must have made an even more shattering impact before the chimneys of the pavilions were shortened. Originally they soared up to the roof-line of the house like great free-standing columns, setting the whole composition in mysterious motion.

There is a distinctly Baroque feeling about this house, and of all the Roman-inspired styles, the Baroque, which like the Elizabethan achievement is a synthesis of the vertical and horizontal, must surely have been the most congenial to English architects and the mode they would have pursued if foreign influences and the whole temper of the age had not militated against it. Even Inigo Jones himself, with all his devotion to Palladio, was half carried away by Baroque fervour when he came to design the famous Double Cube Room at Wilton. For although it is planned according to Palladio's rules of symmetry and proportion, the length being twice its height and width, the coved ceiling, the sumptuous gilded swags and broken pediments and the heroic mantelpiece, the crowning pediment of which is open to accommodate a coronated shield while its curving arms support reclining figures, are closer in atmosphere to the exuberant seventeenth-century rooms in the Royal Palace at Turin than to any interior by Palladio. And before Lord Burlington instigated a return to unadulterated Palladianism, the Baroque spirit was often manifested in the design and detail of English houses, adding to the remarkable diversity of the scene.

Sir William Wilson of Sutton Coldfield used the Baroque form of the classical style to complete and enhance the lively movement of projecting wings, diapered brickwork and tall mullions initiated by a Jacobean builder when he added the dormers, the balustraded parapet, some of the second-floor windows, the cupola and the great centre-piece to Sudbury Hall, Derbyshire, towards the end of the century. The horizontal line of the parapet is offset by the steep pitch of the roof and the high drum of the cupola, and this vertical emphasis is strengthened by the Baroque frontispiece, which has much the same effect in relation to the rest of the house as the porch of Kirby Hall to its long façade. The design is swept straight up to the cupola by two tiers of lofty, high-based, coupled columns supporting huge entablatures and curving pediments in which cartouches seem to float rather than rest. Two of the upper-floor windows exhibit an unusual tracery design which enriches the texture and quickens the rhythm of the façade. Each window shows two round-headed lights crowned by two ovals. This is the horizontal form of a pattern which occurs vertically in the frontispiece, where two arched niches above the door are surmounted, in the head of the narrow window between the first-floor columns, by two upright ovals.

At Raynham Park, Norfolk, the traditional and the classical styles are similarly linked in a design moving both vertically and horizontally. The house is constructed on the H-plan with one side of the H between the cross-wings filled in. The forceful line of the cornice is counteracted by the upstarting, shaped gables of each wing with their swelling Ionic volutes and pediments, and by a central double pediment, the upper of which rises from the broken curve of the lower. Bold dentils give sparkling emphasis to these pointed and undulating forms, and the buoyancy of the volutes is strangely animated by the Ionic capitals in which they end. They are like columns cut loose from their bases, swaying and curling

The Double Cube Room, Wilton House, Wiltshire

Inigo Jones's name was connected with Wilton from 1632, when Philip, 4th Earl of Pembroke, invited him on the advice of King Charles I to lay out the gardens and redesign the south front of the house. The Double Cube Room was part of the new work and was in existence by 1640. In *Vitruvius Britannicus*, Campbell attributes this work wholly to Jones, but Mr Howard Colvin, the Oxford historian, has shown that Jones was too busy with the king's own projects to undertake the rebuilding himself and that he recommended Isaac de Caus. But according to Aubrey, Caus did nothing 'without the advice and approbation of Mr Jones', so Inigo Jones remains the presiding genius of this great creation. After a fire of 1647/8 the state rooms, including the Double Cube Room, were redecorated by Inigo Jones and John Webb. The proportions of this famous room, 60 feet long by 30 feet wide and 30 feet high, and the decoration were all inspired by Jones. The design for the magnificent central doorway with its broken pediment, cartouche and reclining figures can be traced to a drawing he made for Whitehall, and the chimney-piece is based on an engraving from Jean Barbet's *Livre d'Architecture, d'Autels et de Cheminées* (1633), a source to which Inigo Jones frequently resorted. The swirling putti, urns, cartouches and swags of fruit and foliage in the cove were painted by Edward Pierce, and the three central panels of the ceiling, depicting the story of Perseus, were the work of Emmanuel de Critz in *c.* 1650. The large scale of Pierce's bold painting, the shattered pediments, the tilting cartouches, the gilded, light-reflecting figures and the fat plaster ornament, for which closely parallel designs by Jones exist, give this noble room a feeling of life and movement which can best be described as Baroque.

as they float. This smooth, gentle movement contrasts with the sharp, upward thrust of the three outsize keystones pushing through the lintels of the lower windows of the wings. The central entrance of the west front, added, like that at Sudbury, to a house begun much earlier, sustains the Baroque mood of the façade. Broad, shallow steps mount in two short stages to a doorway framed by lofty Corinthian columns and a broken pediment repeating the rhythm´ of the gable volutes, while the cartouche within it echoes the pattern of the scrolly frame of the oval window in the pediment above it.

Another house which is more subtlely Baroque in design than either Raynham Park or Sudbury Hall, is Thomas Archer's splendid creation at Chicheley, which is entirely different from his later work at Hale Park built when he had succumbed to the spell of Palladianism. The composition of Chicheley fires the imagination of the spectator in much the same way as it is kindled by the first glimpse of Hardwick, by its overwhelmingly harmonious yet unexpected and unorthodox character. The façades of white stone and red brick are articulated by gigantic pilasters, the size of which is moderated, however, by the delicacy of the fluting and of the precisely carved, luxuriant Corinthian capitals. The vertical impulse of these prominent members is likewise checked by the ponderous frieze immediately above them; but the frieze turns into a base for further simpler pilasters and itself sweeps upwards on either side of the forward-jutting central feature of the main front, a movement repeated by the line of the parapet which crowns the attic storey. The bold advance of the entrance bay is stressed by the rich adornment of the frieze in this section by carved cornucopias and masks; and at each angle of the house the powerful accent of the projecting cornice is softened by a huge sculptured leafy scroll from which emerge the three-dimensional, ammonite-horned head and forelegs of a ram. The doorway is surmounted by an

Chicheley House, Buckinghamshire

In this house, attributed on stylistic grounds to Thomas Archer and begun for Sir John Chester *c.* 1690, the classical idiom, with which the architect had become thoroughly familiar during four years abroad spent mostly in Italy, is treated in an unorthodox manner which gives it something of the excitement of the great Elizabethan houses of a hundred years earlier, although the angular movement of those masterpieces is here modified by curves. The detail and proportions of the entrance have the exaggerated emphasis of a Baroque conceit, but are unlike anything seen in a classical land; and the upward sweep of the elaborately carved cornice rising to surmount the three tall windows above the strange entrance, the design of the windows themselves and the brick aprons below the first-floor windows are equally individual.

The west front, Raynham Hall, Norfolk

Raynham Hall, of brick and stone like Thomas Archer's house opposite, begun as early as 1622 for Sir Roger Townshend, an amateur of architecture, and completed by about 1632, has some affinities with Chicheley, though the combination of new and traditional forms which so remarkably characterize it has not been achieved with the controlled and highly conscious grasp of all the components which produced the Buckinghamshire design. Raynham may be the work of a local mason, William Edge, who had been taken abroad by Sir Roger in 1620, probably to the Netherlands. Dutch influence is clear in the gable-ends, and such pediment-crowned, curving gables were at that time novelties. The awkward but aspiring central feature, only part of which can be glimpsed in the photograph, comprising a segmental pediment interrupted by a raised pediment, may have been based on an engraving. The façade must have been lacking in cohesion before the addition of the exaggeratedly tall central door, c. 1680. Before that time there were two doors which led into two screens passages at either end of a seven-bay hall. The sash windows date from the Georgian period: the original windows were mullioned and transomed.

extraordinary pediment, a broken segmental arch in reverse like a diminished mirror image of the strange roof-line. The carved stone frames of the windows above this doorway echo these curves, while the windows flanking the door are curiously stepped like Elizabethan gable-ends and like the window in the gable of Haunt Hill House. The step motif occurs in reverse in the design of the brick aprons resembling inverted battlements below each of the first-floor windows. The idea of the looking-glass counterparts may be related to the theme of the broad canals which enclose the great lawn in front of the house on three sides, for it is the reflections in these geometrical expanses of clear, still water which create the enchanted, sequestered atmosphere of Chicheley and calm the restless rhythm of the house. This rhythm, marked though it is, is but a faint reminder of the dynamism of the Baroque in lands where it was the accompaniment of a religious revival of fanatical intensity and the expression of an inherent sense of display and drama.

But there were at least two architects in Britain whose work may be compared for heroic scale and command of contrast and chiaroscuro with developments on the Continent. Sir William Bruce, who held the post of King's Surveyor and Master of the Works in Scotland, was later, and with justice, described by Colen Campbell in his *Vitruvious Britannicus* as 'the best architect of his time in the Kingdom [Scotland]'. But his buildings show little respect for the Palladian module which Campbell so much admired and sought to establish. Indeed they are Baroque in the Elizabethan rather than in the continental tradition, and perhaps Sir William, working in the remote north, should be regarded as a belated Elizabethan. The symmetry and much of the imagery of his designs are classical, but Scottish and wholly individual elements mingle in the most unorthodox way with the classical and the proportions change with each of his vigorously advancing and retreating, aspiring or spreading compositions. Bruce's most ex-

Tilley Manor House, West Harptree, Somerset, and (below) the White Cottage, Claremont, Surrey

Both these houses are surprising for the large scale and Baroque feeling of the ornament which in each case embellishes a severe façade. According to an inscription on an overmantel, Tilley Manor dates from 1659, but it was altered later and the low-pitched roof, which stresses the horizontality of the house, must belong to the later work. The windows are traditional mullions, which intensifies the startling effect of the vigorous decoration over the ground-floor openings, the cartouches breaking through enormous, curving, open pediments and the detached segmental pediments above them. The massive doorway shows another oddity: it is flanked by pilasters which look as though they have been set upside down, for the bases are Ionic capitals. The difference between this house and the White Cottage resembles that between Raynham Hall and Chicheley (pages 172 and 173). If the fantasy of Tilley Manor is partly the result of an incomplete grasp of the classical idiom, the huge and heavy rustications of the White Cottage are entirely intentional. It was built by Sir John Vanbrugh after 1708.

citing house is Drumlanrig Castle in Dumfriesshire, begun in 1675 and finished in 1688 for the Duke of Queensbury. Set on a high podium, continued round two sides of the great forecourt, Drumlanrig recalls Wollaton in its design, for it is a hollow square with huge angle towers soaring up above the rest of the building and rendered yet more conspicuous by fantastic pepper-pot turrets. From the towers bays of graded heights make step patterns on each façade, converging in the main front onto a central upward-moving feature which takes the form of a bold projection approached by a double, curving perron, flanked by tall pilasters and crowned by an open, segmental pediment and a cupola on an octagonal drum. So the most arresting aspect of this impressive pile is its eccentric roof-line, the lively interplay against the sky of the verticals of turrets and chimneys, and the horizontals of strongly defined balustraded parapets, all at different levels and all seen in varying perspectives. The strange character of the house is emphasized by certain details, by the exaggerated, height-promoting width, for instance, of the entablature above each pedimented window, and by the way in which each of these pediments is crammed with heraldic sculpture. This sculpture is remarkable not only for the high quality of the work but for the fact that it was carved *in situ* from the stones of the wall face. This was also the case with the swags of fruit adorning the entrance, with the deeply cut, animated coat of arms in the open pediment and with the giant trefoils so prominently encircling the principal cupola. The relation of sculpture and architecture in this building only hints at the possibilities realized in the fusion of the two arts in extreme expressions of the Baroque. But in his plan for Hopetoun House, his grandest enterprise, altered by William Adam, Bruce intended to complete the movement of the balustrades by gesticulating figures; and his grasp of the role sculpture could play in the architecture of drama and motion is further shown in the fabulous cornucopia of fish over the gate of his own house at Kinross opening onto Loch Leven.

It was, however, in the work of Sir John Vanbrugh, achieved just before the advent of the Burlingtonians, that Baroque feeling allied to a complete grasp of classical form most boldly took possession of English house design. Vanbrugh composed on the gargantuan scale and with the irresistible rhythm of the author of Bolsover. And indeed it is with Bolsover that the blackened ruins of Seaton Delaval, with its vast forecourt, colossal porticoes, stupendous ringed columns and Titanic keystones and rustications, invite comparison. The vivid chiaroscuro, the advancing, retreating and flickering movement of this great house and of Castle Howard and Blenheim, are not so overwhelmingly present in Vanbrugh's smaller houses, but they too are governed by an enthusiasm for mass and unexpected scale which can only be called Baroque. At King's Weston, near Bristol, the façade is articulated by a commanding pedimented and pilastered projection. The pilasters are Corinthian and of prodigious size, so arranged that two of them flank the entrance while the remaining four are coupled at either end of the projecting bay. The pediment contains an arch, the shape of which is dramatically echoed in the arcade springing from the roof to support the six chimney-stacks and to draw the design upwards. The small cruciform brick house, formerly the gardener's cottage, which Vanbrugh built at Claremont, is weighted by heavy, stark horizontal bands to counteract the bounce of high-arched recesses and the pronounced verticality of the tremendous keystones and tall chimney-stacks; and a theatrical note is added by the contrast between the plain little house and the colossal wall enclosing the kitchen garden like an impregnable bastion.

The brick house at Somersby, Lincolnshire, known as Manor Farm, shows that Vanbrugh, if it is indeed by him, was aware of the affinity between his work and that of the Elizabethans, for in the design he consciously alludes to past practice by juxtaposing Gothic and classic motifs. He combines angle turrets and battlements with round-headed windows and a heavily rusticated porch on the north front, while on the south side a central projecting bay with a flight of steps ascending to a narrow door and a pediment rising above the parapet imparts a

The Great Chamber, Seaton Delaval,
Northumberland (left),
Manor Farm, Somersby, Lincolnshire
(below), and (right) Drumlanrig
Castle, Dumfriesshire

All three houses, so diverse in scale
and design, are dominated by a vivid
sense of drama and romance akin to
that which inspired late Elizabethan
mansions. The battlements and
turrets of Manor Farm, which was
probably designed by Vanbrugh,
suggest the Middle Ages in the same
fanciful way as the towers and pointed openings of East Lulworth Castle
(page 110), and as with the Dorset
house, these elements have been combined with classical details. The
impressive red sandstone house in the
Nith valley, built by Sir William
Bruce in 1675-88, is informed with
as bold a feeling for chiaroscuro and
movement as the great Baroque
houses of the Continent, such as
Brühl and Pommersfelden, but incorporates traditional motifs like
pepper-pot domes and corner towers.
There is nothing traditional about the
gigantic arcading, cyclopean masonry
and animated sculpture of the vast
ruined room at Seaton Delaval,
Vanbrugh's last great work, begun in
1718, yet it is informed with a grand,
theatrical castle air which at once
recalls Bolsover and is as peculiarly
English as Webster's two Italian
tragedies, for the violence and passion
of which it would provide a perfect
setting.

Entrance to Clifton House, King's Lynn, Norfolk (left), and (above) Petworth House, Sussex

The rare ascending, spiralling columns of the doorway ascribed to Henry Bell, who built the King's Lynn Custom House in 1685, so suitably framing the further door with its broken pediment, and the long, sophisticated façade of Petworth with its strong horizontal emphasis, show what very diverse influences were at work towards the close of the seventeenth century. The King's Lynn doorway is wholly in the Italian Baroque tradition, while the source of the Petworth design seems essentially French, whether it was actually the invention of an Englishman inspired by French ideas, as Sir Anthony Blunt has suggested, or the work of Pierre Puget or Daniel Marot, both of whose names have been associated with the house. The façade was built for the 6th Duke of Somerset soon after 1686.

marked upward swing to the composition. The interior of the house reiterates the references to the past, for the vaulted hall is entered by a mock screens passage.

Vanbrugh's flamboyant creations represent the climax of a mood which rarely dominated an entire house, but which often showed itself in isolated details, which was not altogether subdued even in Palladian England and which eventually flared up again in another guise in the cult of the Picturesque. A memorable instance of the introduction of exotic Baroque motifs into an otherwise static, heavily horizontal design occurs at West Harptree, Somerset, where the ground-floor windows of a stone house are surmounted by vigorously curving pediments enclosing angel-headed cartouches. The queer detached segmental pediments above these are typical of the period, always inducing a floating sensation. The seventeenth-century addition to a house at Cubley, Derbyshire, is enlivened by a centre-piece flanked by giant pilasters, a curving, urn-topped pediment and by enchanting, quite unexpected scroll ornaments of disproportionate size suggestive of an airy pediment. The doorway of Clifton House, King's Lynn, by Henry Bell, assumes the thoroughly Baroque form of a curved pediment set on spiralling columns; and at Rosewell House, Bath, as late as 1735, the Baroque spirit breaks out in carved window frames which are equalled only by those of Lerici in their wild exuberance.

It is always thought that Vanbrugh's invention was powerfully stimulated by the massive architecture of the Bastille at Vincennes, where he was imprisoned for two years on suspicion of being an enemy agent. Sir William Bruce was also familiar with French architecture. But French influence showed itself more clearly in works which were very different from the colourful architecture of these two men. The rational temper of the age and its bias towards the horizontal materialized in an extreme form in the long, excessively low west front of Petworth, the monotony of which is unrelieved by the exquisitely refined detail and could never have been much mitigated by the vanished saucer dome. William

179

Talman's work at Chatsworth is in the same vein; his composition there embraces an even instead of the customary odd number of bays so that a central vertical accent is ruled out. At Dyrham Park, Gloucestershire, Talman's finest design, shallow projections and a pillared entrance door with a pilastered window above it gently articulate the façade, though the impression is still one of flatness and inordinate length. The strongly horizontal character of this house is, however, extraordinarily effective in its setting, for it stands across the bottom of a deep valley which opens out before the west front into a vast panorama of undulating, wooded landscape, to which it provides the perfect foil.

All the disparate influences embodied in the houses so far described in this chapter, the Palladian, the Baroque, the French, the Dutch and the traditional styles, were gradually welded into a peculiarly English version of the classical and horizontal mode. The process might have taken quite a different course if it had not been for the example of Sir Christopher Wren. Very few purely domestic buildings can be proved to have been his design, but he was none the less the dominating architectural personality after Inigo Jones's death, and the fact that popular opinion, however unfounded, has attached his name to houses which unite the classical and the traditional in a smooth harmony which is immediately recognizable as the precursor of what we know as the Georgian style, is indicative of the strength of his influence. For Wren's genius lay in his astounding ability to assimilate and co-ordinate ideas from widely divergent sources, an ability most clearly displayed, perhaps, in his brilliant designs for the towers of the City of London churches, where even the Gothic past is recalled. However various in their upper stages, these towers rise over a square plan like their medieval predecessors, and, while making endless play upon the Orders, merge the aspiring character of medieval architecture with the language of classical horizontality. In Wren's designs for Chelsea Hospital, Morden College, Blackheath, and the Orangery of

House at Stamford, Lincolnshire

This house has almost achieved the predominant domestic design which emerged at the end of the seventeenth century when various foreign influences had been assimilated and fused with native traditions. A white-painted wooden cornice has taken the place of the projecting eaves of a house such as that at Blandford (page 165), the steep roof takes the form of a truncated pyramid covering the square block of the building, which is two rooms deep instead of the traditional one. It is interrupted by dormers and is surmounted by symmetrically placed chimneys adorned here with classical niches, but often panelled. The first floor preserves the sash windows, set almost flush with the wall, which had been introduced by the late Stuart period. The door, surmounted by a scrolled pediment, should be central, but the façade is here thrown out of balance by an extra bay on the left.

The north front, Belton House, Grantham, Lincolnshire

Belton House was built between 1684 and 1688 for Sir John Brownlow and may have been designed by William Winde or Wynne, the author of the house which once stood on the site of Buckingham Palace. The mason was William Stanton. But the building has always, until recently, been associated with the name of Wren, and the skill and harmony with which tradition and novelty have been synthesized and the clear logic of the design, establishing so many features of the Georgian style, are characteristic of Wren's genius. Belton harks back to the old plan of the principal block with cross-wings, but it is perfectly symmetrical and the nucleus of the house consists of a central hall entered from the south front with the dining-room immediately behind it facing north. All the remaining rooms are grouped round these apartments and are passage rooms. In each wing service stairs give access to the kitchen in the basement.

Kensington Palace, the lines are long and low but the façades are far from monotonous owing to the variegated colour of the fabric, an advancing and retreating movement and the boldness of the ornamental detail. And the houses ascribed to Wren show much the same characteristics of diversity allied to a definite predilection for horizontality. The first impression of Belton House, Grantham, is that it is a flattened version of Ashdown, Berkshire. We are confronted by the same prominent cornice, the same hipped roof and the same balustraded flat out of which rises a cupola, but neither these elements nor the flight of steps impart more than a suggestion of upward movement to this essentially horizontal composition. The *oeils de boeuf* are French in flavour, but the house is actually built on the traditional H-plan, and the central pediment, despite its conspicuous modillions and garlanded cartouches, is constructed more like a gable than any southern pediment. The wings do not end in gables but, like those of Sudbury Hall, are hipped. This was an innovation of the period and a symptom of the tendency towards greater horizontality.

At Honington Hall, another and much more charming house once attributed to Wren, the cross-wings of the earlier tradition have become the merest shallow projections and the alternating segmental and triangular heads of the dormers of Belton have been replaced by straight heads which do nothing to break the roofline. The height of the chimneys, however, adds another dimension to the house, and the whole façade is invigorated by the magnificent doorway and the huge urn bursting through the broken segmental pediment. This idiosyncratic and prominent doorway foreshadows the highly individual evolution of this feature in Georgian house design. Another typical doorway of the last years of the seventeenth century is that of Rampyndene, Burwash, where two richly carved brackets support a semicircular hood carved with birds and a cherub head. Such projecting canopies distinguish many houses of this period from later examples,

181

Door hood, Wootton Wawen, Warwickshire

The semi-circular hood supported on richly carved brackets was a favourite form of over-door in the late seventeenth century. This robust example by a country craftsman is filled with acanthus scrolls, flowers and fruit modelled in plaster and brightly coloured. The panels of the door are as characteristic of the period as the hood; the upper panels are taller than the lower ones, and they all have bevelled edges, the bevels slightly sunk below the face of the panel.

The dining-room, Belton House, Lincolnshire (opposite)

The bolection (projecting) moulding framing the panels and the strongly defined segmental pediments of the door-cases are typical of the style popularized by Wren. The fielded panel projects from the line of the wall and the arrangement of the panelling follows strict rules based on the proportions of the classical column. A moulded dado runs round the room some 2 feet 9 inches from the ground; below it squat panels are squared up with tall panels above it, the panels varying in width to accommodate openings and features such as the chimney-piece. The panelling is completed by a bold, well-moulded cornice. The woodwork is all of oak, left its natural colour and polished. The simply moulded marble fireplace is no longer of two storeys, like the ostentatious compositions of the Elizabethan and Jacobean periods (see pages 131-2), but is surmounted by a panel intended to enclose a portrait. This panel, plain in more modest houses, is here embellished with splendid naturalistic carvings of birds, foliage, fruit and flowers, the richest of several similar decorations. They have always in the past been attributed to Grinling Gibbons, though no evidence of payment to him has come to light. Payment is, however, recorded to have been made to one Edmund Carpenter for three of the carvings (not including the masterpiece in the dining-room), for the most elaborate of which he received £25. The portrait above the fireplace is of Margaret Brownlow.

BELTON HOUSE *ground floor*

A. HALL
B. DINING-ROOM
C. CHAPEL

10 0   50   100

the semicircular hood often taking the form of a shell, as at Crown House, Newport, Essex.

The poetical enrichment of the walls above the ground-floor windows of Honington with classical busts represents the development of an idea originating in northern Italy, but it links the house with others of an earlier period in England, for it occurs at Barlborough and was first used by Wolsey in the great gateway at Hampton Court where the busts, like their Italian prototypes, were of terracotta and were made by Giovanni da Maiano. These stone busts, like that adorning Brick House, Wicken Bonhunt, when seen in conjunction with homely brick and tall chimneys, are piercingly eloquent of the strange metamorphosis of classical antiquity in this northern land. They occur again, with magical effect, on a house at West Green, Hampshire, where they take the place of the first-floor windows; and they invest the otherwise rather forbidding and pedestrian front of Ham House with touch of epic grandeur.

Belton, Honington and West Green House are all related in style and all conform in obvious ways to the type of house which became the established mode both in town and country. This house differed from the traditional dwelling, which was one room thick, with or without wings, in that it took the form of a square or near square block, as at Stedcombe House, Axmouth. It was symmetrical with a central entrance and balanced windows, which normally, on the two principal floors, were all of the same size, as at Lodge Park, Belton and Rampyndene House. The steep roof was hipped and shaped, in the case of the perfectly square house, like a truncated pyramid. The sides of the tall chimneys were usually panelled and the roof was interrupted by hipped dormers, as in the case of a particularly fine example of the period in St George's Square, Stamford. And another characteristic feature is the deeply projecting wooden eaves-cornice with modillions in the bedmould. The upper storey of Rampyndene House, following the vernacular style of Kent and east Sussex, is box-framed and tile-hung, but in general houses of this type were fronted in brick if they were not, like the house

at Stamford, built in a stone region with exceptionally strong traditions. The quoins were often emphasized by the use of rusticated dressed stone, as at Honington and Castle House, Launceston, though sometimes the quoins were of brick made to counterfeit stone, or, more often, were stressed by the use of a special crimson brick of fine texture, laid flush, with very fine joints, putty taking the place of mortar. And occasionally the angles of the house were marked by pilasters carried out in brick and painted to imitate stone, as in a delightfully unsophisticated house at Spaldwick, Huntingdonshire, which has unfortunately lost its original chimneys.

The house at Burwash, like several others shown here, is still lit by the typically seventeenth-century transomed windows with lead glazing and swinging iron casements which towards the end of the period were superseded by the wood-framed, double-hung sash windows such as are seen in the upper floor of the house in St George's Square at Stamford. These windows are set flush with the external face of the wall and are based on the proportions of a double square. Only one sash, the lower, was at first movable.

The interior plan of such houses is extremely simple. They are generally two rooms deep on either side of the staircase hall, though smaller houses might have only one room on each side of the hall, with irregular rear accommodation in the form of a wing or a lean-to. There is a little house of this type in Hill Street, Saffron Walden. The rooms were carefully proportioned and panelled in a way which differed sharply from the small panel style of the Elizabethan Renaissance. There was a low moulded dado with squat panels below it, made to square with the tall panels above it. The proportions of these panels corresponded to those of a classical column. Each panel was framed by a projecting moulding and the panelling was completed at ceiling height by a bold cornice in wood or plaster. The fireplace opening was conceived as part of the design of the room and was quite unlike the ostentatious, monumental overmantel of the Jacobean period, very often consisting of no more than a plain wood, stone or marble bolection moulding without a shelf. Above the fireplace there was usually an oblong panel for a painting or a mirror. In more pretentious houses, such as Belton, this panel was marked by carved festoons of fruit and flowers. Plaster ceilings were much plainer than in the preceding period, though that of the hall might be decorated. The hall of Rampyndene boasts an exceptionally fine example of ornamental stucco, an arrangement of leaves and flowers in such bold relief as to appear to be almost detached from the ceiling. Modelled ceilings do occur in the rooms of larger houses and then the decoration is generally a repeated pattern in high relief of naturalistic flowers and fruit or of ribbon-bound leaves, or it may consist of a number of heavy wreaths built up of separately modelled flowers and leaves surrounded by lesser geometric figures. The most remarkable example of this type of ornamentation occurs at Astley Hall, Chorley, Lancashire, where the central feature of the drawing-room ceiling is composed of four enormous scallop shells and two pendant boys (modelled fully in the round and attached by wires to the design) carrying festoons, all contained within a deep floral garland. Giant roses and fern fronds fill the mathematical shapes occupying the corners of the ceiling. It all looks like a rich, formal garden powdered with snow.

The staircase of the mature seventeenth-century house was of the well-type, when space permitted, with flights at right-angles to each other, leaving a well in the middle and providing intermediate landings. If there was no room for this type of stair, there were only two flights, the second returning in the opposite direction to the first, with one intermediate landing. This so-called 'dog-leg' stair proved ideal for the terrace house, which was beginning to emerge, and has continued in use in smaller houses until the present day. The staircase at Ashburnham House, Westminster, is a noble example of the well-type and of the translation of the Italian marble staircase into English wood. The fluted Ionic pilasters and columns, the arched niches and semicircular pediments over the

FOUR-ROOMED PLAN

A. Alternative position of chimney-stacks

Staircases at Ashburnham House, Westminster, and (below) Castle House, Deddington, Oxfordshire

The staircase at Ashburnham House (*c.* 1660) is in principle of the same form of construction as that at Knole (page 128): it mounts in straight flights at right-angles to each other, leaving a well in the middle. The earlier staircase at Castle House, Deddington, is of the 'dog-leg' type in which the second flight returns in the opposite direction of the first without a well-hole. Here the newel-posts, though less prominent than those of the Elizabethan staircase, still rise high above the handrail, while at Ashburnham House they are heavier, squarer, without the finial, and no higher than the handrail. The balusters in both cases rest upon the strings. At Deddington they are vertically symmetrical and forceful. The baluster form of balustrade at Ashburnham House is an alternative to the Caroline fashion for balustrading consisting of pierced panels of naturalistic carving such as can be seen at Sudbury Hall, Derbyshire, and Thorpe Hall, Northamptonshire. The probable designer of the dramatically lit and domed staircase at Ashburnham House was William Samwell, a Norfolk country squire as well as an architect.

Coxwell Street, Cirencester,
Gloucestershire

The houses in this characteristic
seventeenth-century town street are
not designed as repeating units in
terraces, but classical influence, shown
in the flat façades with rows of
windows of uniform size, give the
little thoroughfare an air of harmony
to which the gables of the house in
the foreground, dating from the early
years of the century, impart a
wayward charm. The windows of the
house on the right are the typical
openings of the mid seventeenth
century, two-light windows,
transomed to make a cross shape,
filled with square, leaded lights and
fitted with iron swing casements.

doors, echo Palladio, and one of Veronese's painted figures would not look out of
place leaning over the balustrade of the enchanting dome. But the material, the
modest dimensions, the foliated keystones and the plaster garlands of naturalistic
flowers are as unmistakably English as the sober movement and the actual design
of the staircase, which is a development of the form found in late Elizabethan
houses. It is of the close-string type, common at the time, with square newels
and a broad handrail in sections, connecting the newels but not passing over them;
and the turned balusters rest upon the string and not on the treads. A comparison
between this staircase and an example from the earlier seventeenth century, that
at Deddington Castle, Oxfordshire, shows that the chief distinction is in the
height and termination of the newel-posts. The newel-posts at Deddington are
carried up well above the handrail and are crowned with balls, a simpler version
of the heraldic finials favoured in grander houses. The balusters are clumsier and
more closely set than at Ashburnham House.

The gradual adoption of the classical manner was accompanied by a revolution
in urban building. English seventeenth-century towns were still predominantly
medieval, although gables were beginning to give way to long elevations topped
by eaves or cornices, as on one side of Coxwell Street, Cirencester, which is so
redolent of the atmosphere of the period. But the character of the Georgian town
house had already been determined in London under Charles I in the building of
the Covent Garden Piazza designed by Inigo Jones for the 4th Earl of Bedford
under the control of the King's Commission for Buildings – the object of which
was to control development in the capital and to insist on certain standards of
construction. The north and east sides of the Piazza were taken up by private
houses, which were arcaded like those in northern Italian cities and presented an
unbroken façade to the square, while behind them were gardens with coach

King's Bench Walk, Temple, London

This fine red-brick range dates from 1678 with Georgian additions. It is much more formal than the Cirencester street and depends for its grand, cliff-like effect on the severity of the façades, the long horizontal lines of the string courses and the repetition of the window units, which in houses of this early date are of the same size on all the principal floors. King's Bench Walk is still not conceived as a complete terrace composition; each house, although designed on exactly the same principles as its neighbour, is individual. The only enrichment of the austere façades is the doors. The two nearest the eye in the photograph are original, and comprise Renaissance arches flanked by Corinthian pilasters, all of brick.

houses and stables at the end. The germ of the terraced house had appeared before this, but here for the first time it was subordinated to a controlling design. Each house contained a parlour and a study on the ground floor, a dining-room and a drawing-room on the first floor and bedrooms above. The rooms were probably panelled and the oak staircase was of the dog-leg type just described. Terrace houses in the Italianate style also appeared during the reign of Charles I in Great Queen Street and the adjacent Lincoln's Inn Fields, again the work of a speculative landlord, William Newton, encouraged by the King. These houses, of which traces survive, were of red brick with the heavy wooden eaves-cornices of the period, steep, dormered roofs and façades adorned with pilasters rising from the first-floor level to the cornice. The windows were casements.

The Civil War put an end to the Italianizing of London, but the opportunities offered to speculative builders after the Great Fire were such as to encourage the terrace-house idea to such an extent that it struck an observer like Roger North as a new invention. And the man greeted as the 'inventor' of this new method of building was the most prominent of the many amateur speculators of the period, Dr Nicholas Barbon, whose singular history has been related by N. G. Brett Young. He was born Barebone, though the *Dictionary of National Biography* calls him Barbon. He lived from about 1640 until 1698 and took a medical degree in Utrecht, though he never practised medicine. He was one of the most audacious speculative builders of his day, and is said, in a letter written just before his death and quoted by Nathaniel Lloyd, to have laid out £200,000 in building, most of which he borrowed. It was Barbon who was inspired by the disaster of the Great Fire to launch the idea of an insurance company in 1682. As a builder he was chiefly active in the two areas to the south of the Strand and in Red Lion Fields, west of Gray's Inn Lane, and he was also connected with the development of

St James's Square. But it was in the Strand that he made his fortune, where the aristocratic owners of the great riverside palaces were unable to hold out against the chance of selling property they were too impoverished by war and exile to maintain. Barbon's purchase and development of the Essex House estate is typical of his character and his methods. He had bought the great Tudor mansion with its elaborate parterres from the executors of the last owner, when Charles II decided to present it to a faithful earl who had done brave work in Ireland and asked to repurchase. Barbon refused, and before the King and Council could press their demand he had pulled the house down and torn up the garden. In less than a year the site was covered with brick houses, taverns, ale houses and cook-shops, the houses as standardized and as mass produced as it was possible for them to be at that age. A few of the Essex Street houses, their façades renovated in the eighteenth century and their original casements replaced by sashes, still stand. The fact that their fronts had to be rebuilt is a criticism of the original workmanship, and Barbon's houses were no doubt as shoddy as they could be at a time when the principles of Tudor craftsmanship were still observed. Yet they are so infinitely superior in proportion and character to their modern counterparts that it is easy to overlook the meanness of the planning and the repetitious style of the detail. Each house contained a basement, a pair of rooms on each of its floors and a staircase hall running from front to back.

This eruption of 'housing' instead of individual dwellings in London was paralleled by a tenement development in Edinburgh which made this northern capital unique in Europe. After the death of James IV at Flodden in 1513, the city's bounds had been defined by a new wall beyond which the people of later generations did not care to risk building. As they increased in numbers, the problem of space became acute, and so they built upwards until, in the seventeenth century, the characteristic block of flats might rise to a height of as much as ten storeys. These lofty structures were mostly the work of speculative builders and were distinguished by vernacular features such as staircase turrets and crow-stepped gables which added to their astonishing appearance. They were known as 'lands', perhaps because they took the place of the land that was lacking for building. These soaring Edinburgh tenements did not only present a visual contrast to the London terraces: there was another even more striking difference between them. In London each house was inhabited by a single family, living vertically, but in Edinburgh each tenement contained as many families as there were floors, living horizontally and using the communal staircase. Furthermore, the 'lands' housed families of varied means and background under the same roof: artisans, merchants, writers and even nobles. The best flats were on the lower floors.

The proliferation of speculative building in the latter half of the seventeenth century is symptomatic of far-reaching changes in the whole attitude to house design at this period, and of the division of the art into two streams, the one still drawing its strength from tradition, however moulded by classical inspiration, the other based on formal canons bearing no relation to local peculiarities; the one guided by craftsmen, very often unknown and of no special culture, the other guided by the architectect who, although possessing a wide knowledge of the classical and continental styles, was not trained at the bench and had sometimes, like Inigo Jones, Sir John Vanbrugh and even Sir Christopher Wren, distinguished himself in other spheres before turning to building. When Sir Balthazar Gerbier, the painter and architect, wrote his *Counsel and advice to all builders for the choice of their surveyors, clerks of their works, bricklayers, masons, carpenters and other workmen concerned therein* in 1663, he took it for granted that a man having his house built for him would pay an architect to design it. The divorce between the architect and craftsman, which was incipient in the sixteenth century, was now accomplished, though the end-results of this separation did not make themselves fully felt until well into the nineteenth century.

Advocate's Close, Old Town, Edinburgh

The striking form taken by these tenements was the result of lack of space in the Old Town and of the strong influence in Edinburgh of tower-house design, the source of the round staircase turrets. An interesting aspect of the 'lands', as these early blocks of flats were called, was that they housed the nobility and the artisan under the same roof and encouraged a spirit of conviviality among the diverse tenants; parties were commonly given to those who shared the same stair. Boswell entertained Dr Johnson in a flat in a similar tenement near by – James's Court (now destroyed), where David Hume lived.

9

The Triumph of the Orders

No style of domestic architecture has been more popular than the Georgian; none seems more familiar and none has been more frequently aped in our own confused and eclectic century. And yet this style is one of the most extraordinary phenomena in the whole history of art. For it represents nothing more nor less than the imposition of the temple architecture of an extinct Mediterranean civilization upon the house design of a northern people. Not only the members of the small governing class but every squire, tradesman and farmer who could afford to modernize or rebuild his house, even the parson, deputy of Christ, lived behind a façade which was conceived in the terms of a Classical Order, entered his home through a doorway deriving from the portico of a pagan shrine and sat at a hearth which resembled a miniature triumphal arch or an altar to the Lares. In sharp contrast to its Italian manifestation, this last, belated expression of the Renaissance of Roman architecture on English soil was primarily, grandly domestic and at the same time, as nowhere else, comfortably middle class and homely.

It has already been observed that this adoption of the classical formula repeated the pattern of a much earlier phase in the history of the English house; and just as the houses erected by the Romans in Britain were modified by local conditions, so the scholarly understanding of pagan practice which obtained in Georgian England was transmuted by tradition, especially in the case of the smaller houses. The two widely separated periods show other affinities. They can be likened to twin eminences of sanity and culture, rising up on either side of the mysterious, Gothic, monkish and, to the Georgians, ignorant and barbaric centuries which divided them. The new natural philosophy had explained Nature's laws and had engendered a feeling of escape from the terror of inhabiting an unintelligible universe. The laws of Nature were the laws of reason and unity, and proportion reigned supreme. This sense of emancipation was accompanied by the relief of living in conditions of security. The upheavals of the Civil War belonged to the past, and by a combination of political and economic causes Britain was advancing to the front rank of European states. The Whig revolution and the victories over the French had re-established Britain's greatness and confirmed her authority. Most of those who were articulate during the first half of the eighteenth century felt they were living in an age of enlightenment. There was a remarkable degree of conscious discernment among the members of the important class of society at the top, who, prompted chiefly by Shaftesbury, displayed a new and keen interest in the principles of critical discrimination. Above all there was a general agreement as to what constituted correct taste. A system of control was inaugurated which endured until the rise of an industrial and more democratic society, but which produced its happiest results in the early and middle years of the eighteenth century. At that time those with aesthetic sensibility and the means to express it must have enjoyed the nearest approach to a Golden Age ever known to such men. We know that the era was marked by horrors which the tender

Walden Place, Saffron Walden, Essex

The red brick and white paint of this symmetrical façade, and the classical, architectural composition of the pedimented doorway, all introduced across smooth lawns by a Roman Doric, ball-surmounted column, sum up the Georgian style as it is embodied in the mansions of country squires all over England. This house, distinguished by its truncated pyramid of a roof, half hidden behind a parapet ornamented with recessed panels and rising above a bold, plainly moulded cornice; by the complete entablature of its doorcase without a glazed light; and by its sash windows with prominent glazing bars, graduated in height, is indeed typical of its period, *c.* 1740. It is equally character-istic that the composition should be marked by details depending on the whim of the builder. The windows immediately above the entrance are emphasized by thick, shouldered casing, which in the case of the uppermost window, projects on square, stepped brackets.

Palladio's Villa Capra, Vicenza (above), Mereworth Castle, Kent (left), and Chiswick House, Middlesex (right)

Palladio's celebrated villa, also known as the Rotonda, built in 1552, was based on the Roman temple architecture of Vitruvius's *De Architectura*. It is planned as a Greek cross, a form not previously used for domestic architecture. It is of brick coated with stucco. Colen Campbell's Mereworth Castle (1723) and Lord Burlington's villa at Chiswick (1729) were both inspired by the Villa Capra, but, as the photographs show, introduce subtle varations into the design to adapt it to English individual requirements (*see* pages 194, 198-9).

doubt until the comparatively recent discovery of the contemporary documents and drawings relating to the villa.

During his Italian travels, Lord Burlington had examined not only Renaissance works, but many surviving Roman buildings. He had also acquired a considerable number of drawings of those buildings made by Palladio and his pupils. His villa at Chiswick is a masterly combination of elements from these studies with a free adaptation of the Villa Capra. The most obvious difference between the two designs is that whereas the Villa Capra, although it crowns a hill, is exquisitely horizontal and exactly like a temple, Chiswick gains height and a sense of domesticity by the addition of obelisk-shaped chimneys, the transformation of the central feature into a raised octagonal dome pierced by semi-circular

The Gallery, Chiswick House,
Middlesex

The rich interior of Lord Burlington's
villa was designed by William Kent.
The walls of the apse at either end
of the Gallery are pierced by arched
openings yielding glimpses into
adjoining rooms, circular at one end
and square at the other, creating an
effect of variety and space although
the apartments themselves are small. It
was in this room that the most
important pictures in Lord Burlington's
collection were displayed. The
handsome doorway, with its broken
pediment, lead into the central,
octagonal, domed saloon.

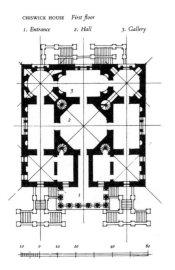

CHISWICK HOUSE   *First floor*

1. Entrance   2. Hall   3. Gallery

windows and by variations in the elevations. Only the entrance and garden fronts
are adorned with stairs, and these, unlike Palladio's, consist of grand double
sweeps, leading in the case of the façade to a Corinthian portico, while on
the garden side the double flights meet in front of a Venetian or Palladian
window (with a semicircular arched central light and side lights framed in an
Order) which can be opened to form a doorway. Such windows became a
feature of Palladian and also, in a modified form, of Adam houses. The villa is
of two storeys, the ground floor of which is of dressed Portland stone carved
with bold vermiculation. The upper storey is much taller. The proportions of
the two floors set the standard for most larger houses of the next fifty years and
are reflected in the arrangement of countless lesser houses.

For the interior the architect drew upon the drawings of Roman Baths by
Palladio, now exhibited on the ground floor of the villa, and created an intriguing
variety of room shapes and vistas, which achieve unexpected grandeur in so small
a building. Some of the rooms are rectangular. The central hall is octagonal and
domed, and on the garden side, where a long dignified gallery with apsidal ends
opens into two tiny chambers, one octagonal, the other circular, the arrangement
appears to play upon the old hall house plan. The decoration of the Chiswick
interior was the work of William Kent, Lord Burlington's talented collaborator
in the establishment of the Palladian style. Originally trained as a coach painter
in Hull, Kent had been sent by a Yorkshire patron to Italy, where he attracted the
attention of Lord Burlington, who became his life-long friend. Kent's imagination moved to solemn, stately rhythms which exactly suited the classic grandeur
of Lord Burlington's architecture, while the vigour and richness of his ornament
provided a perfect counterfoil to his patron's severely controlled framework.

As I have mentioned, Kent had just been editing Inigo Jones's architectural
drawings for Lord Burlington, and his decoration at Chiswick is imbued with the
same dynamic quality which characterizes the Double Cube Room at Wilton.
Doorways are surmounted by broken pediments and circular paintings in volup-
tuous frames held by fish-tailed amorini bursting from undulating foliage;
scrolled, festooned and gilded overmantels sit heavily upon robust marble fireplaces and above bold friezes of masks and garlands; powerful and elaborately
ornamented ribs divide the ceilings into rectangular compartments, while that of
the dome, inspired by the Pantheon, is formed of deeply moulded and profusely
decorated octagonal panels decreasing in size towards the crown. This contrast
between a plain, symmetrical exterior and unexpectedly sumptuous internal
decoration is characteristic of the Palladian style. It is even more marked at
Holkham Hall, Norfolk, planned by Kent and decorated by him with the utmost
magnificence.

Just as the villa marks a new departure in architectural design, so the garden,
largely Kent's work, opens a new chapter in the history of the house in relation
to its setting. The contrast between contrived order and the abhorred and
inimical chaos of nature expressed by the severely formal garden layouts of the
two previous centuries was no longer in key with the romantic attitude represented by such poetry as Thomson's. During his Italian travels, Kent had been
excited not only by Renaissance and Roman architecture, but by the Italian landscape. He was among the first of those who looked at the Campagna through the
eyes of Claude and Salvator Rosa, and who on their return to England set about
reconstructing the classical villas of Virgil and Horace in a garden which was a
three-dimensional interpretation of a painter's vision:

> And scenes like these, on Memory's tablet drawn,
> Bring back to Britain; then give local form
> To each idea; and, if Nature lend
> Materials fit of torrent, rock and shade,
> Produce new Tivolis.

The gardens of Chiswick House, Middlesex

Just as Chiswick House marked the beginning of a new style in domestic architecture, so the gardens of the Villa inaugurated a new Picturesque conception of the house and its environment. They were largely planned by William Kent and were inspired by Italian landscape as seen through the eyes of painters such as Claude, Poussin and Salvator Rosa. The view of the Ionic temple on the left is typical of the sudden encounters at Chiswick of features and scenes evoking classical antiquity in the manner of these painters. The sphinx on the right belongs to an avenue of sphinxes and great urns leading to the three statues in evergreen niches seen in the background of the photograph. They are reputed to have come from Hadrian's Villa at Tivoli, and represent Julius Caesar, Pompey and Cicero.

Chiswick combines something of the architectural quality of the Italian Renaissance garden with a hint of the new Picturesque landscape conception which was soon to give rise to Stourhead, Stowe and many another enchanted park, re-creating with their pillared mansions the scenery of an imagined Golden Age. At Chiswick the formality of long rectangles, ordered vistas, temples, obelisks, sphinxes and terms is softened by the meandering of an artificial river, forerunner of the irregular sheets of water which later graced every country seat; by a wilderness threaded by winding footpaths and the asymmetrical placing of a pool with an Ionic temple on its bank and an obelisk rising from its centre.

Two more English versions of the Villa Rotonda were built later in the eighteenth century, one called Nuthall Temple in Nottinghamshire, now demolished, by Stephen Wright, and another at Foots Cray, Kent; and Sir William Chambers's enchanting little Casino Marino on the outskirts of Dublin, built for Lord Charlemont in 1764, echoes Palladio's villa in its cruciform plan. But as house designs these, together with Mereworth and Chiswick, could never appear other than eccentric, modelled as they were on a building which is itself unique as a piece of domestic planning. Yet there could have been no better advertisement of the Palladian revival than the startling images of these temple-like structures in the English landscape. And the marvels of Chiswick were

extolled by those who saw it. In the fourth of his *Moral Essays*, dedicated to Lord Burlington, Pope commends the Earl's approach to architecture and landscape, his revival of Roman grandeur and his awareness of the importance of nature, and addresses him thus:

> Erect new wonders and the old repair;
> Jones and Palladio to themselves restore
> And be whatever Vitruvius was before.

Lord Burlington and his followers needed no urging, and soon the principles exemplified at Chiswick were incorporated in many other splendid and more orthodox houses, which in general took the form of a single symmetrical block, like Leoni's Clandon Park and the majority of small Georgian houses or of a central building with wings or subsidiary blocks which superseded the E- and H-shaped houses as the most suitable plan for great country mansions. Among them are Stourhead by Colen Campbell; Thomas Archer's Hale Park, already mentioned; Prior Park, Bath, by John Wood the Elder; Eversley, Warbrook, by John James of Greenwich, the designer of St George's, Hanover Square; Holkham Hall, Norfolk, built for Thomas Coke, later Earl of Leceister, by William Kent with the collaboration of Lord Burlington and the owner; Wolterton Hall, Norfolk, of which only one wing was completed, by Thomas Ripley, originally a Yorkshire carpenter; and the immensely spread-out Wentworth Woodhouse by Henry Flitcroft, also trained as a carpenter. These purely Palladian examples were followed by many later houses planned in the same way, Heaton Park and Castlecoole, Co. Fermanagh, by Wyatt; Harewood House, by Carr of York; the entrance front and wings of Kedleston, by James Paine; Kenwood by Robert Adam, and Southill by Henry Holland, to name only a few. Holkham, Clandon, Wolterton and other great houses of the early Georgian period, among them

Stowe House, Buckinghamshire

Stowe began to assume its familiar aspect as the result of improvements made to a late seventeenth-century house by Sir Richard Temple. But the south front, towards which we are looking, only took on its present form after Giovanni Battista Borra had in 1774 altered and executed a design prepared by Robert Adam. In its landscape setting, embellished with sculpture and with classical and Gothic temples, Stowe perfectly embodies the Palladian ideal. The large mansion, a central block with lower wings, recessed here, and tall end pavilions, completes a vista which, with its artificial lake, known as Oxford Water, and its flanking trees, is like an imaginary scene painted by Claude. In the mid Georgian period Capability Brown enhanced and unified the garden design begun by Charles Bridgeman in 1725 and laid out in part by Kent, who in the Elysian Fields and the Grecian Valley developed the Picturesque conceits he had first tried out at Chiswick.

202

Hawnes Park, Bedfordshire, probably by Ripley, were built, like Palladio's villa, and his palaces at Vicenza, and out of respect for Roman practice, of brick, and thus the passion for antiquity fostered the use of a material which had already taken the once universal place of timber in English house construction, and which is associated more than any other with the Georgian style.

It is usually said that the perfection of form and proportion achieved by the Palladians had degenerated into a mere cold monotonous 'correctness' of style by the mid eighteenth century. Nevertheless, the traditions symbolized by Chiswick House was still sufficiently alive to inspire the forceful rhythm of Wardour Castle by James Paine, articulated by giant columns and pilasters, paired and single; and as late as 1830 Sir John Soane was exhorting his pupils in his lectures to 'follow closely the precepts of Vitruvius'.

Furthermore, the innovations in style, of which Adam was the source, were in reality but variations on the original Palladian theme. The development of this theme was effected by the shift of emphasis from the revival of Roman Architecture by the Italian Renaissance builders to the works of antiquity itself. The publication of two books by Robert Wood, *The Ruins of Palmyra* (1753) and *The Ruins of Balbec* (1757), showed the trend of fashion; and they were followed in 1764 by the splendid folio recording Robert Adam's visit to Spalato in Dalmatia, *The Ruins of the Palace of the Emperor Diocletian at Spalato*. The neo-classical movement was quickened also by the excavations which were going on at Pompeii and Herculaneum under Charles Bourbon and Maria Amelia Christine. The style associated with Robert Adam's name reveals the influences of these new discoveries compounded with that of his own studies in Italy, both of Roman and Renaissance works, and moulded by the Palladian tradition. The

The south front, Clandon Park, Surrey

The house stands on the site of an Elizabethan building acquired by Sir Richard Onslow in 1642, and was redesigned by Giacomo Leoni in 1713-29, during the time when Leoni was associated with Lord Burlington. The house is of the rectangular block plan assumed by the smaller Georgian mansion and is built of red brick. For all that Leoni published the first English edition of Palladio, Clandon does not entirely conform to Palladian principles, for each façade is different in design, and the front shown here, with its four giant central pilasters and its swags above the first-floor windows, is French rather than Italian in feeling. Certain characteristics of the design, the brick aprons below the windows, for instance, link Clandon with Baroque houses such as Chicheley (page 172).

originality of the style consists not so much in the characteristic ornament, the garlands, vases, urns, tripods, gryphons, swags, festoons of husks, arabesques and scrolls, as in the lightness and extreme delicacy with which they are treated. This lightness informs not only the decoration but the entire building, as a comparison of Ely House, 37 Dover Street, London, by Sir Robert Taylor, and the house by Adam which still survives in Adam Street makes clear. The rustication on the ground floor of the latter is merely decorative beside the bold treatment in Dover Street, the heavy keystones and massive vermiculation of the arches; and whereas Taylor's façade is ashlared and strongly articulated in its upper storeys by tabernacled or deeply set square windows, Adam's front is of brick enlivened with contrasting stucco to mark the rusticated ground floor and the tall pilasters above it. The windows are without pediments and columns and are set almost flush with the walls, and the proportions (as Palladian as those of

Ralph Allen's House, Bath, Somerset

This was a seventeenth-century house redesigned and enlarged by John Wood the Elder for Ralph Allen, the Bath postmaster, in 1727. It shows the bold chiaroscuro and vigorous character of the Palladian style as embodied in a small town house of the early Georgian period. The ground floor is strongly rusticated, giant Corinthian columns articulate the first floor and support the ornated pediment, the central windows are arched and it is to be noted that the principal rooms in this town house are on the first instead of on the ground floor. The Italianate character of the design is enhanced by the stone in which it is carried out: Bath stone from quarries at Combe Down, which Allen had purchased in the year when the house was built, and which he made famous.

House in Adam Street, London

This house, which was part of the Adelphi scheme planned by the three brothers Adam in 1768, is basically the same design as the example on the opposite page, but it is flat and linear in its elegance beside the strong, almost three-dimensional relief of the Bath composition. The ground-floor rustications have been carried out in stucco instead of stone; and the powerful Corinthian columns have been replaced by thin, stuccoed pilasters adorned with honeysuckle ornament in the shallowest relief. Whereas in John Wood's façade contrast is achieved by the forceful light and shade of heavy mouldings and the great, smooth, cylindrical forms of the columns, here variety depends on the effect of light stucco ornament against dark brick and of extremely refined detail on a flat elevation.

Taylor) are marked, as though by embroidery, with strips of wiry honeysuckle ornament.

One of Adam's latest undertakings, Charlotte Square, Edinburgh, the most complete of his terrace elevations to survive, again illustrates both his dependence on the Palladian ideal and his divergence from earlier expressions of it. If it is compared with the Palladian Queen Square, Bath, of some sixty years earlier, the differences are again seen to lie in the character of the trimmings rather than the form, in the replacing of pedimented windows by Venetian openings and in the introduction of graceful ornament in the Edinburgh terrace, where the blocks are both taller, much more thinly and flatly treated, and of greater elegance than the Bath composition. The distinction is like that which divides the art of ancient Rome from that of Pompeii. Even the most monumental of Adam's works, the Roman Hall at Kedleston, with its columns of green-veined alabaster, gorgeous anthemion frieze of gold on blue and coved ceiling stuccoed by Joseph Rose, is ornate – albeit enchantingly, transportingly ornate – rather than noble beside that most grandly Roman of all English eighteenth-century interiors, the Great Hall at Holkham by William Kent which re-creates the spirit of antiquity more nearly than any purely domestic apartment of the Italian Renaissance, and which, although Kent makes use of actual Roman examples for details such as the glorious frieze taken from the Temple of Fortuna Virilis, is a supremely imaginative work, a fusion of classical inspiration and brilliant adaptation to existing conditions.

Adam and his brother James prided themselves in having broken away from

what they called the rigidity of Lord Burlington and of having brought about 'a greater movement and variety in the outside composition and in the decoration of the inside an almost total change'. They flatter themselves in the first volume of *The Works in Architecture of Robert and James Adam* (1773) on having 'adopted a beautiful variety of light mouldings, gracefully formed, delicately enriched and arranged with propriety and skill' to take the place of 'the massive entablature, the ponderous compartment ceiling, the tabernacle frame'. The first of these claims, as Christopher Hussey pointed out in his classic on the subject, is closely linked with the taste for the Picturesque which will be described later. This is Adam's famous definition of his conception of movement as related to the south front of Kedleston Hall:

'Movement is meant to express the rise and fall, the advance and recess with other diversity of form, in the different parts of a building, so as to add greatly to the picturesqueness of the composition, for the rising and falling, advancing and receding, with the convexity and concavity, and other forms of the great parts, have the same effects in architecture that hill and dale, foreground and distance, swelling and sinking have in landscape; that is they serve to produce an agreeable and diversified contour, that groups and contrasts like a picture, and creates a variety of light and shade, which gives great spirit, beauty and effect to the composition.'

Despite Robert Adam's admiration for Vanbrugh, the kind of movement described here has little in common with the dynamic upward sweeps, the dramatic advances and recessions, the open forms, the strong chiaroscuro and complexity of the true Baroque. It would be impossible to characterize any of Vanbrugh's buildings, still less a building by any of the great masters of the Baroque, Borromini, Bernini or Longhena, as 'agreeable and diversified'. Adam's façade is indeed 'diversified'; but even had the composition been completed by the curving wings designed to echo the crab-pincer, concave shape of the perron,

The library, Kenwood, Middlesex (left), and (right) the Red Drawing-Room, Syon House, Middlesex

Robert Adam completed Kenwood for Lord Mansfield before 1770 and was at work on the transformation of Syon for the 1st Duke of Northumberland from 1762. The Kenwood detail shows one of the apsidal ends of the library and part of one of the screens of fluted Corinthian columns which divide these apses from the centre of the room. A comparison of this photograph with that of the Chiswick gallery (page 198) shows the freedom with which Adam has used the apsidal form. The heavy coffered decoration at Chiswick has been replaced by the rich but delicate arabesques of the stuccoist Joseph Rose. The entablature carried by the columns before each semi-dome brilliantly continues the frieze from which the unusual barrel vault springs. The ceiling at Syon is another typical expression of Adam's style: both coves and flat are sprinkled with octagons and diamonds, each enclosing a decorative paper panel by another of the architect's most prolific collaborators, Angelica Kauffmann.

Drawing-room door, Syon House, Middlesex (above), and (right) view from the saloon into the hall, Kedleston, Derbyshire

The two photographs illustrate the versatility of Adam's genius. The Syon composition depends for its effect on the sumptuousness of its ornament. The doorcase, set against wall hangings of crimson Spitalfields silk, shows an ivory ground with carved and gilded decoration on the lintel and inlaid ormolu on the pilasters. The door itself is of highly polished mahogany with gilded panels. At Kedleston, where Adam worked from 1760, the emphasis is on Roman monumentality, and the great hall is intended to correspond to the atrium of antiquity. The severe Ionic door pilasters and the stupendous Corinthian columns of the hall are of green-veined Derbyshire alabaster.

the building would still have appeared sedate and only intermittently animated, even beside so pale a version of the Baroque as Archer's Chicheley. For Kedleston remains a basically horizontal, Palladian building to which the central feature, based on the Roman triumphal arch, has been added in the manner of a rich ornament. Adam's treatment of this theme, transforming it into something lighter, gayer and more elegant even than anything seen at Pompeii, is irresistible. And the effect of his graceful, projecting columns with their rich capitals supporting classical sculptures posed against a delicately ornamented attic was not lost on his contemporaries and followers. The most memorable element in Robert Taylor's design at Heveningham, built some eight years later than Kedleston, was based on it, and Sir John Soane was inspired by Adam's use of the triumphal arch motif for the façade of his own house, Pitzhanger Manor (1800–3) at Ealing.

In claiming to have achieved lightness and variety Adam was altogether justified. It is in the way in which he adapts ornament to rooms of different character and in his sense of contrast in the designing of the rooms that his genius is most impressively revealed. Chiswick House is remarkable for the pleasing diversity in the sizes and shapes of its rooms, yet Kent's composition appears limited beside Adam's refinement and development of this aspect of interior planning. A completely rectangular room is an exception in a house designed by him, where apses, octagonal shapes, elliptical ends and curving niches create endless spatial variety. Delicious ornament and the brilliant arrangement of space characterize all Adam's houses, large and small, and he is as inventive a designer of medium-sized houses for professional people, like those in the ill-starred Adelphi, as of grand mansions such as Osterley and Syon.

Home House, 20 Portman Square, London, built for the Countess of Home, and now the Courtauld Institute, is much more than the symmetrical arrangement of well-proportioned boxes which makes up the typical Georgian interior.

207

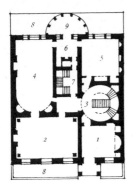

HOME HOUSE *Ground floor*
1. *Hall*   2. *Front parlour*
3. *Staircase*   4. *Back parlour*
5. *Library*   6. *Ante-room*
7. *Servants' stair*   8. *Areas*
9. *Portico*

Attingham Hall, Shropshire

The architect of this noble mansion, built for Noel Hill, 1st Lord Berwick, in 1784, was George Steuart, a Scot, about whom little is known. The austere façade and the giant portico, the starkness of which is relieved only by the elegant Ionic capitals of the surprisingly slender columns, reflect the tendency towards greater simplicity in design which followed on the transference of fashionable interest from Rome to Greece as a source of inspiration. The plain surface and the actual treatment of the stone shows the influence of the researches of the better-known James Stuart at Athens. The plan of the house is still Palladian, with colonnades connecting the main block to low service wings.

Each room introduces and enhances the one beyond it. Thus the hall leads into the circular stairwell, flooded with light from a dome at the top towards which the two steep and airy branches of the stair aspire like pleated ribbons. From the hall also open the front parlour, with its three large windows and unusual angle columns of porphyry, the back parlour, with its Corinthian pilasters and delicate swags of drapery, and the library, with its recesses in the centre of each wall and painted ceiling canvases by Zucchi. Upstairs a sequence of rooms lead one into another, as intimately related yet as fully contrasted as the movements of a Mozart sonata. A delicate boudoir gives on to the highly coloured and geometrically decorated music-room, once adorned with an organ and draped looking-glasses. This yields to a ballroom and through a tiny antechamber into the completely contrasting Etruscan bedroom. Each room depends for its effect on its relation to its neighbour and every detail is important in the creation of the final effect. Adam designed everything himself, even the door handles, and it was impossible to make the slightest change without disturbing his plan.

Among Adam's larger interiors, his most exquisitely contrived counterpoint of space and colour is perhaps Syon, even though this, like nearly all his greater enterprises, was an adaptation of an existing house. The contrast between the exterior of this house, pale and uneventful except for its crenellations (reminders of its medieval history as a nunnery), and the incredibly ornate interior is one of the most striking in all Georgian architecture. The marble floor of the vast, cool hall repeats in black and white the bold, diapered pattern of the plastered ceiling. At one end a great coffered apse houses a cast of the Apollo Belvedere, at the other a Roman Doric screen leads into a square recess which opens into an ante-room so richly coloured that the eye is dazzled. The floor is of highly polished scagliola, yellow, brown and red; and the walls are adorned with gilded stucco reliefs of trophies of arms by Joseph Rose. The oblong shape of the apartment is brilliantly converted into a square by twelve free-standing columns projecting into the room and forming a screen at one end. These columns are of green marble with gilt Ionic capitals and white and gold bases; and each supports a gilded figure based on the antique. The bold compartment ceiling of this room, like that of the hall, is more characteristic of Lord Burlington than Adam. The dining-room is apsidal, screened at either end, and along the walls stand statues in niches. A flat, fluted band runs from the Corinthian entablature all round the walls and above the band are long panels painted in chiaroscuro by Cipriani. This ivory and gold room is a perfect foil to the crimson drawing-room with its damask hangings patterned with ribbons and flowers. The ceiling is ornamented with small octagons and squares, each enclosing a panel painted by Angelica Kaufmann, and the carpet of red, gold and blue was specially woven for the room. The ivory-coloured door pilasters and the white marble surrounds of the fireplace are decorated with inlaid ormolu. But the gallery which runs the whole length of the east front is the most original and elegant room in the house. It of course recalls the traditional long gallery and the long rooms at Chiswick and Mereworth. Robert Adam himself explains the use of the gallery: 'It was finished,' he says, 'in a style to afford great variety and amusement.' It was a concession to eighteenth-century dalliance. The architect has overcome the limitations of the immense length of the narrow room with superb skill by dividing it into four pilastered units, and by concentrating on minute and varied detail, classical arabesques, reliefs of polished stucco, entertaining oval portraits. The deliciously frivolous atmosphere is enhanced by the faded pink and green colouring of the gallery, and by the two little closets at its either end. One is square and decorated with a pattern of exotic birds and trees; the other is circular with a delicate miniature cupola from which hangs a golden bird-cage containing a golden bird.

During the last quarter of the eighteenth century, house architecture was still informed with the harmony deriving from the Palladian rule, though there

209

were many variations on the theme, among them striking attempts to clothe it in different fancy dresses, some of which will be discussed in the following chapter. Meanwhile there was a reaction against the extreme elaboration of Adam's interiors and a predilection for Greek rather than Roman originals as sources of inspiration. Adam himself introduced a thoroughly Grecian feature at Osterley in the beautiful portico, which is the earliest instance, soon to be repeated by Wyatt, of columns rising directly from a pavement at ground level or with a few steps only instead of from a high podium. Adam was a friend of James or 'Athenian' Stuart, and absorbed Grecian detail from the four volumes of *The Antiquities of Athens*, published from 1762 onwards by Stuart and his collaborator Nicholas Revett after they had made an expedition to Greece. As a formative influence this work ranked with Wood's *Ruins of Palmyra* and Adam's *Palace of Diocletian at Spalato*, though its impact was not widely felt until after the beginning of the nineteenth century. Stuart's position was isolated and, irresponsible and dilatory in temperament as he was, he was incapable of the sustained effort necessary to achieve success and power. He introduced the Athenian Ionic Order in a house he designed for Lord Anson, 15 St James's Square, London, disposing the constituents, however, in the Palladian manner. Stuart had in fact imbibed Palladian principles during his early training as a painter, for his master, Louis Goupy, a fan painter, had attended Lord Burlington in Italy. He was the author of the astonishing interior of the chapel of Greenwich Hospital, and of some of the decoration at Shugborough, Staffordshire, where he embellished the park with copies of the Tower of the Winds, the Choragic Monument of Lysikrates at Athens, a Doric Temple and a triumphal arch. Revett too built an imaginative version of the Temple of the Winds for West Wycombe Park, as well as a Temple of Flora and a Temple of Music.

Another architect who exercised a far reaching influence through his pupil Soane and through Nash on the domestic building of the later Greek revival was George Dance. Very few of his buildings survive, but photographs exist of his masterpiece, Newgate Gaol, demolished in 1902, and show the remarkable way in which he was able to create dramatic effects without using columns and pilasters, but merely by juxtaposing plain and many-windowed masses, vivid rustication and sharp, rhythmic recessions.

The tendency towards greater simplicity was shown most clearly at first by the work of James Wyatt, the son of a Staffordshire builder and timber merchant, who in his youth attracted the attention of a local landowner, Lord Bagot, by his talent for all the visual arts and for music. Lord Bagot took him to Italy, where he studied under a pupil of Canaletto, Antonio Viscentini. Six years later he returned to England and astonished London by his sensational design for the domed Pantheon in Oxford Street. From then on Wyatt never lacked patrons, and for eighteen years after the death of Sir William Chambers, Wyatt was Surveyor-General. He was a dissolute character devoid of moral convictions. This is not remarkable, but Wyatt also professed himself to be without aesthetic convictions. And yet he had absolute command of the late Georgian idiom, and while deriving a great deal from Adam, whose most serious rival he became, he created several houses and interiors which are wholly enchanting and unforgettable in their restraint and serenity. Castlecoole in Co. Fermanagh, built for Lord Belmore and completed in 1789, must impress the most casual eye with its severe, almost abstract beauty and sensitive proportions. The composition, a central pedimented block flanked by wings, is essentially Palladian, but the matchless poetry of this white stone building resides in the precise balance of the grey Doric colonnades, rising straight from the stylobate in the Greek manner, and small end-pavilions with the bulk of the house and its Ionic portico. This house is also wonderfully attuned to the green landscape in which it is so closely set that a flower-starred meadow waves beneath its very walls. The interior decoration of Castlecoole admirably illustrates Wyatt's simplification of the

The hall, Heveningham, Suffolk

The restrained harmony of this room, completed by James Wyatt in *c.* 1781, one of the most unforgettable and enchanting creations of the English classical style, owes much to Adam. The very design, a rectangular apartment with a barrel vault divided into compartments by open, columned screens at either end continuing the design of the wall frieze, echoes Adam's arrangement in the library at Kenwood. But Wyatt has varied the theme by introducing fan-vault penetrations, and the decoration shows the same predilection for greater simplicity that characterizes the façade of Attingham Hall (page 208), although the influence is Pompeian rather than Greek and the colour is gorgeous. The stone floor is inlaid with red and black marble, the walls are apple-green, the chaste stucco decoration white and the scagliola columns brownish-yellow.

Adam style, and it is significant that the artists who carried out the designs for this Irish mansion were a plasterer from the workshop of Joseph Rose, Adam's great collaborator, and Domenico Bartoli, a relative of Giuseppe Bartoli, who had made the scagliola pillars at Kedleston. The circular saloon is the richest of the rooms, articulated by black, grey and white Corinthian pilasters of scagiola and with delicate stucco swags and garlands above the doors and on the frieze and ceiling, much more sparsely distributed than in Adam's elaborate designs. The lobby on the first floor, serving the bedrooms, is an even more chaste and graceful room and an inspired interpretation of the Greek style. It is lit by a dome and surrounded by a gallery, the ceiling of which is supported by coupled columns. The four stoves which heat this apartment are set in semicircular niches above floor level and assume the delightfully unexpected form of fat, garlanded pedestals surmounted by casts of Greek poets.

Other celebrated interiors by Wyatt include that at Heveningham, probably the dining-room at Crichel, Dorset, Heaton Park, Lancashire, and the dining-room at Westport House, Co. Sligo. The stucco decoration in all these interiors is always much more scattered and much less highly coloured than Adam's work. The patterns consist of circles, semicircles, and segments of circles, outlined by fragile husk chains and reeding and enclosing urns and branching, spiralling foliage, roundels, swags, and oval and circular wall plaques containing figures painted or in relief, and festooned with husk chains describing loops and circles above and around them.

The most outstanding protagonist at the close of the century of the severer

Philipps House, Dinton, Wiltshire

This house, formerly Dinton House, was not built until 1813–16, but it still shows Palladian ancestry, though here the style is modified by the extreme neo-classical simplicity encouraged by Greek influence. The architect was Jeffry Wyatt (1766–1840), nephew of James Wyatt, who changed his name to Wyattville when he was knighted in 1828. The gigantic portico of plain Ionic columns rises directly from the pavement instead of from a stepped base as at Hale (page 194) and Attingham (page 208). The severe façade is otherwise unrelieved, except

212

for the plain entablature below the eaves and a string course.

At Attingham Hall, George Steuart's rich interiors finely contrast with the austerity of the exterior, but here, as with Henry Holland's houses, with which Philipps House has obvious affinities, the apartments are as sparsely adorned as the outside. The house is built of white Chilmark stone quarried in the neighbourhood and the material emphasizes the idyllic aspect of the building in its undulating park. It is the idealized landscape setting in the style of Capability Brown or Repton which makes Philipps House so poetical an evocation of the Palladian theme.

Attic mode, besides Wyatt, was Henry Holland (1746–1806), a builder's son who married the daughter of Capability Brown, the landscape gardener. The sources of his intensive classical studies were Desgodetz's *Les Edifices Antiques de Rome* (1682) and Stuart and Revett's *Antiquities of Athens*. His design for Carlton House, built for the Prince of Wales in 1783, which was demolished in 1826 but which is pictured in Pugin's *Microcosm* and Pyne's *Royal Residences*, is impressively individual and yet maintains the spirit of the established tradition. It is very long and low, rusticated like Dance's Newgate, with a Corinthian portico and an Ionic colonnade of coupled columns shielding the façade from the street. Holland's best-known surviving work is Southill, Bedfordshire, which he re-modelled for Samuel Whitbread. The house, like Castlecoole, repeats the traditional composition of the main block and wings, connected here by loggias with coupled columns, a feature which takes the place of the portico in the projecting centre elevation. The effect here is of sharp angularity and the treatment is austerely plain except for light rustications on the end-pavilions and the lower storey of the main block.

Whereas earlier eighteenth-century houses, as we have seen, exhibit the greatest possible contrast between the exterior and interior, the interior of Southill is closely related to the exterior in its fastidious elegance and extreme restraint. The ceilings are in some cases very gently vaulted, but very often they are quite plain except for narrow ribs or bands of plaster adorned with Greek key patterns or delicate running Greek foliage. Holland's severe treatment of surfaces, the precision of his design, the dignity and reticence of his neo-classical ornament are

213

characteristic of the last phase of the tradition which began with Lord Burlington, the phase we know as the Regency.

★

Turning now from the architecture of the leading masters of Palladianism to the ways in which the style was handled and developed by local builders, one of the most fascinating aspects of the subject is the influence of printed books in spreading knowledge of the classical mould. Palladianism was established not so much by actual example as by the publication throughout the century, and particularly during its first half, of books of plans, designs and practical instructions for builders which encouraged laymen to concern themselves with design and provided craftsmen with a rule of thumb. Colen Campbell's *Vitruvius Britannicus* has already been mentioned, and another important work of this kind was Kyp and Knyff's *Noblemen's Seats* published in 1709. One of the ways in which an architect sought to establish himself was to persuade his patron to publish sumptuous volumes of the plans of individual great houses when they were being built. The designs by Campbell, Ripley and Kent for Houghton appeared in 1735 and Isaac Ware published a further volume on the plans, elevations and sections, chimney-pieces and ceilings of this great house in 1760. But more influential than these was the appearance of innumerable text-books for the guidance of provincial builders and craftsmen. The most prolific author of such productions and the most widely read was Batty Langley (1696-1751), the son of a gardener, the writer, in addition to his other works, of four books on gardening and one of the most fashionable landscape gardeners of the period following the creation of Stourhead by Sir Henry Hoare. The list of his manuals includes *A Sure Guide to Builders* (1726 and 1729); *A Young Builder's Rudiments* (1730); *The Builder's Compleat Assistant* (1738); *The City and Country Builder's and Workman's Treasury of Designs* (1740); *The Builder's Jewel* (1741); and *The London Prices of Bricklayers' Materials and Works* (1747). Many editions were sold of all these publications, which contained practical instruction in building and surveying, mechanics and hydrostatics, drawings showing the proportions of the different Orders with comparisons between those of Vitruvius, Palladio, Scamozzi, Vignola, Serlio, Perrault, Brosse and Angelo; a summary of Acts of Parliament relating to building, plates of designs for doors, windows, chimney-pieces, ceilings, and even of bookcases; and details of mouldings. Batty Langley also set up a school of architecture in Soho together with his brother Thomas, an engraver. Their pupils were chiefly carpenters.

Another prolific author of textbooks was William Halfpenny, who described himself as 'architect and carpenter'. *Magnum in Parvo: Or The Marrow of Architecture* (1722) and *The Art of Sound Building* (1725) contained instructions on how to set out geometrically brick arches, niches, columns and pilasters, and designs of various buildings and staircases. Halfpenny collaborated later, in 1742, with the Scottish architect and carpenter, Roger Morris, author of the romantic, turreted Inverary Castle in Argyllshire, with his brother John and with 'T. Lightholer, carver' in the production of *The Modern Builder's Assistant*. *The British Carpenter* by Francis Price (1733), Clerk of the Works and Surveyor of Salisbury Cathedral, was another popular work which showed how to set out roof timbers, staircases, etc., and was furnished in the second edition with a supplement illustrating the Orders according to Palladio and showing Palladian doors and windows; this work went into four editions and was recommended by Hawksmoor, John James and James Gibbs.

A more comprehensive and more influential publication than all these was Isaac Ware's *A Complete Body of Architecture* (1756) dealing with terms and

Broad Street, Ludlow, Shropshire

This memorable street with its cobbled slope is steeped in the serenity which unites any eighteenth-century row of houses even though they are of different dates and vary in detail. The houses at the end of this row, set back behind white railings, display the steep roofs, dormers and characteristic doorways of *c.* 1700. Neither of these façades is perfectly symmetrical, probably because space did not permit of double fronts. The next house has the quoins of rubbed brick of a deeper colour than the rest of the façade and the sash windows set flush with the external face of the wall which marked the Queen Anne and early Georgian period. Its neighbour exhibits a doorcase with a broken entablature and triangular pediment framing the fanlight, which dates it about 1750; the windows are slightly recessed in accordance with a London building regulation of 1708 affecting country districts considerably later. The house nearest the camera is distinguished by Venetian windows on all its floors, a legacy from the Palladians and a feature made popular by Adam in the late eighteenth century.

materials, the siting of the building, foundations, drainage, the shell of the house, the ornament, the use of the Orders, proportion and design. According to the author of the *Life of Nollekens*, J. T. Smith, who was told the story by Nollekens's father, Ware was a poor sickly little chimney sweep who attracted the attention of a 'gentleman of considerable taste and fortune', who happened to be passing one morning when the child was amusing himself by drawing a Whitehall street-front upon the building itself with a piece of chalk. The gentleman was so interested that he purchased the rest of the boy's time, educated him, sent him to Italy and upon his return employed him and introduced him to his friends as an architect. This generous patron may have been Lord Burlington himself; in any case Ware was closely connected with the Palladians. His best-known work was Chesterfield House, now demolished, and he designed No. 5 Bloomsbury Square in London for his own use. But it is upon his book, tedious reading though it is in parts, that Ware's fame rests. It was instrumental in forming the taste of builders in remote counties and in helping to inculcate the Palladian principles of design and building that determined the marvellously harmonious domestic style of the eighteenth century. Ware's thorough exposition of these principles remained a standard textbook until the early nineteenth century, and the matter in it was repeated in a number of other manuals for village craftsmen such as

Pallant House, Chichester, Sussex, and (left) Rutland Lodge, Petersham, Surrey (since gutted by fire)

Pallant House was built in *c.* 1712 for Henry Peckham, whose crest showed an ostrich, which may have determined the form of the birds on the gatepiers, though they have been called dodos and even swans. This brick house displays all the familiar characteristics of the early Georgian style: a hipped and dormered roof half hidden behind a brick parapet varied by recessed panels, symmetrical chimney-stacks, bold quoins marking the angles of the house and the projecting centre, sashed windows of the same height on both floors, basement offices and a broad doorway flanked by Corinthian columns and crowned by a segmental pediment. Rutland House, which was built in 1660 and altered *c.* 1720, is a fine and more modest version of the style seen at Clandon Park, in which an attic storey is added above the modillioned cornice, continuing the plane of the façade upwards and finishing with a parapet. The tall, handsome doorcase shows the unusual design of Doric pilasters against a rusticated background.

Clarence House, Thaxted, Essex

This house dates from about the same as Rutland House, *c.* 1718, according to the information on a rainwater head, and presents a different but equally characteristic early Georgian façade to the street. The windows are segmental headed and are furnished with large keystones in the stone that sometimes took the place of rubbed brick for dressings. The doorway, again with a segmental pediment, is based on the Corinthian Order, common at this time. The entablature curves gracefully in the middle, a form also associated with this period. Although there is no eaves-cornice, the parapet, which had come into general use even in the country by the second decade of the century, does little to mask a traditional roof and dormers. These dormers are also typical of their decade in that they are alternatively triangular and segmental and are fitted with casements instead of sashes.

those by William Pain, 'architect and joiner', whose *Builder's Golden Rule* (1781) and *The British Palladio* (1786) once more set out the details of the Orders, the proportions of elevations and the use of ornament according to the Italian master.

The smaller houses built according to these textbooks and the Palladian rules follow the same of development as their more stately contemporaries, the essentially classical design becoming lighter, more elegant, flatter and simpler towards the end of the century. But owing to the slow rate of change in fashion in many country districts, it is seldom possible to date a small Georgian house accurately from its elevations alone. The so-called Great House in the corner of the Market Place, Lavenham, for instance, is late Georgian according to the Greek Doric doorway and thin glazing bars, but the steep pitch of the hipped roof suggests the Queen Anne period. The house might have been built then and altered later, or the local wheelwright, working in the last quarter of the eighteenth century, may have constructed the roof in the earlier style. A strong under-current of traditional craftsmanship, adjusted and modified to suit the ever-changing details of fashion, yet always controlled by classical laws of proportion, produced a distinctive, insular, vital style, always in a state of flux, never stereotyped yet immediately recognizable.

Of the recognizable characteristics of the Georgian house, the foremost are the symmetry of the façade and the sense of balance and repose imparted by well-placed windows of exactly the right proportions. The typical elevation shows a central entrance and two principal floors with an attic and the basement which had been introduced in Elizabethan times. Sometimes in streets where space did not allow for the double front, semi-detached houses are combined to present a symmetrical façade, with the two entrances centrally placed beneath a single pediment, as in Upper Cheyne Row, Chelsea. The steep, truncated pyramidal roof of the late Stuart period, which tended to counteract the classical aspect of the elevation, was now half-hidden by a parapet with a cornice of brick, or later of stucco. The practical reason for this was the vulnerability to fire of the pro-

minent wooden eaves cornices which were such a noticeable feature of late seventeenth-century houses, and which were prohibited in London by a statute of 1707. Visually the parapet gave more prominence to the façade; and this emphasis was still more marked when, by about 1720, the square block of the house was covered by two parallel roofs of gentle pitch which from the ground were completely hidden by the parapet. Both types of parapeted roof can be seen in North Brink, Wisbech.

Though always in classical dress and always reticent, the aspect of these Georgian façades is extraordinarily diverse. Very often the parapet is no more than a simple cornice concealing nothing of the attic dormers; sometimes the tops of the dormers peer over a higher parapet; sometimes, following Leoni's example at Clandon Park, a parapeted and pedimented attic storey continues the plane of the façade upwards above the cornice, as at Rutland House, Petersham. Frequently the house soars up, as in many Dublin terraces and as at High House, Bawdsey, with no articulation on its plain cliff-like front other than the openings. Often, in country districts, it stands fatly, of comfortable height, perhaps with neither basement nor attic. Sometimes tall pilasters frame or enliven the façade instead of the more usual stone or brick coins, seen at the well-known Pallant House, Chichester.

Palladian motifs are handled with the most delightful freedom and are found in the most remote and unlikely places. An arched, rusticated doorway with a

Ormsby Hall, Lincolnshire

Ormsby was designed by James Paine in 1752–5. Paine began as a Burlingtonian and the Lincolnshire house shows Palladian influence, though it is quite individual. The south front, facing the camera, was not intentionally asymmetrical: the canted bay was the centre of Paine's composition and the extension upsetting its balance dates from 1803. The house of 1755 was boldly animated, as now, by its central bay, while the side-bays jutting north and south took the place of wings. A giant pediment emphasized the Palladian aspect of the house and contrasted with the severity of the walls and the three-light windows under blank arches. The Roman Doric porch was part of the later addition, perhaps by John Carr.

218

heavy keystone, like the entrance Kent designed for Lady Isabella Finch's house in Berkeley Square, looks out on the churchyard at Stamford; central Venetian windows with Tuscan porches on either side of them grace the small limestone village of Winster, Derbyshire, in a design embracing two houses. Pilasters rise from a frieze running above the ground floor and Ionic columns frame the central, triangular-headed light of the first-floor Palladian window. Between the pedestals of these columns runs a row of crude little balusters, an arrangement peculiar to the local builder of this engaging elevation, which he repeats, with a variation in the shape of the balusters, beneath the plain rectangular windows. At Bradford on Avon open triangular pediments emphasize the windows of the important first floor of a seven-bayed house with a massively rusticated door, while adjoining it the central window of a façade articulated by a bold cornice above each floor and by an emphatic, pedimented, pillared doorway, is distinguished by a segmental pediment. At Withersdale Street, Suffolk, the Palladian theme of the central block with wings is echoed by curving screen walls on either side of the façade, each pierced by an arched door and terminating in brick, ball-topped piers. And at Clare in the same county this same theme takes the form of a Georgian front added to a sixteenth-century house with screen walls terminating in tiny pavilions with round-headed doors and bulls-eye openings above square-headed windows. At Burford, Gloucestershire, a seventeenth-century cottage hides an oddly placed dormer and a detached chimney-shaft behind a Georgian

Red House, Withersdale Street, Suffolk

In this rustic, mid-Georgian version of the Palladian ideal, the parapet only half conceals a steep, pantile roof, the curving walls, pierced by round-arched doors echoing the round-headed window above the entrance, play the part of wings, and behind the balanced, one-room-thick block and at right-angles to it is part of an older, traditional house. The façade, like that of most houses of the mid eighteenth century, is no longer enlivened by quoins but has become a blank expanse, relieved only by the openings, and classical detail is limited to the doorcase.

The Circus, Bath, Somerset (opposite), and (right) The Crescent, Buxton, Derbyshire

The monumental Circus dates from 1754–8 and was the last great work of the elder John Wood, who died in the year it was begun. It was the first circus to be built in England, and when it was new it stood isolated like a Roman circus and the space it enclosed was paved for spectacles and tournaments. The design was intended to emphasize the shape and unity of the Circus, for the elaborately ornamented architraves are continuous and the powerful rhythm of the three tiers of coupled columns, Tuscan, Ionic and Corinthian, is broken only where three streets enter the Circus. If the house has become externally a repeating unit in one great palatial façade, it remains internally an individual composition. There is no uniformity behind these splendid façades: they conceal rooms differing widely in number, shape, size and decoration.

The waters of Buxton, like those of Bath, were known to the Romans, and in about 1780 the fifth Duke of Devonshire conceived the idea of following the example of Bath and reviving the use of the springs. John Carr's Crescent was thus built close to St Anne's Well and, based on a more exact classical knowledge than the Bath Circus, consciously and nobly, if rather prosaically, reflected the spirit of antiquity.

parapeted front with heavy quoins and classically arched windows with big key-stones.

Apart from a vivid expression of the Palladian conception in individual houses, there is a further variation on the theme in the terrace. Terrace houses, as we have seen, existed at least as early as the sixteenth century and the brand of terrace house built by Barbon has already been discussed. But the terrace imagined as one grand architectural composition, not as a row of individual or even repeating units, is the creation of the eighteenth century. The square had already come into existence as the nucleus of planned improvements in towns. Inigo Jones's Covent Garden piazza, the only instance before Wood's achievements at Bath of a consistent scheme in terrace design, had been followed by Bloomsbury Square, St James' Square, Red Lion Square and Soho Square. But there had been nothing like the stupendous plan by John Wood the Elder for Bath. The real precursor of his grandiloquent conception was the ancient Roman city of Bath, and one of the most fascinating episodes in this story of repeating patterns is the building of Palladian Bath above the actual ruins of classical antiquity celebrated by the Saxon poet. Wood's conscious intent was to revive the splendours of Aquae Sulis. The Circus, indeed, the earliest of its kind in England, was directly based on the design of the Roman circus and has been compared by Sir John Summerson to the Colosseum. Wood even intended the enclosure to be used for an 'Exhibition of Sports'. Queen Square is so designed that each of its ranges is seen as a single palatial composition articulated by attached columns with a central pediment spanning five bays.

At the time of Wood's death, only Queen Square and the Circus were completed. His son built a whole quarter round them, crowning his father's work

with the noble, monumental sweep of the Royal Crescent (1757-65), in which the great elliptical terrace is treated as a single composition facing a grassy open space like one vast Palladian mansion. The sonorous and magnificent curve of the Crescent is set in momentum by a hundred giant Ionic columns rising above a completely plain ground floor and reducing the incidence of door and window to faint shadows of these usually forceful elements in the Georgian façade.

The vision of the terrace as a monumental façade persisted well into the nineteenth century. The grand crescent at Buxton by John Carr of York, built less than ten years after Wood's Royal Crescent, is a more scholarly interpretation of the classical mode, reflecting the antiquarian interests of the second half of the eighteenth century. The ground floor is taken up by a rusticated arcade from which Roman Doric pilasters rise to support a metope frieze, deep cornice and balustraded parapet. Robert Adam's Charlotte Square, Edinburgh, has already been mentioned. Bedford Square, London, perhaps by Thomas Leverton, the son of a builder of Woodford, Essex, is a handsome version of the Adam manner; each side is treated as a single composition with a pedimented, stuccoed and pilastered centre bay. The broadly spaced vermiculated rustications of the wide-arched doorways, the bearded faces on the keystones and the capitals of the pilasters appear to be made of stone but are fashioned of a species of terracotta, the famous Coade Stone, the precise composition of which remains a mystery. It was manufactured at Lambeth from about 1770 when, as Mrs Esdaile revealed in two articles in *Architect and Building News*, published in 1940, Mrs Eleanor

Charlotte Square, Edinburgh

By comparison with the Circus and the Crescent shown on the preceding pages, Robert Adam's Edinburgh terrace is strikingly elegant and even gay. Yet it is conceived in the Palladian tradition and, carried out in stone instead of brick and stucco, it has a far greater solidity than the house shown on page 205. It was in 1791, towards the end of his life, that Adam was invited by the Edinburgh Town Council to design the Square as part of the scheme for the New Town. It differs from the grand terrace compositions of the earlier Palladians in detail, in its greater simplicity and in the lightness of its ornament - circular panels and festoons - rather than form. It is treated as a single pedimented façade, though the relentless rhythm of both the Bath Circus and the Buxton Crescent is here replaced by a composition like that of a grandiose mansion with a central feature and projecting wings. Charlotte Square is almost unique in retaining its original lamp standards with their pretty glass bowls.

Coade, 'the daughter of the person who discovered the composition', took over an unprofitable business concerned with the production of artificial stone. Under Mrs Coade's skilful management and with the aid of a young sculptor, John Bacon, the business prospered so well that most of the architectural ornament in the West End of London, in the neighbouring counties and even farther afield, came from the Lambeth factory. Excellent and durable as it proved to be, Coade Stone was a fake material and furthermore the ornaments made of it were mass produced. The rustications, keystones, mouldings and capitals of Bedford Square occur in other places in London, in Mansfield Street, Devonshire Street and Harley Street. They were chosen from a pattern book instead of being designed for a specific purpose in an individual setting, and, already breathing the air of make-believe and standardization which together with other influences were eventually to destroy the house as a work of art, they mark a definite decline from Burlingtonian principles.

Among later interpretations of the terrace composition, the east side of Mecklenburgh Square, London, by Joseph Kay, with a stuccoed central feature with Ionic pilasters, is in the same tradition as the work of the Woods, but with all the grandeur and solidity changed to prettiness. At Wilmington Square, a version of the Adam style with a central pedimented feature and stuccoed ground floor with mock rustications, the design, though well conceived as a whole, betrays its late date by the close spacing and mean proportions of the openings.

When, as so often happens, the façade of the Georgian house is quite plain, the success of the design depends very largely on the character and disposition of the door and windows. From the time of Queen Anne the double-hung sash was an essential feature of the classical elevation. At first the upper sash was fixed, and in cottages it was rare for both sashes to lift even as late as the nineteenth century. Many examples survive all over the country of cottage windows with fixed upper sashes. The lower half when raised is kept at various heights by means of a series of notches and a catch to hook into them. The form of sash suspended by a weight and line and moving over a pulley with a groove for the weight in the solid, moulded frame is thought to be of Dutch origin. This was followed by the box frame containing counter-weights attached to cords for raising and lowering both sashes, and towards the end of the eighteenth century sash fasteners, attached to the meeting rails, were invented.

The proportions of these tall sash windows were at first based on those of the double square, and the windows were of the same height on each floor, though occasionally the upper windows might be shorter as at Creech Grange, Dorset, where a Palladian front was added to the family seat of Sir Thomas Bond, speculative builder, of Bond Street, by Francis Cartwright in about 1740. The attic windows, when they occurred in the same plane as the ground and first floors were invariably shorter and usually square as at Clandon Park, thus effectively preventing the composition from taking on a predominantly vertical aspect. In later houses the windows were graduated in height: in mansions, where the reception-rooms were on the first floor, they were marked by the tallest windows, but in smaller houses the ground-floor openings were the tallest. The window heads might be semicircular or straight, and although the latter were most commonly seen in the individual small house throughout the century, different rhythms were imparted to façades by diverse arrangements of the two types, especially in terrace architecture. The window above the entrance was often distinguished by special treatment; it might be a three-light Venetian or a round-headed window in contrast to its neighbour, or the opening might be treated as an alcove for sculpture. Bow windows, descendants of the oriel, became common about the middle of the century and assumed many forms. They might sweep round in a gentle curve, they might project as half-hexagons as in houses at Saffron Walden, Newport and Tenterden; sometimes they were corbelled out like the true oriel and sometimes they were adorned with columns

and pilasters. The window-sills of some houses are emphasized by brick aprons,
as in examples at Ludlow and Harleston, and occasionally the head of the window
may be accentuated by decorated brickwork. The openings of a house at
Ampthill, for instance, are surmounted by wavy pelmets of brick constructed
and designed with incredible ingenuity.

The broad wooden frames of late Stuart windows were, as we have seen, set
flush with the outside face of the wall, but a building regulation of 1708, motivated like the statute prohibiting wooden eaves cornices by fear of fire, enacted
that frames should be set back four inches. But this law did not affect country
districts until towards the end of the century, when another statute of 1774 led to
the concealing of all the boxing of sash windows in the brick-work. By this time,
the fat glazing bars of Stuart and early Georgian houses had become thin. The
glazing bars of Wren's time were two inches thick; by 1820 they were only half
an inch thick. White-painted window frames containing a white grill of from
twelve to as many as twenty-four panes contrast with the warm red brick in
which they are set in the façade, which in our imaginations is most typical of the
Georgian house; and which, though its formal source is in classical antiquity and
Palladio, is so utterly unlike either, combining them with a vernacular tradition
which was in itself a guarantee that the academic formulas of the textbooks
would seldom produce sterility. The white paint associated with Georgian houses
was first used not for aesthetic but for practical reasons. Oak had become even
scarcer in the eighteenth century than it had been in the previous period, but now
that the timber-framed house had become obsolete there was no need for wood
of such great strength and softwood was imported from Scandinavia. Although
this was easily worked it could not withstand the moist English climate like oak,
which hardened with age and exposure. Oil paint had been used by artists since
the late fifteenth century, but it was only now that scientists discovered that it
could serve as a protective skin on the surface of wood. They experimented with
lead oxide applied with an oil media, and factories for the manufacture of lead
oxide were opened along the Thames estuary. Thus the painted timber of both
the windows and door of the Georgian house was invariably white. For although
the masons in some of the stone regions carried out the whole façade composition
in stone, the doorways of the vast majority of lesser Georgian houses were chiefly
of wood, no matter where they were situated.

The door frame of the Georgian house is its most individual feature, and nowhere else is the local builder's fertility of invention more eloquently displayed. The door, above all, was the expression of his mastery of the fashionable classical style, and of his client's up-to-dateness. If the owner of a sixteenth- or seventeenth-century outmoded hall house could not afford to have it refaced, he would at least indulge in a pilastered and pedimented doorcase, and even the cottage was embellished by a miniature, simplified version of the temple portico. Although the proportions for external doorways were laid down in the pattern books as a double square, the heights were generally more than twice the width of openings, and designers permitted themselves every degree of latitude in their interpretation of details.

It has already been remarked that at the close of the seventeenth century the most prominent feature of the door was the projecting hood carried on elaborately carved brackets. Country builders were still devising new variations on this theme at the end of the last century and a few miserably attenuated and timid ghosts of the idea can still be seen on some of the standardized brick boxes of today. But in the centres of fashion the projecting hood gave way in the early Georgian period to the pedimented entablature on engaged columns or pilasters. The pediment was either curved, as at Pallant House, Chichester, and 3 High Street, Harleston, or triangular, as at 42 West Street, Harwich. The compositions are based on one of the Orders; the Corinthian in the earlier part of the eighteenth century followed by a predilection for Renaissance Ionic, and even more for Doric in the middle and later years of the period. The Greek Ionic Order with fat columns and a heavy entablature, became popular in the years following the Napoleonic Wars. But no doorway exactly repeats another, and the endless, unexpected ways in which column, capital, abacus, entablature and pediment have been harmonized and decorated by individual craftsmen in every part of the country are among the sharpest of the many pleasures to be derived from the English vernacular. Scarcely ever does one come upon a doorway which exactly reproduces an example in one of the pattern books. The Tuscan door in Langley's *Builder's Jewel* has materialized between two bulging bays in Saffron Walden High Street, but even here the proportions of the door at the head of a flight of

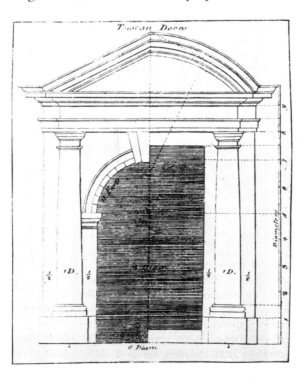

Doorway, 74 High Street, Saffron Walden, Essex

This doorway, carried out in painted wood, as were most Georgian doorways, even in stone districts, shows how a country craftsman used one of the most popular of the many pattern books which established classical principles of design in every district. It is an interpretation of the Tuscan door (reproduced alongside it) from Batty Langley's *Builder's Jewel* (1741).

sixteenth century. An inventory made in 1536 at the Monastery of St Syxborough on the Isle of Sheppey mentions a set of chamber hangings of painted paper, while a fragment of block-printed paper dating from the same century was found in the Master's Lodge, Christ's College, Cambridge. The pattern is large in scale and adapted from contemporary damask. Two block-printed papers dating from about 1580 were found early in the present century on the walls of Borden Hall, Kent, tacked to the filling between the timbers, the designs consisting of small conventional flowers on brightly coloured grounds. Similar patterns were used during the seventeenth century, and on some papers the devices were painted in oils or tempera, sized with gold and then dusted with powder colour, producing a rather rough texture. Flock papers, in which the design is printed with an adhesive, then sprinkled with finely cut pieces of silk or wool to stand out like damask or velvet against the plain background – an English technique – also made their appearance during the seventeenth century. Towards the end of that period merchants and missionaries brought back from China sheets of paper painted with gay designs, and gradually these, made up into sets for the walls of rooms, became a fashionable though costly form of wall decoration. As Lady Mary Wortley Montague wrote to her daughter from Louverne in 1749: 'I had heard of the fame of paper hangings and had some thought of sending for a suite, but was informed that they were as dear as damask is here, which put an end to my curiosity.' These Chinese wallpapers were painted with designs which fell into three categories: landscape, bird and flower and scenes of domestic life. A characteristic Chinese landscape paper, combining lofty peaks, pines and rivers, still adorns a room in Ramsbury Manor, Wiltshire.

In the mid eighteenth century John Baptist Jackson of Battersea was producing paper imitating stucco as well as what he called 'chiaroscuro' printed papers, offering such subjects as 'The Appolo of the Belvidere Palace, the Medicean Venus and other antique statues, landscapes after Salvator Rosa, Claude Lorrain, views of Venice by Canaletti, copies of all the best painters of the Italian, French and Flemish Schools, in short every Bird that flies, every Figure that moves upon the Surface of the Earth, from the Insect to the Human, and every vegetable that springs from the Ground, whatever is of Art or Nature, may be used for fitting up and furnishing rooms.' This description, taken from a book published by Jackson in 1754, is daunting, yet Horace Walpole used some of these papers on his walls and wrote of them: 'When I gave them the air of barbarous bas reliefs, they succeeded to a miracle. It is impossible at first sight not to conclude that they contain the history of Attila or Totila done about the very era.' Jackson's papers were advertised in the London *Evening Post* of 8 January 1754 thus: 'The new invented paper hangings for the ornamenting of rooms, Screens, andc., are to be had by the Patentee's direction of Thomas Vincent, Stationer, next door to the Waxwork in Fleet Street. *Note.* These new invented paper hangings in Beauty, Neatness and Cheapness infinitely surpass anything of the like nature hitherto made use of.'

In minor houses, needless to say, papers of a much simpler design than these were favoured, often a perfectly plain, unprinted paper was used, blue being the preferred colour. Marbled and varnished papers were also popular because they were more durable.

The method of hanging wallpaper by this time was to paste it directly on to the bare wall. Before the middle of the century the paper was pasted on to strips of canvas or thick rice paper and then tacked or stuck on to the plaster, a procedure which superseded an earlier method of applying the paper to wooden frames stretched with canvas and set up over the brick or stone walls. Prior to our own century there was seldom any idea of stripping off previous papers, and in old houses as in the case of that at Harpenden mentioned earlier in this book, as many as twenty layers of paper have sometimes been found, revealing a whole historical sequence of designs.

10

The Gothic and Picturesque

The Rococo extravagances in plaster and carving described in the last chapter were contrasted with the disciplined and often austere elevations and plans of Georgian houses. They never actually jeopardize the Palladian framework of these structures, but in extreme cases, such as the interior of Isaac Ware's Chesterfield House, now only to be enjoyed in photographs, the arabesques, scrolls and curves of the Rococo ornament, undulating about the Renaissance forms of doors and mantelpieces, hint at a reaction against the Classical Order. And when the Rococo mingles with the Oriental taste, creating a sense of mystery and outlandishness entirely alien to the Vitruvian Rule, the hint becomes a threat. At Ramsbury, as in other instances where the Oriental fashion is expressed by no more than a wall-paper, the outlandishness is subordinated to the proportions and symmetry of the room. But there exists one example of the Chinese mode, the most memorable and probably the most complete in England, which shows how easily the Orders could be swept aside by this particular form of fantasy. The fireplaces and door-heads in the extraordinary lilac, white and yellow Chinese Room at Claydon look as though they are awash in petrified waves breaking about the pale frowning masks of drowning Chinamen. But dazzling though these are, the eye is distracted from them by a greater marvel, the enormous pagoda-like alcove occupying a whole wall and vividly, minutely carved with fretwork, scrolls, rocks and waves and hung with white-painted wooden bells. This is the setting for an amazing, eternal tea-party. A Chinese man and woman sit at a table laid with a fringed cloth and a tea-set and perched on a dripping, shell-encrusted rock. Their two children stand on either side of them, each raising an arm in a wild gesture of greeting, a gesture echoed with startling intensity by the squat figures at the table, who seem about to clap their hands as part of a compelling ritual which the onlookers cannot ignore. This remarkable tableau is the work of a local Buckinghamshire woodcarver, unknown apart from this one brilliant example of his talent, his recorded surname, Lightfoot, and a description of him by Sir Thomas Robinson, the architect of the house, as an artist with 'no small trace of madness in his composition'. There is nothing to compare with Claydon in this country and although William Halfpenny included *New Designs for Chinese Temples* and *Rural Architecture in the Chinese Taste* among his pattern books and although Sir William Chambers published *Designs of Chinese Buildings, etc.* in 1757 and was the author of the Pagoda at Kew, *chinoiserie* remained an indoor and decorative rather than an architectural style, its influence being limited externally to an occasional feature such as a trellised porch like that of Reydon House, Harleston, or the frieze on an otherwise classical doorway. Lightfoot's work at Claydon is nevertheless symptomatic of an attitude of mind which eventually proved to be incompatible with the classical ideal.

It was inevitable that the desire to break through the limits imposed by Palladianism should find its most prominent expression in the revival of the style it had originally ousted, the Gothic, but, as we shall see, it took other wayward forms including the Egyptian, Moorish and Indian modes, was fostered by a widespread interest in the antiquities of the British Isles as opposed to those of Rome and Greece and was encouraged above all by a passion for the Picturesque which subjected every style, even the classical, to its requirements.

The name of Horace Walpole and that of Strawberry Hill, the house he purchased from Mrs Chevenix in 1747 and reconstructed as a miniature Gothic castle, have been associated with eighteenth-century neo-Gothic by every writer on the subject, and the building of the completely Gothic Strawberry Hill certainly established the style as a fashion. But Gothic trimmings had appeared before this. The embattled house at Somersby, Lincolnshire, ascribed to Vanbrugh, has already been described, and Vanbrugh had built a huge sham fortification at Castle Howard as early as 1709, thus already uniting the Gothic and the Picturesque, as in his great Baroque houses he had combined the Picturesque and the classical. Another early instance of medieval detail occurs in Ivy Lodge, one of the adornments of Cirencester Park, built for Lord Bathurst, possibly by Kent in the 1720s. If these and other examples of the delight taken by individual architects in Gothic forms are considered in conjunction with the persistence of medieval traditions in much regional building during the sixteenth and seventeenth centuries, it might appear and has been ably argued that the Gothic style had never died. But the architectural character of all the houses mentioned in the previous chapter is the very antithesis of Gothic, which the arbiters of taste rejected as barbaric. And whether Ivy Lodge be by Kent or not, it most clearly demonstrates that the Palladian version of Gothic is as little related to the architecture of the Middle Ages as are most Elizabethan versions of Renaissance forms to the work of Palladio. The eighteenth-century situation reverses and exactly balances that which obtained in the sixteenth century. Ivy Lodge conforms to the classic pattern of a central block with wings, although the main building suggests a fat tower and the end pavilions are adorned with crow-stepped gables. Battlements and pointed openings are part of the same composition as a Renaissance

frieze, a Palladian window and *oeils de boeuf*, an assemblage as charmingly
incongruous as the juxtaposition of battlements, Ionic pillars and gables in the
Elizabethan manor of Snitterton, Derbyshire.

The Georgian style was so basically hostile to the Gothic mode that when
pinnacles, pointed arches and battlements became popular, they had no immediate effect on the insistent symmetry of domestic architecture. Despite the
serious antiquarian enthusiasm of the age, Georgian Gothic strikes the eye sobered
by acquaintance with the academic approach of the Victorians as deliciously
artificial, a high-spirited interpretation rather than an imitation. And this view
of it was later endorsed by Humphrey Repton, who in 1806, in his *Inquiry into the
Changes of Taste in Landscape Gardening*, pointed out that the Gothic house could
only avoid being a copy of a castle or abbey by using a travesty of the medieval
style and that 'a house may be adorned with towers and battlements or pinnacles
and flying buttresses, but it should still maintain the character of a house of the age

243

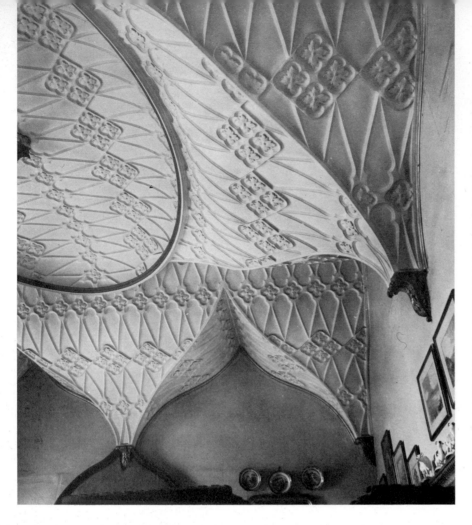

These gigantic fan vaults are coarse in
detail beside those of Arbury, and of
a shape, an exotic ogee, peculiar to
the Gothic Revival. The principle
component of the decoration, the
mouchette or dagger, is one of the
most popular motifs of the mock-
Gothic stuccoist. The work belongs to
the last quarter of the eighteenth
century, when the brilliant precision
of early Gothic Revival work, still so
remarkably evident at Arbury, was
beginning to give way to a more
sketchy approach.

The same spirit which animates the
brilliant Rococo work of the great
continental eighteenth-century
stuccoists, such as the masters
responsible for the decorations at
Sans Souci or the Amalienburg at
Munich, is manifest in the superb
Gothic fantasies in plaster at Arbury.
There is the same playful relationship
between Rococo forms and their
classical sources as between these
mock-Gothic fan vaults, ribs,
pendants and clustered shafts and their
medieval prototypes. Stucco replaces
stone and a round arch consorts with
Perpendicular-inspired details, which
are elaborated and mingled in
patterns unlike anything found in
true Gothic architecture. The use of
trefoil cresting, for instance, to adorn
the inner and outer edges of the arch
framing the bay window, is entirely
original. This great window belongs
to the last stage in the gothicizing of
Arbury, which went on from 1746 to
1793. It was probably designed in the
1760s by Henry Keene, but was
carried out by his successor, the local
craftsman Henry Couchman. The
plasterwork was done by William
Hanwell in 1786.

and country in which it was erected'. Classical proportions are usually firmly
retained in the façade and plan of the average Georgian family house exhibiting
Gothic influence, an influence which is for the most part confined to the windows
and entrance externally and inside may appear only in the design of a door and
chimney-piece here and there. The central light of a Venetian window may assume
the form of an ogee, as in houses at Porchester and Woburn, or the tracery of a
fanlight may echo the interlacings the quatrefoils and mouchettes of medieval
glass. The effect is always animating and sometimes adds just that touch of variety
necessary to redeem symmetry and severity from dullness, as in a plump, em-
phatically horizontal façade at Hatfield Broadoak where ogee-headed lights
playfully relate rounded bays to turrets. Rarely does the introduction of Gothic
elements disturb the prevailing symmetry, though this does happen at Well
Walk, Hampstead, where it is only the pretty, toy-like character of the jutting
oriel which prevents it from entirely ruining the balance of the tall narrow front.

The owners of houses which were originally built at a time when medieval
traditions were still alive were naturally often attracted by the idea of gothicizing
them. Simple examples of this tendency can sometimes be seen in East Anglia
where, as in a house by the Stour at Clare, pointed lights (much too regularly
disposed to be original) replace the straight-headed windows which must once
have graced the jettied façade, imparting an irresistibly fantastic and picturesque
air to a genuinely sixteenth-century structure. But the most splendid instance of
such gothicizing is Arbury Hall, Warwickshire, a Tudor house transformed for
Sir Roger Newdigate over several decades, beginning in 1750, probably by
Sanderson Miller, Robert Keene and a local architect called Couchman. The
exterior is strictly symmetrical and evokes rather than reproduces the Perpendicular style with its gay battlements and fretted parapets. The cusped and

crocketted interior superimposes Gothic detail on classically proportioned rooms
with brilliant staccato intensity and a meticulous rhythm wholly unlike the
irregular movement of true Gothic. And whereas the forms of Gothic architecture, however richly they were ornamented, were dictated by function, the
groined and barrelled ceilings, the elaborate fan vaults, the shrine-like chimney-
pieces, the white and gold bosses, ribs and pendants, the chamfers and ogees, the
trefoil crestings and filigree tracery of Arbury, the very arches and fluted pillars
are pure decoration, all fashioned of plaster. The make-believe constitutes half
the charm of these ravishing interiors, the effect of which was described by George
Eliot as 'petrified lacework'.

In two of the rooms at Arbury the essentially classical habit of mind of the
designers is apparent in more than the proportions: in the dining-room, with its
mullioned windows in pointed embrasures and its huge fan vaults, copies of well-
known classical statues stand in Gothic canopied niches; and the Gothic book
recesses and cusped panelling in the library are combined with a coved ceiling
painted with Renaissance arabesques and medallions in the manner of Angelica
Kaufmann.

Gothic and classic appear side by side in a yet more astonishing manner at
Castleward House, Co. Down. The house, originally, like Arbury, a sixteenth-
century building, was first improved and enlarged for Michael Ward during the
first half of the eighteenth century, perhaps by Richard Cassels, who had come to
Ireland in 1728 to design Castle House, Co. Fermanagh, for Sir Gustavus Hume.
But the building we see now was only assuming its present unforgettable appearance by 1772 at the hands of an unknown architect. The south-west front is an
exercise in the Palladian manner with a projecting centre block with three arches

surmounted by four Ionic columns and a pediment bearing the Ward arms. There is nothing particularly exciting about this design in itself. The originality of Castleward is only revealed when the Palladian front is considered in relation to the north-east façade. For this confronts the delighted spectator with an array of battlements and Gothic windows. The unique arrangement is expressive of a disagreement between Bernard Ward, son of Michael and First Lord Bangor, and his wife, Lady Anne, over the rival merits of the two most fashionable styles of the period. They finally resolved their difference of opinion by giving one front a Gothic dress and building the other in the classical mode. Inside the house Lady Anne insisted on Gothic detail while her husband maintained his preference for the Palladian convention. A classical hall leads into a Gothic saloon and the dining- and music-rooms are uncompromisingly classical. The sitting-room exhibits perhaps the most eccentric Georgian Gothic decoration in existence. So exaggerated, so inflated are the fan vaults of this apartment that they dwarf all else, and yet, recognizably of plaster, they seem to the affrighted eye buoyant rather than weighty and about to swell to an even more nightmarish size. Here, as at Claydon, fantasy has run riot and obscured the classical proportions of the room.

There is another far more unassuming instance of this mingling of the Gothic and the classic under the same roof at Beccles in Suffolk. St Peter's House stands

Interior of St Peter's House, Beccles, Suffolk

As at Castle Ward (page 244), some of the rooms of this house are decorated in the Classic, others in the Gothic taste. The preference of the Gothic Revivalists for ogival forms again apparent. The fireplace is conceived as a shrine with plaster statues of saints in the canopied niches.

building. The former abbey had already been made into a house soon after the Dissolution when the property was acquired by Sir William Sharrington. The south front remains much as he left it and shows that he was inspired by the new feeling for Renaissance architecture (*see* pp. 79 and 80). The classical tendency of Sharrington's conversion was reversed by the work carried out at the abbey in the neo-Gothic manner by Sanderson Miller for John Ivory Talbot, a descendant of Sharrington's niece, in 1754-60. The pretty ogee-headed windows of the hall, the doorway between them approached by a two-armed flight of steps and the polygonal angle turrets; and inside, the tunnel vault adorned with coats of arms, the Gothic chimney-pieces, Gothic niches and crested doorheads light-heartedly and superficially refer to the truly medieval survivals at the abbey, the perpendicular cloister and two rooms in the former west range of the cloister garth.

At Butley in Suffolk the possibilities of the abandoned but miraculously well-preserved gatehouse of the former Augustine priory were splendidly realized by its various eighteenth-century owners. The priory was surrendered in 1538 and after brief tenures by the Dukes of Suffolk and Norfolk passed to William Forthe, a clothier of Hadleigh. Forthe built a Tudor house on the east side of the gatehouse while the rest of the monastery was allowed to disintegrate and to become a quarry for road repairs and local building. On the death of Elizabeth Devereux, descendant of William Forthe, the priory was inherited by her husband John Clyatt. In 1737 the gatehouse was acquired by George Wright through his

Mendham Priory Lodge, Suffolk

The Gothic aspect of this typically Picturesque cottage has been encouraged by the use of fragments from the former Early English Cluniac Priory of Mendham, founded in the twelfth century.

Butley Priory, Suffolk

The fourteenth-century gatehouse of the former Augustinian priory was converted into a house after the Dissolution and reconverted again by successive eighteenth- and early nineteenth-century owners, beginning with George Wright in 1738. The heavily buttressed structure, with its rich ornamental façade, already satisfied most of the requirements of the Picturesque architect. It was irregular, it united different styles in one building, it was full of variety in colour and texture, it was Gothic (and partly ruined when Wright acquired it) and it made conspicuous use of traditional materials. These qualities were recognized by Wright and encouraged by later owners, the Marquess of Donegal and Lord Rendlesham.

marriage to the Clyatt heiress. By that time the Tudor attachment was a ruin and Wright demolished what was left of it when he decided to turn the gatehouse into a residence. As it stands today the building is the product of several periods harmonized by the Picturesque taste. Fourteenth-century cusped and canopied niches, traceried windows and moulded arches consort with square-headed windows, whose sills have been cleverly adapted to accommodate the pointed tops of the sham, flushwork windows below them, and with roofs and chimneys of Georgian and nineteenth-century origin. The curious proportions and the astonishingly lively and diversely patterned texture of Butley make a staggering impression. A great central gable shoots up between two projecting bays which were once the towers of the medieval gatehouse but which George Wright truncated and provided with the steep, sloping roofs, narrowing oddly towards the eaves and adding much to the unusual aspect of the house. Behind loom tall chimneys, a hipped roof and the shaggy outline of buttressed walls. The former passageway through the gatehouse, consisting of a narrow pointed pedestrian entrance cheek by jowl with a wide depressed arch for vehicles, at once challenges the idea of symmetry, as indeed does the richly vaulted living-room now occupying the passage. The spandrels of the taller, broader arch are filled with flushwork in the shape of large trefoils, while the pedestrian opening is surmounted by a curvilinear flushwork panel more like a Georgian fanlight than any other flint and freestone ornament of the fourteenth century, when this peculiarly East

255

Milton Abbas, Dorset

Milton Abbas was laid out for Joseph Dormer, later Earl of Dorchester, perhaps by Sir William Chambers in *c.* 1790 to replace the original village which intruded too closely on the calm vista seen from the converted abbey. It is not a fully developed Picturesque village, for the cottages are formally designed and regularly disposed in their valley setting. Milton Abbas does, however, mark the appearance of the Picturesque in a simple form, the rustic. The cob and thatch of the cottages illustrate the architect's regard for traditional building construction, the balanced relationship between the village and its surroundings show his appreciation of the rules of Picturesque composition, and the grouping of the cottages in pairs may be considered as the first instance of one of the most enduring legacies of the Picturesque style, the semi-detached house. There are many model villages scattered about England, most of them Picturesque, whether they make use of the classical idiom, like Lowther, in Westmorland, where the square stone cottages stand in fine contrast to the sham Gothic Castle, or whether their thatched roofs and mud walls follow a meandering path on a tree-clad slope, as at Selworthy, Somerset. A complete Picturesque village with church to match was built at Sulham, Berkshire, in 1838, and many other examples of this peculiarly English conception were created throughout the nineteenth century and greatly influenced the design of building estates in the present age.

Cottage near Hales, Norfolk
Round house, Hatfield Heath, Essex
Lodge, Wivenhoe Park, Essex

The Picturesque view of architecture did not only give rise to complete villages, but to innumerable isolated, romantic cottages adapted to the park scenery of great estates and set off by their own bursting flower gardens and box-edged paths. Such cottages, entrance lodges or casemented keepers' dwellings might be circular, oval or polygonal as well as rectangular; one design might resemble nothing so much as a Gothic umbrella, another (that near Hales) could caricature the human face with exaggerated eyebrow arches in its thatch and a bonnet porch like a bushy moustache. The windows tended to be pointed, the roofs were preferably of emphatically steep, ornamental thatch, while the chimneys were almost invariably tall, central and of a Gothic or Tudor flavour. Early nineteenth-century examples of these cottages ornés are often constructed of local materials. The cottage near Hales stands on a tarred brick and flint base with walls of plastered clay lump. Countless publications by professional designers and amateur authors contain illustrations which might have served as models for the cottages shown here. Among them may be mentioned Pocock's *Architectural Designs for Rustic Cottages, Picturesque Dwellings, etc.* (1807) and *Rural Residences . . . consisting of Designs for Cottages, Decorated Cottages, Small Villas and other Ornamental Buildings* (1818) by J. B. Papworth.

Cast-iron veranda-balcony, Pershore, Worcestershire

The elegant display of black-painted cast-iron, usually found on the fronts of those Regency houses not affected by the Gothic or Fancy styles, adds an exotic note to the pale, severe façades. The veranda, a development of the great overhanging, lattice-enclosed window of Saracenic architecture, appeared among the Picturesque cottage and villa designs of late eighteenth-century publications such as Plaw's *Rural Architecture* and Charles Middleton's *Picturesque Views for Cottages, farmhouses, villas*. The cast-iron designs were taken from pattern books and mass produced, so that although there was considerable choice, repetition was inevitable. The veranda at Pershore has its counterpart at Cheltenham, where every combination of the standardized cast-iron units of the period, sometimes intruding in a wrought-iron design, can be studied.

or fretted bargeboards, these enchanting little houses are rendered yet more picturesque by the forest of giant evergreens planted by Loudon to embrace the whole village, protecting it and casting over it a dense infinity of reposeful shade.

In contrast to Milton Abbas and Great Tew, the hamlet of Blaise near Bristol, laid out by John Nash for John Scandrett Harford, the Quaker banker, in 1811, shows little if any feeling for local style. The cottages, mostly constructed of rubble, are distributed about an undulating, curving green, each one differing wholly from its neighbours. Some of the roofs are thatched, with exaggerated ridges, some are stone-slated, while others are pantiled; some of the chimneys rise in Tudor clusters and others stand in rounded or polygonal isolation. In the villages Nash designed some thirteen years later on the edge of Regent's Park, Park Village East and Park Village West, the rustic element is barely present at all. Here the idea of the Picturesque village is applied to suburban development with such success that suburbs have ever since been Picturesque to a greater or lesser degree. The Park Villages exhibit all the diversity of style advocated in the pattern books and may indeed have prompted some of Robinson's and Loudon's designs. Italian, Gothic and chalet-like villas with fanciful gables and balconies are irregularly and closely set amid trees with the canal, which was part of the layout of the Regent's Park scheme, running between them, thus conjuring up the countrified atmosphere so dear to the Englishman in an environment that was anything but rural.

These Park Village houses are stuccoed and the name of John Nash is associated more than that of any other architect with the use of this fake material which, since it was intended to counterfeit stone and create a *trompe l'oeil* effect, was an essentially pictorial medium and which was also the first of those synthetic productions which have destroyed regional traditions and which have since come

Cumberland Terrace, Regent's Park, London, by John Nash

John Nash laid out Regent's Park, the terraces surrounding it, Park Crescent, Park Square, Regent Street planned as a 'Royal Mile' from Carlton House to the park), Carlton House Terrace and St James's Park for the Prince Regent between 1811 and 1835. Although the scheme, disrupted by the destruction of Regent Street in the present century and by the refusal of the Treasury in the architect's own day to subsidize the whole of the original plan, represents only a part of Nash's grandiose conception, it remains one of the most visually satisfying creations of the Picturesque imagination. The terraces are the supreme example of the Picturesque taste expressed in the classical idiom. For though it is Grecian and Ionic, this architecture is of stucco, not stone, and the triumphal arches, statues and columns, the pediments and huge pavilions, so effective scenically, and so lacking in finish, rise like stage sets from the surrounding green, palatially exaggerated in size, their air of sham reinforced by the mean and careless design of the service quarters at the back.

to be used almost exclusively for domestic building. Nash used Parker's Roman cement on its introduction in 1798 and changed to Hamelin's mastic in about 1820. He was mentioned earlier as one of those architects who composed with equal readiness in the classic or medieval styles. But whatever the forms he used, his work is always Picturesque. His Regent's Park terraces are among the grandest and are perhaps the noblest examples of the style. Like all Picturesque buildings they are exquisitely attuned to their surroundings, rising like fabulous palaces from the landscaped park, yet suggesting their proximity to a great metropolis by their superb urbanity. Although the language of these terraces is classical, it is only necessary to compare them with the Bath crescents to realize how superficial is their connection with the Palladian concept. Instead of the continuing and conspicuously horizontal lines of façades and parapets and the symmetrically disposed chimney-stacks of the Bath houses, which even when they are forced to go uphill mount the slope with the regularity of a flight of steps, the Nash terraces advance and retreat more dramatically than Adam's composition at Kedleston, and the diverse shapes of balustrades, sudden uprearing attic storeys, enormous pediments and groups of sculpture break up the skyline. The execution is careless, the detail summary; all that matters is the pictorial effect, which reaches the height of its splendid, spectacular expression in the Ionic triumphal arches, giant columns, statues and abrupt variations in height of Cumberland Terrace. This stucco group in particular makes an impression of vast size and Burke had proclaimed size as an indispensable quality of the sublime. Nash's command of the colossal is yet more overwhelmingly demonstrated at Carlton House Terrace, which looms above the trees of St James's Park like a stupendous glittering cliff, the very image which, according to Price, grand Picturesque architecture should bring to mind. Not even the Brighton Pavilion, with its exotic mixture of Indian domes, crimped Islamic arches and Gothic friezes of cusped lozenges, is more expressive of Picturesque principles than these London terraces, though the

Bow window, Hastings, Sussex

Cronkhill, Shropshire (right)

The form of this romantic stucco house, built by John Nash for the agent of the Attingham estate in 1802, is entirely dictated by Picturesque principles. The round tower is purely scenic, for it does not contain a single circular room; and it is contrasted with a big square tower (not visible in the photograph) to which it is joined by the colonnade, which runs on two sides of the little rectangular block squeezed between them.

CRONKHILL Ground floor
1. Entry   2. Hall   3. Drawing-room   4. Dining-room
5. Study   6. Offices   7. Modern addition

264

Pavilion remains the most striking statement of these principles in Oriental guise. Nash expanded an idea already present in the design Repton had made for an extension to the original Pavilion by Holland. Repton had previously been laying out the grounds of Sezincote in Gloucestershire, a house built by S. P. Cockerell in 1805 for a retired Indian nabob. It is a gorgeous Indian palace with Saracenic arches and a single huge bulbous dome hovering above a wooded park, an irregular sheet of water and a miniature Oriental temple. But Nash's Pavilion far outshines Sezincote and the scheme Repton based on it as a composition in the Picturesque manner, not only in its variety, but also in its use of stucco instead of stone and in its exuberantly arbitrary mingling of styles to create an illusion instead of an interpretation of Far Eastern architecture.

The results of Nash's application in stucco of the full register of Picturesque effect to cottage, villa and urban architecture can be seen all over Britain. The white and cream façades of Regency houses display delightfully sketchy and unorthodox versions of the Greek, Gothic, Moorish, Egyptian and castle styles. They may be battlemented, gabled, turretted or parapetted, their windows furnished with flimsy dripmoulds; or sashed or pointed and casemented, with tracery in the heads and margin lights; or they may be arched and fantastically glazed to suggest the Orient. The door, occasionally panelled in the Gothic mode, may be set in a porch of medieval character flanked by clusters of narrow engaged shafts; it may be approached between squat pillars recalling the entrance to an Egyptian temple; it may be announced by huge, heavily Greek, Doric or Ionic columns supporting a swelling projection in accordance with the cult of the colossal as in a notable terrace, Albemarle Villas in Plymouth; or it may, in a most theatrical manner, merely hint at a style with a few grooved lines in the stucco head and jambs, as in the case of a little house in Church Street, Saffron Walden.

Egyptian House, Penzance, Cornwall
House in St John's Wood, London

The Picturesque did not always assume a Gothic character. Many publications of the first quarter of the nineteenth century provided a choice between Gothic, Grecian, Swiss, Italian, Egyptian and Oriental styles of domestic building. The Egyptian style became fashionable after Napoleon's campaign in Egypt. The example at Penzance (left) is an extreme instance of the style. It is all carried out in brightly coloured stucco irresistibly combining solar discs, lotus flowers, terms and window tracery showing eccentric winged, obelisk and hexagonal patterns with the Royal Arms and a Napoleonic eagle. The St John's Wood house is Moorish in flavour, and again even the window lights are in key with the exotic style.

Lighthouse keeper's lodge, Cromarty,
Ross and Cromarty, and toll house on
the Bath Road, between Hungerford
and Newbury, Berkshire

The low tower of the lighthouse is
fused with the one-storeyed lodge,
which takes the form of a small
temple in the Egyptian manner. This
lodge was not built until 1846, but is
still, in this remote place, in the
stuccoed style of the Nash period.
Perhaps the common root of the
words Pharos and Pharoah prompted
the architect in his choice of style. He
included in his design a little altar (not
visible in the photograph) dedicated
to Aesulapius, physician to the
Argonauts.

In the charming Berkshire toll house
(now demolished), the stuccoed style
takes the shape of a toy castle with
fat turrets and emphatic, black-
outlined battlements, a form copied
by Staffordshire potters a little later in
the century.

Even when it remains perfectly plain, the Regency house, light and insub-
stantial looking with its low-pitched roof, wide eaves, lightly recessed windows
and excessively thin glazing bars, has the air of being part of a scenic design, and
the classical ideal, still faintly and exquisitely manifest in its simple, box-like
proportions, trembles on the brink of dissolution. Frequently the pictorial element is enhanced by the intricate cast-iron verandas, balconies and porches which
are such distinctive features of the Regency period. Such verandas and balconies,
sometimes covered by Oriental-looking, up-curving or shell-shaped canopies,
though widely distributed, are especially associated with seaside houses, for the
development of the coastal watering-places as well as of some inland spas coincided with the age of stucco and the Picturesque. Another noticeable characteristic of Regency seaside architecture is the frequent occurrence of the curved
bay window. Two, three and sometimes four storeys high, these windows billow,
one after another, along whole terraces and crescents, echoing in true Picturesque
fashion the element they confront.

Cast iron, like stucco, was a substitute material which helped to weaken the
strong sense of the special qualities and varieties of stone, wood and metal which
had persisted throughout the earlier Georgian period and to encourage the facile
creation of Picturesque effects. Cast iron had been used by the Adam brothers for
the mass production of fanlights, and it was used structurally for the first time in
1771–81 for the famous bridge over the Severn at Ironbridge. William Porden
created a fantastic display of cast-iron Gothic tracery at Eaton Hall in Cheshire,
designed in the Perpendicular style for the Marquess of Westminster in 1803, and
by the Regency period this material had captured the market for balconies,
verandas, stair balustrades, bootscrapers, doorknockers and much else besides.
The veranda, a development of the great overhanging, lattice-enclosed windows
of Saracenic architecture, appeared among the Picturesque cottage and villas
designs of such late eighteenth-century publications as the already mentioned
Plaw's *Rural Architecture* and Charles Middleton's *Picturesque Views for Cottages,
farmhouses, villas, etc*. The cast-iron designs were taken from pattern books and
mass produced, so that although there was considerable choice, repetition was
inevitable. There is no better place for the study of every possible combination
of the standardized cast-iron units of the period than Cheltenham. The chief
architect of the town, J. B. Papworth, expressed his satisfaction that in view of
the cheapness of cast iron it could be expected that richly embossed work would
come into frequent use, 'particularly as this method is now generally substituted
for other materials'. His expectations were fully realized, for the filigree designs
of the early Regency soon gave way to a coarse flamboyance achieved by the
addition of embossed ornaments such as adorn the exuberant balustrades and
porches of many a Victorian villa.

The close connection between the Picturesque and later suburban development
has already been noted. One of the most persistent components of the suburb, the
semi-detached villa, first became established through Picturesque example. The
cottages at Milton Abbas could be called semi-detached, and in his *Georgian
London* Sir John Summerson refers to a map of the Eyre Estate, St John's Wood,
showing a complete scheme of development, dated 1794, based entirely on semi-
detached houses. The originator of the plan may have known Milton Abbas, but
it was revolutionary to apply the semi-detached idea to a district which was
regarded as an extension of the metropolis. When the Eyre Estate came to be
built up in *c*. 1820, it consisted largely of semi-detached villas. Paired stucco
houses are common in other developments of the period, often, despite their
enchanting fragility and elegance, presaging in the variety of their ornament
applied to a repeated plan, the semi-detached excesses of the present century. The
substitution of semi-detached villas in urban architecture for the terrace, conceived as a single classical composition, completed the conquest of the Palladian
Order by the Picturesque style.

11

Victorian Dilemma

Nathaniel Lloyd ends his great work on the English house with a few examples from the first half of the nineteenth century to show 'the trend of taste – or lack of it . . . . The sight is a melancholy one, and when the course of the degradation is realized, pursuit of the theme can profit little.' We, half a century farther removed from the Victorian age and in the midst of a housing revolution which is more alarming in its implications than any of the changes of the past, view the last century with more sympathy, and even on occasion with nostalgia. It is a period of peculiar fascination for us, for it is in relation to what happened then that we now realize the disastrous potentialities, aesthetic as well as social, of past tendencies, many of them going back to the sixteenth century. They came to fruition in the Victorian era and are seen in retrospect to have exerted a malignant, disruptive influence from which there has been no recovery.

The architect and craftsman were now irrevocably divorced from one another; and in an industrial society the craftsman was replaced by the general contractor, who became a dominant figure in the profession – one, moreover, whose only interest was financial. The emphasis on economics was underlined also by the entry of a new figure on the scene: the quantity surveyor, who provided the information, calculated from the architect's plans and specifications, on which different contractors based their competitive prices. It was inevitable that standards of execution should fall and that quantity should be preferred to quality. And other factors hastened the decline. The expansion of industry and the spectacular explosion of the urban population gave tremendous opportunities to the speculative builder. The population of London alone increased from just under a million to four and a half million between 1800 and 1900, and that of the whole country was trebled by 1850, most of the growth taking place in the northern or midland towns of Birmingham, Manchester, Leeds and Sheffield, where new housing (a word first used in Victorian England to describe workers' dwellings and tenements for the poor) created mile upon mile of mean, squalid streets devoid of architectural merit. Furthermore, the revolution in transport, the elimination of distance brought about with such extraordinary rapidity by the advent of the steam railway, meant that the close, traditional relationship between the house and its environment was broken, that one of the most vital ingredients in domestic architecture was lost. Local materials no longer dictated the texture and colour of the house: the builder had to make a conscious choice of materials and this choice was usually decided by cost. Thus Welsh slates found their way almost everywhere, creating harsh discords in regions of half-timber, brick and limestone.

Many writers have pointed to affinities between the Victorian age and that of Elizabeth I. In both periods society was undergoing dramatic changes, in both patronage was passing into the hands of a new class. The sixteenth and nineteenth centuries were equally characterized by astonishing vitality, power of invention and individuality. Architecturally they are alike in their love of ostentation and bigness of scale and in their confident use of motifs from diverse styles to enhance a predominantly vertical image. But the resemblances only shed a more glaring light on the gulf that divides the two ages. The difference is that so acutely felt by Matthew Arnold and expressed in his comparison of Glanvil's Oxford Scholar who had 'one aim, one business, one desire' with the men of his own time:

> O born in days when wits were fresh and clear
> And life ran gaily as the sparkling Thames:
> Before this strange disease of modern life
> With its sick hurry, its divided aims,
> Its heads o'er taxed, its palsied hearts, was rife.

Although Elizabethan prosperity was based on commerce, Elizabethan civilization was based on an imaginative ideal, the ideal, as we have seen, of breeding a nation of men who were Christian, chivalrous, valiant, merciful and generous, just and free. The consciousness of this ideal, which implied a morally responsible society, redeemed the preoccupation with wealth and property which then, as in the nineteenth century and in all periods of violent change, was much in evidence. Thus the Elizabethan artist, whether architect, writer or musician, did not regard commercial enterprise as a dangerous, hostile development, but as a glorious adventure, a parallel in the world of action to his own endeavours. His age was one of vivid contrast, but these contrasts were united in a view of life and reflected in an art remarkable for their strength and cohesion. The Victorians, on the other hand, failed conspicuously to synthesize the conflicting forces of their age. They failed because they were dominated to a terrifying extent by their single-minded pursuit of wealth. Their very attitude to the wretchedness and depravity of the new factory towns and the new working-class districts reveals the degree of their obsession and their blindness to their responsibilities. In their subscription to the belief, stemming from Adam Smith, that their prosperity depended on the unimpaired operation of economic law, and that to alleviate the sufferings of the poor would be tantamount to interfering with sacred economic processes, they acquiesced in the appalling misery of a growing percentage of the population as part of the price that had to be paid for the nation's wealth. Instead of pitying the poor as victims of a fate which might have been their own, they feared and despised them.

The Victorians' worship of property is epitomized in their glorification of 'the Home'. For while many of the objects with which they crammed it - the wax fruit, the feather flowers and stuffed birds under glass domes, the scrap screens, the shell-framed pictures of ships and seaside scenes, the ships in bottles, the sand bells, the pictures of cut paper and dried seaweed, the narrative paintings, the paper-weights through whose convex glass a building or townscape leaps into three-dimensional life, the albums and mementos - conjure up for us a vision of snug, secure domesticity, their superfluity in the Victorian house turned it into a personal museum, the deathly, stifling character of which was the antithesis of the concept of the home. Many descriptions of Victorian interiors by those who knew them confirm this strange dichotomy:

> The Dormer drawing room was, in some curious way, reminiscent of a mausoleum. The vault-like air, the white marble mantelpiece recalling tombs; the wreath of wax camelias made by Mrs Velindre in early youth and by her jealously treasured; the heavy curtains of purple cloth and the immense valence weighted with balls and fringe, that concealed their union with the curtain-rod as if it were an indecency - all these and the solemn hush that pervaded it, slowly gathering Sunday by Sunday like a rising sea, made it less like a sitting room than a grave.

The quality of creative imagination which gives individual relics of the

Victorian period an independent vitality even when they are hideous, is belied by so obsessive a reverence of the keepsake and souvenir. Not only the ostentatious villas of south London, Hampstead and Edgbaston but the little houses and cottages of respectable and thrifty artisans and farm labourers partook of this museum and shrine-like character. The various palaces of the Queen were supreme examples of the home as a memorial not of personal taste but of personality. After the death of Albert, Victoria retained all his rooms as he had left them and slept with a wreath above her head in the bed where her dead husband had lain. Possessions were an expression of individuality and a guarantee of its importance and survival in a period already threatened by the impersonality of the modern world.

At a time when the outward forms of wealth were cherished beyond all else, the English middle classes were pious as never before. The manufacturer or mill-owner whose main concern on weekdays was to get rich regardless of those whose labour he hired, took over the role of chaplain to his household on Sunday, unconscious of the hypocrisy of his behaviour. The contrast, as Taine drily observed in a description of the head of an English family conducting prayers at home, was not just that between commercialism and piety, but between faith and unbelief. In a period in which more churches were built than in any other century since the Middle Ages - a period in which one of the foremost exponents of the Gothic style could write that 'everything grand, edifying and noble in art is the result of feelings produced by the Catholic religion in the human mind' - religious faith was being ceaselessly undermined. After the publication in 1859 of Darwin's *Origin of Species*, it was impossible for the thinking man to pay more than lip-service to the theological history on which he had been nurtured. The scientific revelation accorded too well with the gospel of the materialist to permit of doubt in its turn, or to arouse an answering realization of the eternal, imaginative truths, more important for men's understanding of his predicament than any discernible facts, which underlie every mythology.

The position of the architect, as of all artists, was fraught with difficulty in this century of paradox. Something of the dilemma which confronted him is summed up in a book of essays by leading architects such as G. F. Bodley and R. Norman Shaw, painters and designers such as W. B. Richmond and William Morris and teachers such as W. R. Lethaby, published in 1892 and entitled *Architecture: a Profession or an Art?* For in a commercial society it was natural that 'the client' (as the patron had now significantly come to be called) - generally an industrialist or tradesman, who with rare exceptions was devoid of both taste and feeling - should want value for money and should therefore insist on evidence of his architect's ability. So, in 1855, the Architectural Association, which had been formed in 1847, put forward a proposal that the Institute of British Architects (founded in 1834) should organize examinations and issue a diploma to distinguish qualified architects from others. Despite the protests of many eminent figures throughout the latter half of the century, and despite the excellent case presented by the writers of the collection of essays just mentioned, architecture finally became a closed profession. However great a genius a man might be, he could not practise unless he had passed an examination which could not possibly put artistic originality to the test. The multiplication of the numbers of men who became 'architects' after the institution of the qualifying examination is sufficient proof that the system could not produce artists. By 1900 more than 1,500 qualified architects were members of the R.I.B.A. alone. The number of members practising architecture at the beginning of Victoria's reign was eighty-two.

The architect was caught up in this conflict between the profession and the art of architecture, and affected, moreover, by the social emphasis placed on his professional standing. He was also faced with the antithesis of architecture as an art and as a structural science. The Institute of Civil Engineers had come into being as early as 1818 and had received its Royal Charter in 1828. But at that time, the

Thomas Hopper, the architect of
Penrhyn Castle, had built an
enormous Gothic conservatory at
Carlton House for George IV, and
Decimus Burton and the engineer
Richard Turner had designed the
elegant ogee-shaped Palm House at
Kew in glass and cast-iron in 1844-8,
but the essentially Victorian vogue for
the conservatory was stimulated by
the fame of Paxton's Great
Conservatory at Chatsworth, completed by 1849, by the unique
specimens of tropical and rare plants
with which he filled it and, above all,
by the giant greenhouse he designed
to house the Great Exhibition of 1851.
Soon the smallest villa was not
considered complete without a
conservatory in which to cultivate
some of the exotic plants and shrubs
which, owing to the adventurous
botanical expeditions of the
nineteenth century, in which Paxton
played a notable part, had become all
the rage. The glass used for the
Crystal Palace was thin, polished
sheet glass which was cast and not
blown, as earlier glass had been, and
which it had become possible to
produce commercially by 1838.
Without this cheaply produced glass,
the conservatory could never have
achieved its popularity. This humble
example, attached to a house in the
Grecian style, has Gothic cast-iron
lights of a standardized pattern.

architect and engineer were scarcely conscious of rivalry. The architect indeed,
as we have seen, made ample use of the engineer's material: cast iron. And though
the purposes to which he put it were very often decorative, the material was also
used structurally in house design. The two staircases at either end of the corridor
in the Pavilion, Brighton, are of cast iron, as are the four slender columns ending
in palm fronds which support the kitchen ceiling. The Duke of Portland was
making lavish use of cast iron combined with glass for the fantastic underground
palace he was hollowing out of the ground at Welbeck Abbey in the second half
of the century. And no Victorian villa was complete without its miniature version
of the glass-houses at Chatsworth: the conservatory. But by then the professions
of architecture and engineer were sharply divided. For even though Scott in his
Remarks on Secular and Domestic Architecture (1858) proclaimed that 'metallic
construction is the great development of our age', the architect continued to
conceive his projects in terms of brick and stone, while the engineer was supreme
in the domain of glass and iron. And although traditional building methods had
been distorted and undermined by nineteenth-century developments, the
architect still clung to what was left of them, while the engineer carried out his
work by means of prefabrication. Art historians have rightly stressed the impor-

Cast-iron railings, Cavendish, Suffolk

These exuberant, billowing railings are composed of standardized parts which were still being advertised by O'Brien, Thomas & Company at the end of the nineteenth century. The filigree elegance of the veranda at Pershore (page 262) has given way to a coarse flamboyance, encouraged by the addition of solid, embossed ornaments. But in this example the inherent vulgarity of the new technique is disciplined by a vigorous sense of design which has triumphed over the condition of prefabrication.

tance of the brilliant technical achievements of the Victorian engineers – their bridges, railway stations and exhibition buildings – in relation to the products of our own age, but the widely held view that Victorian industrialized building was the most significant aesthetic expression of the period is surely open to question. The economic advantages of factory-made buildings ensured the eventual triumph of the engineer in the architectural field but at the same time relegated the architect in his true role of artist to a minor position. The situation was already foreshadowed in the partnership of Brunel and Matthew Digby Wyatt in the building of Paddington Station. Brunel saw himself as the principal partner who was 'to build a station after my own fancy which almost of necessity becomes an engineering work', while Wyatt was fitted for nothing more than the 'detail of ornamentation for which I neither have time nor knowledge . . .'. The spread of this attitude, and its application in due course to domestic architecture, gave rise to the pitifully limited conception of the house as 'a machine for living in'. The fact that the originator of that phrase was one of the most celebrated architects of the present century shows the extent to which the functions of engineer and architect came to be confused. But I am looking too far ahead: this substitution of structural science for building art in the domestic field was a reaction against the development of the Picturesque in the Victorian period. Unchecked by the controlling influence of a standard of taste imposed by a cultured minority, the Picturesque reached disastrous proportions, the effects of which are with us still.

Newcastle steel-master, where the chimney-piece is so vast it becomes the whole wall and where the riot of strapwork and arabesque ornament and the carved alabaster rivals the decoration at Langleys (pp. 132–3) in its robust abundance; and, entirely different, but as forceful, Bryanston (1899), in the Wren manner. With some of these houses the seriousness with which the chosen style has been emulated is, as might be expected, more in evidence than the spirit of adventurous reinterpretation. Such are George Devey's Jacobean Betteshanger, Kent (1856), W. E. Nesfield's Kimmel Park, Derbyshire, in the William and Mary manner, and Sir Ernest George's Shiplake Court, Oxfordshire, a richly textured mansion which is notably close in feeling to the Elizabethan Lake House, Amesbury. In an account so necessarily superficial and inadequate as this, it is more profitable and more interesting to dwell briefly on one or two of those mansions in which the element of the Picturesque underlying them all erupts, as it was bound to do from time to time in a situation so fraught with contradictions, in an architecture so bizarre as to stun the beholder into astonished silence.

Among these tremendously exciting and monster houses, Harlaxton comes first to mind. It invites direct comparison with Burleigh and is reminiscent also of Montacute and Wollaton but is at the same time a distinct and unforgettable monument of the Victorian imagination at its greatest pitch of intensity. The vast golden stone building recaptures and develops to a new degrees of drama and intricacy the aspiring, advancing and retreating pattern of the great Elizabethan houses. Flanked by octagonal turrets, crowned with banded and spired cupolas, the main façade moves to the flicker of strapwork ornament, the flame-like upsurge of ogee gables adorned with spiralling finials, to the curve of an ornate two-storeyed oriel and the angular thrust of square and polygonal bays, the rhythm quickening and culminating in the central arcaded turret and elaborate cupola on its lofty octagonal base, to which is attached a gargantuan clock. The ringed pillars of the turret arcade and the tapering, banded cupola are more academically Baroque in their detail than any Elizabethan form; they define the mood of the whole building and at the same time confirm the latent Baroque character of Elizabethan architecture. The interior of this extraordinary house states explicitly what the exterior suggests and what so many Elizabethan houses suggest: it is wildly, outrageously and entirely Baroque. The inspired architect was William Burn, a Scot and a pupil of Robert Smirke. The opulence of the original dining-room, now a chapel, and of the present dining-room recalls that of Pelagio Palagi's apartments at Turin and Naples, it is so superbly confident, but Burn's work is more intoxicatingly alive and more preposterous. The first of these rooms is dominated by its colossal frontispiece of a marble fireplace with its strange waisted pilasters, by the Baroque terms like those at Pommersfelden supporting the roof trusses and by a stone screen which is a free and ebullient transcription of the one at Audley End Mansion; the sumptuous dining-room is resplendent with another gigantic chimney-piece, this time of black and red and white mottled marble, and with overdoors crowded with shields and putti above pink and white marble surrounds. But it is the hall which is the artist's masterpiece, the great hall with its cedar staircase embellished with bowed and kneeling Michelangelesque figures of youths and statues of vestal virgins holding aloft richly ornamented candelabra. Even in southern Italy there is little to rival the overwhelmingly theatrical effect of this composition. The hall soars up to a balcony resting on giant scrolly brackets and the backs of vigorous Atlas figures. From the brackets, attached to them by real cord, swing plaster swags of flowers and fruit, and from the balcony itself hang billowing plaster curtains looped with cords from which depend huge plaster tassels lightly swaying with every current of air. Writhing, trumpet-blowing putti struggle to free themselves from the folds of the curtains. Higher still, an arcade hung with counterfeit drapery supports yet another balcony articulated by six Cyclopean plaster pendants and swarming with putti, while two Father Time figures

The Tower Room, Cardiff Castle, Glamorgan, Wales

This opulent room is as overpowering and even more staggering in its concentration on detail than the interior of the hall at Harlaxton shown on the previous page, with which, curiously enough, it has clear affinities, although, because William Burges, the author of Cardiff Castle, was exclusively a medievalist, it is carried out in a totally different idiom from that of William Burn's masterpiece. Both rooms are remarkable for a wholly intoxicating air of fantasy and dazzling splendour, based in the one case on spectacular and partially illusory effects of perspective and in the other on amazing contrasts in scale.

The entire south-west sector of the castle, which dates from the twelfth century and stands on the site of a Roman fort, was reconstructed for the 3rd Marquess of Bute during the years 1870–5 by William Burges. The proportions and decoration of the Tower Room, also known as the Summer Smoking Room, represent the most violent protest against Georgian canons of taste. Elegance and uniformity are deliberately spurned for the sake of dramatic impact, and abstract or formalized ornament is eschewed in favour of figurative and narrative decoration. As the room is at the top of the lofty Clock Tower, the main theme of the ornament is the firmament. The large chandelier takes the form of sun-rays and the dome above it is lined with mirrors to reflect its light. A bronze model of the world is inlaid in the centre of the tiled floor with the words '*Globus hic monstrat microcosmum*', and the enamelled tiles themselves depict the spheres encircling the globe. The huge, unusually fresh and vigorous corbel figures beneath the gigantic capital of the pillars supporting the gallery symbolize the winds coming from the four corners of the earth. They were carved by Thomas Nicholls, who was Burges's chief sculptor in all his later undertakings. Nicholls also carved the figure of Cupid with a love-bird on the extraordinary hooded chimney-piece and the frieze showing summer lovers and the state of matrimony, represented by two dogs pulling in opposite directions and a dog barking at a cat in a tree (cynical enough images, though Burges himself was unmarried). The capitals of the pillars are painted with portraits of great astronomers of the past. The hand-painted tiles covering the walls illustrate themes drawn from classical mythology. Every detail of the room was designed by Burges himself.

The hall, Adcote, Shropshire

The house was built by Norman Shaw in 1879 and is externally in the Elizabethan style. The hall is based entirely on that of the medieval manor house, fitted with a wooden screen with a screens passage behind it and a minstrels' gallery above it. The dais end is lit by a large bay window. The exaggerated height of the hooded fireplace between the stone arches of the roof is reminiscent of the hall fireplace at Bolsover, which alludes in a similar romantic vein to the past, and which, though less severe than Shaw's striking design, is notably plain beside most of the elaborate compositions in the keep. The panelling of the Victorian hall marks the beginning of a later, suburban practice: it is carried out in thick, embossed paper.

Interior of the keep and (opposite, below) the entrance, Castell Coch, Glamorganshire

William Burges built Castell Coch for Lord Bute in 1875–81. These two photographs show that he was not only able to translate fantasy into unforgettable, spectacular, forceful reality by means of his concentrated, unique conception of ornament, but that he could also conjure up a world of impregnable strongholds and dungeons, as solid and of a more romantic character than any actual medieval remains, in an architecture of noble simplicity and bold geometry. The roofs of the cylindrical tower and the gatehouse (based on French example) give Castell Coch a fairy-tale air which is particularly picturesque and effective in contrast to the severity of the rest of the building.

The drawing-room fireplace,
Penrhyn Castle, Caernarvonshire, by
Thomas Hopper (*see* page 292).

which confront the eye on every side; and the Saracenic ceiling of the dining-room with an eight-pointed central star surrounded by a swirl of three-dimensional pattern surpasses the most extreme of Baroque conceits. There are some exquisite passages among all this accumulated richness of ornament. The panels of the ceiling of Lady Bute's bedroom at Castell Coch, for instance, are painted, every one differently, with enchanting naturalistic coils of foliage among which sport monkeys and birds. But such quiet undertones hardly make themselves felt amid the brassy, battering and sometimes incoherent onslaught of Burges's mosaic of gold leaf and bright colour and of the exaggerated bulk and weight of his architectural units.

Burges's two Welsh castles are extreme expressions of individuality. And no matter what style the Victorian architect adopted, the key-note of it was always individuality and variety, two qualities which were clearly threatened by the mass culture of which industrialism was the harbinger. The terrace house, which already existed, was obviously suited to the increasingly industrial and urban society of the age, but for this very reason it was the least desirable of all houses to the individualist and the romantic. The history of the terrace in the nineteenth century is therefore particularly illuminating. The appearance of the semi-detached villa in an urban environment was recorded in the preceding chapter, but for a time the subversive effect of this phenomenon on formal street architecture was checked by the strongly established terrace tradition of the Georgian period. In Scotland, especially in Glasgow, the classical terrace theme continued to inspire inventive treatment long after it had vanished from the scene in the south. Alexander Thomson, for instance, designed Great Western Terrace as late as 1869 as a long row of two-storeyed houses broken by massive three-storeyed blocks, jutting forward as far as the coupled Ionic porticos of the two-storeyed units. The design would be drab and uneventful were it not for the drama of these forceful porticos, a heavy string course, and immensely wide eaves, casting deep, purposeful shadows. A touch of spontaneity is added by the

North side, Buckland Crescent, near Swiss Cottage, London

These detached stucco villas, built in 1843, faced by paired houses of slightly different design on the other side of the Crescent, still make a unified composition, but the Georgian idea of the terrace as a single palatial façade is already giving way to the preference for individual houses, just as the stucco style is becoming heavily Roman and Renaissance instead of Greek. The characteristic design of the broad, bracketed eaves is quite different from that of the Queen Anne eaves-cornice with modillions in the bedmould. In the latter the rain-water gutter was contained in the upper part of the lead-lined cornice. Here the guttering is separate.

294

cast-iron balustrading, where pointed arches enclose crisp anthemion ornaments. 'Greek' Thomson also adorned the severe little houses of Moray Place with pretty cresting and with chimneys like Egyptian columns topped by palm-leaf capitals, though this flight of fancy would have been better expressed in stucco than stone.

The glittering, plastered mass of Hesketh Crescent, Torquay, designed in 1846 by the brothers W. and J. T. Harvey, rises palatially above a fringe of palms and oleanders with as grand a flourish as the Nash terraces in London; and Chichester Terrace, Brighton, is still firmly Greek, only the aggressiveness of its huge Doric porticos supporting pagoda-like verandas, only the coarseness of its detail proclaiming its late date. Buckland Crescent, near Swiss Cottage, London, shows the beginning of the substitution of the Italian Renaissance style for the Greek or Roman manner in the arched or heavily pedimented windows of its south side and its broad, bracketed eaves. It is more ponderous and more solid than any Regency terrace, but at the same time its great height, the bold articulation of its cornices and outsize quoins and the prominence of its balustraded porches, make a splendidly scenic display. On a misty autumn morning or in the lamp-lit dusk of early spring the curve of stucco façades, romantically blurred, becomes one of the most eloquent of all the Picturesque realizations of Claude's seaport palaces. The crescent is still conceived as one huge sweep, but the houses no longer form part of a single composition. The scribble of laurels and laburnums fills the intervals between the single or paired houses, which thus mark a stage in the transformation of the terrace into a collection of suburban villas.

A further step in the process can be seen in Gilston Road, Kensington, in a more

Gilston Road, Kensington, London

This pair of semi-detached villas show the 'Italian domestic' style which probably made its first appearance in John Nash's Cronkhill (page 264). The villas represent one unit in a varied composition of alternating detached and paired houses which is a stage further removed from the Palladian conception of the terrace than Buckland Crescent.

graceful interpretation of a style already present at Edensor, that known to some of the pattern-book writers as 'Pisan Romanesque' and to others as 'Italian domestic'. Here the houses are only partly stuccoed, in deference to the growing scorn of all superficial imitations of ashlar, and take the shape of paired and detached villas in which single, two- and three-light, arched windows play a prominent part. The paired houses are conceived as a central block with separately roofed recessed wings containing the entrances at either end, and with parapeted bays enlivening the ground floor; while the detached villas are distinguished by square, stuccoed campaniles adorned with arched niches and crowned by low flat roofs rising alongside a rectangular block with its gable-end facing towards the street across a small balustraded garden. A loosely formal arrangement imparts a certain rhythm to the group, but this can no longer be called a terrace.

It was clearly difficult to reconcile the conception of the medieval house, as extolled by Pugin, with its essential variety and irregularity with the formal idea of the terrace. But there is at least one instance of a Pugin enthusiast using an earlier vernacular style as the basis of a street design as regular as any Georgian composition despite its utterly different feeling. Lonsdale Square by R. C. Carpenter no longer presents those flat façades to the street which Scott found so distressing in the Bloomsbury area. The plan of the individual dwellings, like that of most Victorian terrace houses, much resembles that of its Georgian counterpart, but Carpenter emphasizes the asymmetrical arrangement of the individual façade by the projection of the rooms leading from the left or right of the narrow staircase hall, which is thus deeply recessed. Each projection is surmounted by a strikingly steep pointed gable, which, together with the repetition of bold Tudor mullions and the extreme narrowness of each house, makes an impression of spiky, restless verticality which is the negation of the harmony achieved by the classical terrace. The Tudor style of this little square is reflected, as we have already observed, in countless small houses built all over the country before the middle years of the nineteenth century. But they do not take the form

Terrace housing at Newcastle upon Tyne, Northumberland

This characteristic example of the nineteenth-century speculative builder's housing for industrial workers shows none of the flamboyance and individuality of the Victorian mansion or villa. It is a mean and diminished version of the Georgian terrace composition in which each house consists of a cellar, a living room and scullery and two bedrooms. The front door opens into a narrow passage and at the back there is an enclosed yard with outside sanitation.

of terraces, and if they do not stand detached they are grouped in pairs or at most in threes or fours. The mode, like all romantically inspired conceptions, demanded individual treatment. The terrace proper only survived in the housing erected by speculative builders for renting to factory-workers and in the houses designed for the middle classes, again by speculative builders, to combine pretention with density. The rows of workers' back-to-backs with their squalid yards and outdoor lavatories were debased, shrunken versions of the Georgian terrace in which the front door might lead straight into the parlour and where there was sometimes no through access except by means of an arched passage in the middle of the row serving all the houses. The details of fireplaces, doors and ceilings were of the meanest. Although factory-made ornament could be cheaply supplied to suit every type of Victorian house, it was limited in these working-class dwellings to the barest minimum. The exteriors were usually severely plain, except for the shutters of the front, ground-floor window, which in rough districts were an absolute necessity. Poor but respectable terrace houses were occasionally enlivened by a scattering of ornament. Argyll Terrace, Dunstable, is provided with arched doors and windows which have prominent, rusticated keystones, miniature cast-iron balustrading (surviving only in part) running along the sills and trefoil cresting along the ridge. Inside such little houses there might be found a meagre version of the florid plaster cornice and foliated ceiling centre-piece which adorned the principal rooms of wealthier homes, but there would be no glass doors or windows with pretty margin lights of deep blue and scarlet.

Terraces intended for the middle classes were, by contrast, loaded with ornament both inside and out. The heavy marble mantelpieces of the period, at first classical, with a broad, moulded shelf supported on scrolled brackets, but later grotesquely Gothic, Tudor or Italianate, survive in such large numbers that they need no description. Catalogues issued towards the end of the century by manufacturers of household fittings, such as Pfeil, Stedall & Son or O'Brien, Thomas & Co., convey something of the confusing variety of fantastic designs

A terrace at Weymouth, Dorset

This late Victorian terrace was intended by the speculative builder to house working-class families with more pretentions than the occupants of the little dwellings shown on the opposite page. The bay windows, the rough-cast panelling and the polychrome brickwork were all designed to impart an air of respectability to this last degraded and distorted phase of the noble, architectural theme of the terrace. The step-movement occasioned by the hilly street imparts a spurious vitality to the grim, mechanical rhythm of the repeating units and accentuates the stark monotony with which the bays project one after another directly on to the drab street.

Semi-detached houses in Lea Bridge Road, Tottenham, Middlesex, and (below) terrace in Manilla Road, Bristol

The Tottenham houses are part of a row of semi-detached villas erected by a speculative builder for middle-class tenants in the 1870s. The Gothic porch, with its pretty but incongruous bargeboards (of a design closely resembling that at Downham Market (page 281)) and Venetian Gothic pilasters, and the pointed arches and Early English ornament of the ground-floor bay windows are no longer part of a design which is the logical expression of the interior, as in the houses shown on pages 277-80, but mass-produced trimmings appealing to a sentimentality nourished by the Picturesque attitude and intended to give consequence and an air of individuality to standardized houses which have no greater practical advantages than the straightforward terrace design. The internal planning does not differ in essentials from that of the Georgian terrace house: each villa is two rooms deep above basement offices. The difference is all in the character of the rooms, the proportions and style of decoration. The monstrous dwellings in Manilla Road are still conceived as a terrace, but purely for economic and not aesthetic reasons. The restless bulges and projections of the tortured façades and the encrustations of factory-made terracotta forms and ornament wildly confusing Gothic and Renaissance motifs from disparate sources are all intended to blur, for the sake of ostentation, the despised and basic terrace plan, which in the individual house results in an arrangement differing only in detail from that of the Tottenham houses.

Houses in Fitzjohn's Avenue,
Hampstead, London

The terrace house, even in the
bedizened, pretentious form it
achieved in Manilla Road, Bristol
(opposite), was eschewed by every
Victorian who could afford to build
his own house, and thus the conception of the street as a unified
architectural composition gave
way to the Picturesque notion of a
leafy thoroughfare lined with
individual houses, each standing in its
own garden. Of the two houses
shown here, one assumes the form in
brick and stone of a gigantic Scottish
tower with corbelled turrets,
inappropriately furnished with an
oriel window and twin Gothic
entrance arches and combined with a
tall block in the French Renaissance
style; while the other, built for the
painter P. F. Poole, R.A., by T. K.
Green in the 1870s, is a blown-up,
sprawling, multi-gabled cottage orné
of variegated brick with prominent
bargeboards of contrasting designs,
elaborate ridge-cresting and patterned
tiles.

in all conceivable styles which covered every surface and which were translated into cast iron, glass, cast brass, ebony, oak or pottery according to whether they were applied to bolts, door handles, lock plates, finger plates, casement fasteners, chimeny-pieces, grates or the engraved tiles which flanked them and which patterned the hearth.

Externally the Gothic ornament crowding about porches and bay windows yielded to Venetian and French Renaissance influences. The climax of this development in the deliberately ostentatious terrace is well represented by Manilla Road, Bristol. Built of rough yellow stone and decorated with slippery-smooth yellow terracotta, these houses are of formidable ugliness. They are of irregular heights, crowned by steep French mansard roofs liberally festooned with cast-iron cresting and projecting in ample hexagonal bays and huge square porches with banded terracotta columns ending in Venetian capitals. Fussy battlements adorn the ground-floor bays, while those on the first floor are surmounted by classical cornices; and beneath each bay run bands of varied and intricate decoration based on classical motifs. Shallow flights of steps go down from the porches between stone walls which shut off the basement area and at the same time seem to be reaching out like clutching tentacles. For these houses make a definite assault on the spectator. They have no connection with architecture in the sense of that word as building art; forms and ornament are merely there in order to impress: what the whole crushing image expresses is the combative attitude of the Victorian materialist and its triumph over inherited canons of taste.

But except when, as here, it was economically profitable, the terrace house had come to the end of its days. Street architecture had become a collection of houses of various design standing, isolated or in pairs, each in its own garden. The Victorian suburbs of all our larger towns show this development. I will describe a road in one of them. The extremely individual compositions of which it is composed belong mainly to the 1870s. The exaggerated solidity and bulk

Annesley Lodge, Hampstead, London

This L-shaped house, built by C. F. A. Voysey for his father in 1895, shows the salient characteristics of the style of an architect, no less romantic than the builders of the houses shown on the previous page, who turned for inspiration to English regional domestic architecture instead of to the great historical and continental styles. The walls of Annesley Lodge are roughcast (a practice which later become one of the hallmarks of the suburban style), and supported by sloping buttresses, one of which can just be made out in the photograph, under the creeper, and the windows are mullioned and perfectly plain. The placing of the long, low, first-floor windows immediately beneath the eaves recalls the façades of many sixteenth- and seventeenth-century timber-framed houses. Annesley Lodge already embodies many of the attributes of the typical twentieth-century suburban house, whether islated or semi-detached.

Houses at Bedford Park, Middlesex

Bedford Park was laid out by
Norman Shaw for J. T. Carr from
1875, and the architects included
Shaw himself, M. Adams, E. J. May
and E. Godwin. The estate was a
descendant of Edensor and Nash's
Park Villages and prepared the way
for the vast surburban developments
of the present century. The Bedford
Park houses are rural in flavour,
fenced and hedged and set in tree-
shaded winding streets, each with its
front and back garden, most houses or
pair of houses differing from its
neighbours. The pair shown here are
conceived as a single structure unified
by the wide, bracketed porch
embracing the two entrances and by
the tall battered chimney-stack rising
immediately above the porch. The
mock half-timber work, like the
tile-hanging on some of the other
Bedford Park houses, is already nearly
as flimsy and indeterminate as the
decoration of later suburban houses
and suggests no more than vague
traditional associations.

of these houses and the confusion and abundance of detail from mixed styles
which adorns them so thrust themselves on the eye that years of daily familiarity
have failed to soften their fierce impact. Pointed and curly gables; ornate bargeboards; oriels and bays filled with lancet, ogee-headed or shouldered lights, often
divided by Gothic columns with richly carved capitals; towers and campaniles;
conical turrets corbelled out from the wall in the Scottish baronial style; tall,
clustered chimney-stacks; gargoyles; crested ridges; porches flanked by Early
English columns; contracted versions of the castles and mansions raised by
wealthy magnates in the country; immensely blown-up version of the cottage
orné – each powerful image demands and competes for the attention of the
passer-by. Between each house and the road is a garden, usually planted with
shrubs and protected by a wall of banded brick or stone. An elaborate cast-iron
gate or occasionally a form of heavy field gate, filled with massive Gothic
openwork instead of bars, hangs between sturdy pillars, which may be square or
rounded and which are encrusted with ball flowers, dog-tooth moulding or
some other medieval ornament. Very often either the gate or the piers bear a name
such as The Towers, The Laburnums or The Laurels. This was the beginning of
that passion for giving houses names instead of numbers, another pathetic
expression of the desire for individuality, which is so typical of modern suburbia
and of which more will be said later.

Among the hundreds of roads lined with violently contrasting villas of this
kind, Melbury Road, Holland Park, where Burges and Shaw built next to each
other, should not go unmentioned. Some reference has already been made to
the stylistic range of Shaw's work. He was one of the designers in a scheme of
suburban development which was of particular significance for future estate
building. Bedford Park, Chiswick, initiated by Jonathan T. Carr in 1876, was

Fireplace at Seaview, Bawdsey,
Suffolk

Art Nouveau, the style which capti-
vated Europe in the 1890s, sprang
from the same desire as that which
motivated the authors of the Arts and
Crafts Movement, of whom Voysey
was one, in their return to the
simplicity and honesty of traditional,
pre-industrial vernacular building
styles, the desire to break away from
Victorian historicism. Viewed in
perspective, both attempts seem to
belong wholly to the Victorian
period, to represent but two more
phases in a whirlwind sequence of
changing fashions which by the end
of the century had all become confused and unreal. Art Nouveau is, in
fact, not as novel as its name suggests,
for it reflects mingled Rococo,
Japanese and Celtic influences and is a
development of the sinuous decorative style of such designers as Walter
Crane and A. H. Mackmurdo. It was
essentially a decorative and not an
architectural style, and its most
obvious characteristic was its use of a
flowing line which undulated and
coiled like waves, flames or plant
tendrils to create an asymmetrical
image. The name 'Art Nouveau' was
that of a shop which a Hamburg art
dealer, M. S. Bing, had opened in the
Rue de Provence, Paris, in 1895, and
it is significant that, apart from a very
few remarkable buildings, such as
those of Victor Horta in Brussels, it
was in the ephemeral rooms of the
great exhibitions of applied arts which
were becoming ever more popular
that the Art Nouveau style was most
completely expressed. In the private
English house the principal traces left
by the short-lived style are in door
and fireplace designs, of which this
modest example is characteristic.

laid out in streets and avenues of small cottagey villas in gardens and was the first
example of an entire suburb planned with winding roads, carefully preserved
trees and irregular and individual exteriors. The houses are of red brick and they
boast Dutch and tile-hung gables, casement windows, balustraded oriels and
rustic porches, and the paintwork is gleaming white. These modest houses have
considerable charm, and after the horrors of Manilla Road their simplicity is
deeply affecting. Many of them were bought by aesthetes who hung them with
Morris wallpapers or who furnished them in the new Anglo-Japanese manner
which captured the imagination of designers at the end of the century rather as
the Chinese fashion had excited Georgian artists and craftsmen. It gave rise to a
vogue for pottery tubes, shaped like the gnarled trunks of the trees in Japanese
gardens or painted with Oriental scenes, which served as umbrella stands in the
hall; for blue and white plates and Japanese fans fastened to the walls above dados
of Indian matting; for bamboo tables and chairs. The style reached its zenith in
the Peacock Room at 49 Princes Gate, London (now in the Freer Gallery,
Washington), painted by Whistler for F. R. Leyland, the shipowner and art
collector. But like Art Nouveau, the sinuous, flowing character of which
imparted a new, langorous rhythm to the stained-glass imagery of many a front
door and to the ornament on many a mantelpiece, this was a decorative and not
an architectural style. The Bedford Park houses are neither Anglo-Japanese nor
Art Nouveau: they represent the final phase in the feverish quest of the Victorians
for escape from urban industrialism in one form of the Picturesque after another,
and of their impassioned and romantic partiality for vanishing traditions. In the
face of the break-up of the regional styles, there was now, at the end of the
century, a rediscovery of all the elements of old farm and cottage architecture,

half-timbering, weatherboarding, tile-hanging and pargework together with ingle-nooks and catslide roofs. The simplicity of the houses at Bedford Park is due not only to a revulsion of feeling against the pomposity and over-elaboration of High Victorian architecture, but to the fact that the sources of this new enthusiasm were themselves simple and unpretentious.

The vernacular style inspired two kinds of activity: the close reproduction of local methods and new syntheses of these methods. At Bourneville, a suburb of Birmingham laid out for George Cadbury by W. Alexander Harvey from 1894 onwards, some of the houses are astonishingly faithful copies of the Warwick-shire half-timbered style, and at Port Sunlight, built for Lord Leverhulme, the Cheshire black-and-white style with its idiosyncratic patterning has been carefully followed; the houses have even been given stone-slated roofs at a time when Welsh slate was universal. Both these estates contain many more houses of the other kind, in which a vague feeling for tradition is conveyed in a Picturesque fashion by overhanging eaves, dormers, rustic porches and pleasant rough-cast irregularity. The author of the craze for rough-cast, which is now firmly associated with suburban development, was C. F. A. Voysey, who, with Ernest Gimson, was one of the most original designers in the new manner, and who also designed the wallpapers and fabrics, the furniture and fittings and even the spoons and forks for every one of his houses. Annersley Lodge, at the corner of Platt's Lane,

Entrance to a house in Belsize Avenue, Hampstead, London

Art Nouveau influence is seen here in the typical design of the coloured glass filling the upper half of the door and in the improbable asymmetrical ornament above the lintel. Although, with its bold freestone decoration against red brick and the breadth of the coarse arch spanning the fantastic door and triangular oriel, it is far more robust in feeling than any twentieth-century suburban house, this semi-detached villa shows the same insensitively eclectic character as its modern successors.

Hampstead, built for his father in 1895, is a typical example of his art. It is an L-shaped house with buttresses and a long, horizontal band of low first-floor windows just under the eaves. The walls are coated in Voysey's favourite rough-cast. Gimson's White House, Leicester, has one distinguishing feature: a tall, windowless, oddly canted wall with an external chimney-stack which is as dramatic as the east wall of Parsonage Farm, Stebbing (p. 123). The house is of brick, plastered white and otherwise unremarkable.

All these houses, however cosy, however well designed, form the prelude to the vast suburban development of the present century. It became increasingly rare for the revival of a regional style to be carried out in the district to which it belonged. The materials of which suburban houses were fashioned counterfeited those of all parts of the country indiscriminately, and the beginning of this development can already be seen at Bedford Park. This, and the proliferation of houses like those of Voysey, which are anti-urban and yet which belong to no special region, encouraged that annihilation of the distinction between the urban and the rural dwelling and the collapse of domestic architecture as an art which will be briefly described in our concluding chapter.

The White House, Leicester

Built in 1897 for Arthur Gimson by Ernest Gimson.

12

The End of an Art

Houses at Port Sunlight, Cheshire

Port Sunlight was a factory estate planned by the Lever Brothers in 1888 as a garden suburb. The houses are stone-slated in the regional style of the district, and the one in the foreground is, by comparison with twentieth-century allusions to vernacular styles, a remarkably solid evocation of the earlier 'black-and-white' work of the district in which it stands.

This last brief chapter in the story of the English house, told from the point of view adopted in these pages, cannot be anything but disquieting, for it must record the final disintegration of a long and great tradition. It is one of the most disconcerting paradoxes in a history full of contradictions that a rise in the material standards of living so prodigious that the factory worker is more comfortably and conveniently housed than the wealthiest baron of feudal England, has been accompanied by the rapid decline of all that differentiates a house from mere housing.

In the first place, the kind of house which is aesthetically important because it gives the widest scope to the architect – the large country house – can play no part in the modern state. Many of the most splendid historical examples of domestic architecture have become museums. The few country mansions built, chiefly by Sir Edwin Lutyens, in the early years of the present century, were survivors of a way of life which was doomed before the reign of Victoria was over. These Lutyens houses are brilliantly eclectic, embracing the full, romantic range of Picturesque interests, the predilection for mixed period styles and the

305

return to vernacular practices advocated by Voysey, Gimson and the supporters of the Arts and Crafts Movement. Tigbourne Court, Surrey, begun in 1899 for Edgar Horne, is an impressively free interpretation of the Elizabethan style; it even displays that touch of classical fantasy which imparts such intense poetry to the great houses of the sixteenth century. Curving screen walls, tall, diagonally-set and crisply severe chimneys and three adjoining gables are combined with pedimented windows and a Doric loggia. And it is all carried out in Burgate stone, quarried locally, near Godalming, galletted throughout like the fabric of cottages seen in the neighbouring villages of Thursley and Hascombe, and articulated by thin, horizontal bands of tiles. 'Orchards', also in Surrey, near Munsted, is another most inventive variation on period and traditional themes. This is a quadrangular, courtyard design of local brick and tile, with some tile-hanging. One side of the courtyard has been extended in the form of a buttressed, barn-like structure to make an L-shaped entrance and to harmonize with the tall, barn-like opening into the quadrangle.

In his knowledge of local materials, shown not only in his own imaginative use of them, but in his reconstructions and restoration of old houses, such as Great Dixter (p. 48), and in his sense of the relationship of the house and its environment, Lutyens surpassed his immediate predecessors, but he was returning to a tradition from which the roots had already been cut. This gives all his work a depressing air of lifelessness and unreality. It is only necessary to compare any house by Lutyens (not just indifferent examples like the feeble neo-Georgian, Chussex and 'Dormy House' of Walton-on-the-Hill) with the most brutally ugly Victorian villa, such as those in Manilla Road, Bristol (p. 298), so frankly at one with the materialistic, ostentatious spirit of the age, to realize the loss of vitality. Lutyens's houses are nevertheless works of art. It is when the absence of the sensibility so affrontingly proclaimed in Manilla Road and the absence of a burning immediacy (which so flattens the impact of Sir Edwin Lutyens's evocations of the past) are merged in confused and imprecise suggestions of period and locality that art is extinguished. The process can be observed in the vast spread of suburbia, by far the most prominent embodiment of twentieth-century domestic aspirations.

Little Thakeham, Sussex

This house, built by Lutyens in 1902, is a free adaptation of the symmetrical Tudor manor house, E-shaped with the huge polygonal bay taking the place of the Tudor entrance porch. Despite the material of which Little Thakeham is built – local sandstone – and the originality of Lutyens's interpretation of a traditional theme (even more apparent in the skilful internal planning where the hall is entered through a screens passage) the effect is curiously lifeless.

306

Modern suburbia is the logical outcome of developments like those of Bedford Park, Bournville and Port Sunlight, mentioned in the previous chapter, of later garden suburbs, of which the best known is that at Hampstead, planned by Parker and Unwin from 1907 with Sir Edwin Lutyens as consultant; and of the garden cities, inspired by Ebenezer Howard's *Tomorrow* (1898), of which the first was Letchworth, Hertfordshire (1903). Although many of the individual houses in the Hampstead Garden Suburb or Welwyn Garden City are well planned in neo-Tudor or neo-Georgian brick, with an occasional late seventeenth-century feature, and although these developments make a conscious pattern of tree-lined roads and squares instead of sprawling haphazardly or in ribbon outgrowth, the distinction between them and surburban Hendon, Edmonton or Edgware is one of degree rather than kind. All are products of a final eruption of the Picturesque, growing ever weaker and more diffuse, of the antagonism to mechanized industry preached by the Victorian medievalist and of a reaction against the drab uniformity of the back-to-backs of Victorian working-class areas. The rash of semi-detached and detached villas, bedizened with Tudor gables, mock half-timber work, rough cast and bay windows of every shape which disfigures the outskirts of all our towns; the council estates in 'cottage' modes; the new towns, which, like the garden cities, are suburban in character although provided with factories and shopping centres; the recent 'architect designed' housing estates, usually planned by a firm of businessmen who happen to have qualified as architects and who in some cases never visit the site – all express the same uneasy state of mind: a vague romanticism, a dimly sensed nostalgia for the past, for a lost rural existence when house and home were at one with their environment.

A very cursory glance at some of the common features of suburbia will confirm this. First, the bosky, irregular aspect of developments like Bedford Park has been doggedly maintained, despite shortage of land and the frightening speed with which it is consumed by such extravagant use of it. Twentieth-century suburban roads are the antithesis of town streets. They are seldom quite straight, they often become cul-de-sacs, and footpaths are sometimes of shingle instead of paved and are edged with grass and ornamental trees, the most popular of which is the acid pink, alien almond. Roads are rarely called by that straight-forward name; the typically urban *Place, Terrace, Crescent* and *Square* are not popular, while *Street* is universally avoided. Instead, *Drive, Avenue, Way, Lane, Grove, Close* and *Ride* conspire to excite rural memories. The effect is reinforced in most instances by the names of the individual houses, which tend to have even less connection with the actual buildings than those of Victorian suburbs: *The Leas, The Garth, The Barn* (where none is to be seen for many miles), *Dormers* (though there are no attics), *Woodlands, Meadowcroft, Tanglewood, Wychwood* and *Birchfield* all occur in two or three adjacent roads of a north London suburb. Where the names of the drives, lanes and ways are not affectedly countrified (Orchard Close, Manor Ride, Oakhill Grove, Clover Leas), they may commemorate a popular idol and incidentally provide a clue as to the date of the housing (Valentino Way, Mollison Avenue, Sinatra Rise), or create an ambience of gentility (Beverley Drive, Chatsworth Grove) or of high romance (California Close, Manhattan Chase, King Alfred's Ride). The house names, when not of rural connotation, usually celebrate the scene of a successful holiday or honey-moon, consist of words coined from the Christian names of the happily married owners, or make a parade of some commonplace witticism. Whatever the names of houses or thoroughfares, they seldom bear any relation to their particular geographical situation and still more seldom do they celebrate local traditions, personalities, activities or landmarks, as do the names of town streets and those of farm houses, cottages and country mansions of the past. The number unaccompanied by a name is hardly ever found. Where its use is unavoidable, it may be given an arty twist. *One 2 Six* appears in bold Egyptian characters on a wooden gate framing an optimistic rising sun, and *Forty-Nine* slopes in wiry metal italic across a flimsy ironwork structure divided into asymmetrical, rectangular compartments, like a skeletal Mondrian.

The houses themselves exhibit a basic, semi-detached, two-storeyed, bay-windowed plan, and though, in examples of the last two decades, bay windows have been replaced by flat 'picture' windows and slight variations in grouping occur, the general design remains much the same whether it is adorned with details from the vernacular and period styles or whether it wears the flat-roofed, metal and concrete dress of the continental manner. The slates of the Victorian era have yielded to tiles, very often pantiles, which may be green, red or brown; and the bricks, where they are not hidden beneath a coating of pebble-dash, range from salmon-pink to yellow or purple-brown. The upper and lower polygonal or rounded bays of houses built between the wars may be divided by some form of ornamentation, an indeterminate spattering of plaster scrolls and swags of fruit and flowers faintly echoing the vigorous pargework of East Anglia, or an array of fish-scale tiles in mechanical imitation of the tradition peculiar to Kent and east Sussex. The gables may be furnished with plain, anaemic versions of the bargeboards, so energetically patterned and diversified by the Victorians, and they are frequently filled with thin, branching timbers recalling the black-and-white work of Cheshire, while the newest, flat-fronted versions of the suburban house often boast a band of white-painted clapboarding, reminiscent of the charming rural architecture of Kent and the coastal districts of Essex, or of cedarwood cladding in the Scandinavian fashion. The minute gardens which separate these houses from the road may be enclosed by rustic palings or low walls of brick or of coarsely pointed limestone. Whether they are dictated by economics, personal choice or the whim of a speculative builder, these variants are never decided by regional practice: they are as common on the fringes of Liverpool as of Leicester, Nottingham or Newcastle.

The entrances to these houses, which in the semi-detached pair may be set side by side or flung to either end of the shared façade, perhaps reveal more transparently than any other feature the confusion of ill-digested detail and the random character of the twentieth-century suburban dwelling. The doors of the earliest semi-detacheds in a Middlesex suburban area embracing Cricklewood, Dollis Hill and Queensbury, put up some time in the 1920s, each show six cushiony panels surmounted by a glass roundel encircled by belatedly Art Nouveau, spoon-shaped depressions and flanked by leaded oval windows in deeply moulded frames. A disproportionately broad canopy projects over the lintel, apparently held in position by two iron chains fastened to the wall on either side of a Georgian-style fanlight, which seems to perch on the canopy. Across the road, a few yards further on, tiled, round-arched brick porches shelter half-glazed doors decorated with jazzy designs in toffee-brown and lemon-coloured glass, while a turning to the right yields a glimpse of tiled and gabled overhangs jutting out on brackets above limed, studded oak doors fitted with spidery iron hinges and lock plates. Irregularly disposed lozenges of plain glass set in a metal frame fill the openings of a pair of houses erected in about 1960, while the most recent of all the additions to the development display absolutely plain, smooth doors shaded by thin, slab-like canopies resting on non-committal metal posts.

These variations attempt to provide meaningless, mass-produced designs with a reassuring suggestion of individuality. In the names they choose, in the irrational design of their gates, the varieties of hedging they grow, in their sudden indulgence in a splash of mauve or orange paint, in their weakness for crazy paving, concrete gnomes and rabbits crouching on the rims of bird baths or peering from miniature caverns in the rockery, for concrete windmills and wheelbarrows filled with primulas, the occupants themselves make faint, despairing gestures of personality in a world deprived of those attributes of period and locality which once gave precise definition to every house and thus furnished a firm framework

Houses in Hebar Road, Cricklewood (left, top and bottom), in Geary Road, Dollis Hill (top right), and in Mollison Way, Queensbury (bottom right), all in Middlesex

If these villas are compared, even with such decadent examples as those at Tottenham and Bristol shown on page 298, it is at once apparent how much these twentieth-century descendants have lost in vigour and precision. They show the same mixture of styles, they are equally divorced from any connection with a particular place, but these houses, three of which date from the first thirty years of our century, while the last was built only in 1961, show a diffuse, anaemic version of the mixture. Insipid pebbledash (deriving from Voysey's example) plays a prominent part in the twentieth-century suburban composition, and where a reference to a particular region is attempted, as in the ornament on the uppermost Cricklewood house, which recalls East Anglian pargework, it is as vague and misplaced as the muddled allusion to the Gothic Revival in the pointed lights of the casements and the pathetic imitation of the Georgian fanlight. Bargeboards and a bit of bogus half-timber work in the gable, wooden palings or walls of random rubble suggest a distant, unspecified countryside; steep roofs, cavernous, round-arched porches and leaded lights dimly hint at bygone ages; a flat roof and large windows with hideous metal frames and horizontal lights daringly suggest the 'Modern' style, some thirty years after it first appeared, the flat roof a ludicrous mannerism on a house which completely ignores the structural possibilities of steel and concrete and retains the traditional convention of weight-bearing walls. No matter what these façades seek to convey, they all exhibit the basic, semi-detached, bay-windowed plan first created by the Victorian speculative builder allied to the rural flavour of the first garden suburbs. All are eloquent examples of the anonymous architecture of no-man's-land.

for each individual life. For not only does the suburban dweller belong to no particular part of England, but his house is never entirely and whole-heartedly of its own time. If it follows new trends, it does so timidly, fifteen or twenty years late, grafting them on to the familiar suburban convention. And if, as it mostly does, it harks back to the past, the essentials are so feebly grasped, and interpreted with so little conviction and invention, that the imitation can rarely be more than approximately dated.

The most up-to-date of these estate houses are designed on the 'open plan' which was first introduced by Shaw and Lutyens in emulation of the medieval hall house. Although this plan may impart a feeling of space to a small interior, it represents a further attack on individuality, a return to a communal form of living which belonged to a period when the sense of autonomous identity had still not reached the stage of evolution when privacy was considered essential for its expression. In one of the most penetrating essays in his *Language and Silence*, Mr George Steiner has shown how dependent the very concept of literary form is upon privacy, and how long and painful was the struggle which eventually produced the man reading alone in a room with his mouth closed. This crowning triumph of western civilization can scarcely be maintained in modern housing conditions. Marshall McLuhan has given a vivid account of the retreat of the read sentence before the assault of our mass culture and the electronic media of communication, television, the photograph, the comic strip, the advertisement. At the moment when hundreds of thousands, or rather millions, of human beings are for the first time literate, the graphic mass media are taking precedence over the printed book. And at the moment when almost every family in Britain is provided with material comfort, their home is changing from an expression of individuality into a standardized, anonymous unit.

It is in the form of housing which has rightly been hailed as an architecture attuned to modern life, in the multi-storeyed blocks of flats constructed of pre-sectionalized concrete and steel, that the movement towards collectivity,

Copper Coin House, Englefield Green, Surrey, and (right) house on the Green, Queensbury, Middlesex

These two houses illustrate the ability of the suburban builder to clothe a dwelling in the 'Modern' style without in any way altering its basic, impersonal character and its alienation from the realities of place and period. Both houses derive from foreign example. That on the left feebly, belatedly apes Frank Lloyd Wright's high romanticism without any attempt to follow the master's combination of the picturesque with the structural techniques of the age. Exactly the same design can be seen in many different parts of the country; there is an identical house, for instance, on a new estate at Barrington, Cambridgeshire, displaying the same giant, 'primitive' chimney-stack and dry-stone construction (as bizarre a phenomenon in Cambridgeshire as in this part of Surrey) associated with brick, the same green pantiles and the same large plate-glass window. The house at Queensbury, with its long windows immediately under the eaves exaggerating Voysey's mannerism, is of brick with cedar-wood cladding in the Scandinavian fashion, introducing a nostalgic, forest-glade atmosphere among the surrounding bay-windowed, semi-detacheds of thirty years earlier.

already implicit in the uniformity underlying the pathetic trimmings of suburbia, is most starkly expressed. The style of these buildings is not just a negation of local, but of national traditions. It is essentially international, and evolved on the Continent before it established itself, slowly and with many setbacks, in the country where the idea of individuality had been more prized and more aesthetically fruitful than anywhere else. The very notion of a home on one floor of a towering block, long familiar on the Continent, and for three centuries accepted in Scotland, is outrageously alien to the traditional English concept of the house.

'New Ways', Wellingborough Road, Northampton, designed by the German architect Peter Behrens, appropriately enough for an engineering industrialist, in 1925, was the first house in Britain to assume the cubic, rectilinear shape of the modern manner. This was followed by a scattered number of other small, privately-built houses, among them the austere, box-like structure with horizontally banded walls of alternating glass and concrete erected in Frognal, Hampstead, in 1937-8 by Amyas Connell, Basil Ward and Colin Lucas; a similar flat-roofed elevation incorporating a thin balcony projecting on concrete cylinders over a terrace at Farnham Common, Buckinghamshire, by Harding and Tecton (1935), who were also responsible for 'Six Pillars', Crescent Road, Dulwich, built in the same year; and the house by Denys Lasdun (1938) which introduces glass and concrete so incongruously among the small Regency villas of Newton Road, Paddington.

The earliest instances of housing (as distinct from individual houses) in the cubist style are to be seen at Silver End, Essex, a village estate laid out from 1926 by Lord Braintree for disabled men who had been provided with work in a new factory on the site. But here suburban influence can already be seen at work on the abstract, formal conception in arty little triangular windows which recall the cinema buildings of the period. The semi-detached, flat-roofed concrete houses already mentioned show the way in which the new style was eventually fully absorbed into the suburban milieu, its alarming severity dulled by the familiar plan and scale. The style cannot in fact achieve its full expression in the small house. It deliberately eschews one of the most significant components of the language of architecture - ornament - and therefore relies for articulation exclusively on the relation of wall space to window space, of one storey to another, of block to block and of solid to void, and as it is based on the mass production of parts, it is only in a building of great size that a compelling rhythm can be created. Size, indeed, is the only form of grandeur within the range of the engineering work which has taken the place of traditional architecture in the present century, and it is suggestive both of its intrinsic nature and of the exclusive preoccupation with materialism which has produced it that its most representative and impressive examples are factories, office buildings and skyscraper flats. The latter may show slight variations with changing fashions. Heavy, chunky balconies may give way to white rails, windows may become more dominant; or unbroken sweeps of concrete may take on the guise of an impregnable fortress, as in the daunting Lawn Road Flats, Hampstead; aggressive cubism may be replaced by smooth curves, but the inhumanity of the scale, the forbidding, impersonal character of the building remain. There is a striking relationship between these blocks of flats which serve masses instead of individuals, and contemporary literature, music and the arts of sculpture and painting. Just as the architect has limited himself to mass-produced components and has rejected the ornament, rendered meaningless by suburban caricatures of past practice, which formerly distinguished one style from another, articulated form and related it to life, so the writer has turned away from language sullied and made empty by the cliché and has taken refuge in obscurity, non-style or even silence, the composer has moved away from the classical forms of organization which once gave logic and precision to his developing themes, and the painter and sculptor have retreated from their century-long involvement with visual reality into a restricted concern with mediums and an abstraction which has no verbal equivalent.

It is becoming increasingly apparent that in the face of present population trends building methods may have to be even more intensively industrialized than they are at present. Factories for the production of whole houses instead of for the component parts of houses may have to be created. One designer already speaks of concrete as an outmoded material and proposes Thermoplastic as the ideal construction material of the future and the 'Archigram Group of forward looking architects' have advocated 'throwaway buildings'. A growing realization, eloquently expressed by Professor Peter Collins in his *Changing Ideals in Modern Architecture*, that the creation of a humane domestic setting is the architect's most urgent task, has had little influence on the many thousands of new houses and flats which go up every year, a great proportion of them part of private estates or the work of local authorities. Instances of brilliant adaptations and conversions are not lacking but they are scarcely characteristic of the general trend and only accentuate the sad aesthetic incoherence, monotony and mediocrity of the debilitated suburban idiom and the nightmarish size and chilling impersonality of the slab-tower block which dominate the scene, annihilating the sense of place and continuity so vital to man's well-being and establishing an environment which has to be endured rather than enjoyed. A change of direction can come only with an unimaginable revolution in social and economic as well as architectural attitudes. Meantime the story of the English house as an individual work of art has virtually come to an end.

Golden Lane Housing, City of London
New Ash Green, Kent

Planning permission for New Ash Green, a Span development designed by Eric Lyons and Partners, was granted in 1965 and at that time, though within easy reach of London, this upland stretch of North West Kent was still completely rural. The photograph shows what was beginning to replace scattered vernacular red brick, tile-hung or weatherboarded farmhouses and cottages four years later. The short two storey terraces are informed with a more conscious feeling for grouping than the suburban houses already seen, but the idiom remains basically the same. The boarding, though vertical instead of horizontal, vaguely alludes to the local tradition of weatherboarding, but is no more than a meaningless ornamental overlay.

These houses are at least scaled to man's stature and emphasize by contrast the crushing inhumanity of the giant monolith of concrete, steel and glass in Golden Lane which dwarfs even the seven storey block it confronts. A comparison of the two buildings forcefully illustrates the advantage of great size in the establishment of a compelling pattern with prefabricated parts. The curtains and drapes behind the glass units of the small block bear pathetic witness to human occupancy without humanizing the design: they merely spoil it. The proportions of the mammoth block are too vast to be disturbed by traces of human habitation. The effect of the precipitous vertical movement of the twin towers on the short side of the structure and the dark chasm between them, boldly offsetting the strong horizontal articulation of the façade, the rhythmic alternations of glass and concrete and the bands of light and shade created by balconies jutting forward like half open drawers, is wholly dependent on a precision of repetition which only the machine could achieve. The building is indeed literally 'a machine for living in' with no more aesthetic distinction than a well designed refrigerator. It diminishes the human being.

Bibliography

GENERAL WORKS *(including works dealing with regional styles and traditional materials).*

Addy, S. O.   *The Evolution of the English House* (revised and enlarged by John Summerson), 1933

Allen, A.   *The Story of your Home*, 1949

Ambler, L.   *Old Halls and Manor Houses of Yorkshire*, 1913

Archibald, John   *Kentish Architecture as influenced by Geology*, 1934

Architectural Publications Society   *Dictionary of Architecture*, 1848–92

Aslet, Clive   *The Last Country Houses*, 1982

Atkinson, T. D.   *Local Style in English Architecture*, 1947

Ayrton, Maxwell and Silcock, Arnold   *Wrought Iron and its Decorative Use*, 1929

Bankart, G. P.   *The Art of the Plasterer*, 1923

Barley, M. W.   *The English Farmhouse and Cottage*, 1961

Barley, M. W.   *The House and Home*, 1963

Batsford, H. and Fry, C.   *The English Cottage*, 1938

Billett, Michael   *Thatching and Thatched Buildings*, 1979

Bouch, C. M. C. and Jones, G. P.   *The Lake Counties, 1500–1830*, 1961

Braun, Hugh   *The Story of the English House*, 1941

Braun, Hugh   *Old English Houses*, 1962

Briggs, Martin S.   *A Short History of the Building Crafts*, 1925

Brunskill, R. W.   *Illustrated Handbook of Vernacular Architecture*, 1970

Brunskill, R. W.   *Traditional Buildings of Britain*, 1981

Clark, Sir Kenneth   *The Gothic Revival*, 1928

Clifton-Taylor, Alec and Brunskill, R. W.   *English Brickwork*, 1977

Clifton-Taylor, Alec   *The Pattern of English Building*, 1962

Colvin, H. M.   *Biographical Dictionary of English Architects, 1600–1840*, 1954

Cook, O. M. and Smith, E.   *English Cottages and Farmhouses*, 1954

Cook, O. M.   *English Cottages and Farmhouses*, 1982

Cook, O. M.   *The English Country House*, 1974, reprinted 1980

Dauber, E. G.   *Old Cottages and Farmhouses in Kent and Surrey*, 1900

Dauber, E. G.   *Old Cottages in the Cotswold District*, 1904

Davy, Norman   *A History of Building Materials*, 1961

Dutton, Ralph   *The English Country House*, 1935

Evans, E. Estyn   *Irish Folk Ways*, 1944

Gibberd, Sir Frederick   *The Architecture of England from Norman Times to the Present Day*, 2nd edn, 1947

Girouard, Mark   *Life in the English Country House*, 1975

Gloag, John   *The Englishman's Castle*, 1945

Godfrey, W. H.   *The Story of Architecture in England*, 1931

Godfrey, W. H.   *The English Staircase*, 1911

Godfrey, W. H.   *Our Building Inheritance*, 1945

Gotch, J. A.   *The Growth of the English House*, 2nd edn, 1928

Henderson, Andrew   *The Family House in England*, 1964

Hill, Oliver   *Scottish Castles of the Sixteenth and Seventeenth Centuries; with an Introduction by C. Hussey*, 1953

Hoskins, W. G.   *The Heritage of Lancashire*, 1946

Hussey, C.   *The Old Houses of Britain: the Southern Counties*, 1928

Hussey, C.   *The Picturesque*, 1927

Innocent, C. F.   *The Development of English Building Construction*, 1916. New impression, 1971

Jones, S. R.   *English Village Homes*, 1936

Jourdain, Margaret   *English Interiors in Smaller Houses, 1600–1830*, 1923

Kidson, Peter, Murray, Peter and Thompson, Paul   *A History of English Architecture*, 1962

Lenygon, F. and Jourdain, Margaret   *English Decoration and Furniture from Tudor Times to the Nineteenth Century*, 4 vols, 1914–24

Lister, Raymond   *Decorative Cast Ironwork in Great Britain*, 1960

Lloyd, Nathaniel   *A History of the English House*, 1931

Lloyd, Nathaniel   *A History of English Brickwork from Medieval Times to the End of the Georgian Period*, 1925

Lloyd, Nathaniel   *British Craftsmanship in Brick and Tile and in Stone Slates*, 1929

MacGibbon, D. and Ross, T.   *The Castellated and Domestic Architecture of Scotland*, 5 vols, 1887

Mercer, Eric   *Houses of the Gentry Past and Present*, 1954

Mercer, Eric   *English Vernacular Houses*, 1971

Messent, J. W. Claude   *The Old Cottages and Farmhouses of Norfolk*, 1928

Oliver, Basil   *Old Houses and Village Buildings of East Anglia*, 1912

Oliver, Basil   *The Cottages of England: A Review of their Types and Features from the 16th to the 18th Centuries*, 1929

Oswald, Arthur   *Country Houses of Kent*, 1935

Oswald, Arthur   *Country Houses of Dorset*, 2nd edn, 1959

Peate, I. C.   *The Welsh House*, 1944

Pevsner, Nikolaus   *The Buildings of England*, 1951–

Powell, H. J.   *Glass-making in England*, 1923

Richards, J. M.   *A Miniature History of the English House*, 2nd edn, 1960

Richardson, A. E. and Gill, C.   *Regional Architecture of the West of England*, 1946

Richardson, C. J.   *Old English Mansions*, 1839

Rural Industries Bureau   *The Thatcher's Craft*, 1961

Shore, B. C.   *Stones of Britain*, 1957

Shuffrey, L. A.   *The English Fireplace*, 1912

Sinclair, C.   *Thatched Houses*, 1953

Sitwell, Sacheverell   *British Architects and Craftsmen*, 3rd edn, 1947

Stratton, Arthur   *The English Interior*, 1920

Summerson, Sir John   *Architecture in Britain, 1530–1830*, 1956

Tanner, H.   *Interior Woodwork of the XVI–XVIII Centuries*, 1902

Tipping, H. Avray   *English Homes*, 9 vols, 1921

Turnor, Reginald   *The Smaller English House 1500–1939*, 1952

Victoria County Histories

Watkin, David   *The English Vision*, 1982

William-Ellis, Clough and Eastwick-Field, J. and E. *Building in Cob, Pisé and Stabilized Earth.* Revised edn, 1947

Wright, L. *Clean and Decent. The Fascinating History of the Bathroom and Water Closet*, 1960

Yarwood, Doreen *English Houses*, 1966

FROM PREHISTORIC TIMES TO THE MIDDLE AGES

Banks, M. *British Calendar Customs: Scotland, Vol. I*, 1937

Boon, G. C. *Roman Silchester*, 1957

Boumphrey, Geoffrey *Along the Roman Roads*, 1935

Childe, V. G. *Skara Brae: A Pictish Village in Orkney*, 1931

Collingwood, R. G. *Roman Britain*, 1923

Collingwood, R. G. *The Archaeology of Roman Britain*, 1930

Collingwood, R. G. and Myres, J. N. L. *Roman Britain and the English Settlements*, 1936

Grimes, W. F., ed. *Aspects of Archaeology in Britain and Beyond*, 1951

Harden, D. B., ed. *Dark Age Britain*, 1963

Harden, D. B. Domestic Window Glass: Roman, Saxon and Medieval, *Studies in Building History*, ed. E. M. Jope, 1961

Haverfield, F. *The Romanization of Britain*, 4th edn, 1923

Haverfield, F. and Macdonald, Sir George *The Roman Occupation of Britain*, 1924

Hawkes, Jacquetta *A Guide to the Prehistoric and Roman Monuments in England and Wales*, 1951

Hewitt, Cecil *English Historic Carpentry*, 1980

Lethaby, W. R. *London Before the Conquest*, 1902

Radford, C. A. Ralegh The Saxon House, a review and some parallels, *Medieval Archaeology, I*, 1957

Rahtz, P. A. The Saxon and Medieval Palaces at Cheddar, Somerset, *Medieval Archaeology, VI-VII*, 1962-3

Richmond, Ian *Roman Britain*, 1955

Richmond, Ian Roman Timber Building, *Studies in Building History*, ed. E. M. Jope, 1961

Rivet, A. L. F. *Town and Country in Roman Britain*, 1958

Stenton, F. M. *Anglo-Saxon England*, 2nd edn, 1946

Walton, J. The Development of the Cruck Framework, *Antiquity, XXII*, 1948

THE MIDDLE AGES

Andrews, Francis *The Medieval Builder and His Methods*, 1925

Braun, Hugh *An Introduction to English Medieval Architecture*, 1951

Burnett, H. S. *Life on the English Manor*, 1937

Clapham, A. W. *English Romanesque Architecture after the Conquest*, 1934

Coulton, G. G. *The Medieval Village*, 1925

Crossley, F. H. *Timber Building in England*, 1951

Dollman, F. T. *Analysis of Ancient Domestic Architecture*, 1863

Faulkner, P. A. Domestic Planning from the 12th to the 14th Centuries, *Archaeological Journal, CXV*, 1958

Forrester, H. *The Timber-Framed Houses of Essex*, 1959

Harvey, John *Gothic England, a Survey of National Culture*, 1947

Hewett, C. A. Structural Carpentry in Medieval Essex, *Medieval Archaeology, VI-VII*, 1962-3

Jope, E. M. and Dunning, G. C. The Use of Blue Slate for Roofing in Medieval England, *Antiquaries Journal, XXXIV*, 1954

Knoop, D. and Jones, G. P. *The Medieval Mason: an economic history of English stone building in the later Middle Ages and early modern times*, 1933

Pantin, W. A. Medieval Priests' Houses in South West England, *Medieval Archaeology, I*, 1957

Pantin, W. A. Some Medieval English Town Houses, a Study in Adaptation, *Culture and Environment*, ed. I. L. Foster and L. Alcock, 1963

Radford, C. Ralegh The Bishop's Palace, Lamphey, Pembrokeshire, *Ministry of Works Guide*, 1959

Radford, C. Ralegh The Bishop's Palace, St. David's, Pembrokeshire, *Ministry of Works Guide*, 1953

Rouse, E. Clive Longthorpe Tower, *Ministry of Works Guide*, 1957

Salzman, L. F. *English Life in the Middle Ages*, 1929

Salzman, L. F. *Building in England down to 1540*, 1952

Simpson, W. Douglas Bastard Feudalism and the later Castles, *Antiquaries Journal, XXVI*, 1946

Smith, J. T. Medieval Aisled Halls and their Derivatives, *Archaeological Journal, CXII*, 1955

Smith, J. T. Stokesay Castle, *Archaeological Journal, CXII*, 1956

Thompson, A. Hamilton *Military Architecture in England during the Middle Ages*, 1912

Thompson, A. Hamilton Tattershall Castle, Lincolnshire, *National Trust Guide*, 1937

Turner, T. H. and Parker, J. H. *Some Account of the Domestic Architecture of England during the Middle Ages*, 3 vols, 1859-71

Wall, J. C. *Medieval Wall Painting*, 1914

Wood, Margaret Norman Domestic Architecture, *Archaeological Journal, XCII*, 1935

Wood, Margaret *The English Medieval House*, 1965

THE TUDOR, ELIZABETHAN AND JACOBEAN PERIODS

Black, J. B. *The Reign of Elizabeth, 1558-1603*, 1959

Dickins, Margaret *A History of Chastleton*, 1938

Gage, John *History of Hengrave*, 1822

Garner, T. and Stratton, A. *Domestic Architecture of England during the Tudor Period*, 1929

Girouard, Mark *Robert Smythson and the Architecture of the Elizabethan Era*, 1966

Girouard, Mark The Development of Longleat House between 1546 and 1572, *Archaeological Journal, CXVI*, 1961

Harrison, William *Description of England in Shakespeare's Youth*, ed. Frederick T. Furnivall from the first two edns of *Holinshed's Chronicle, 1577-1587*, 1877-8

Harvey, John *An Introduction to Tudor Architecture*, 1949

Jope, E. M. Cornish Houses, 1400-1700, *Studies in Building History*, ed. E. M. Jope, 1961

Knoop, D. *The Genesis of the Speculative Builder*, 1931

Knoop, D. and Jones, G. P. *The Bolsover Castle Building Accounts, 1613*, 1936

Lees-Milne, James *Tudor Renaissance*, 1951

Mackie, J. D. *The Earlier Tudors*, 1957

Mercer, Eric *English Art 1553-1625*, 1962

Nichols, John *Progresses and Public Processions of Queen Elizabeth*, 2nd edn, 1823

Oswald, Arthur Tudor Outlook Towers, *Country Life Annual*, 1957

Pevsner, Nikolaus   Double Profile (Wollaton), *Architectural Review*, March, 1950

Rowse, A. L.   *The England of Elizabeth*, 1950

Salzman, L. F.   *England in Tudor Times*, 1926

Shaw, H.   *Details of Elizabethan Architecture*, 1839

Shute, John   *The First and Chief Groundes of Architecture*, 1563

Stallybrass, Basil   Bess of Hardwick's Building and Building Accounts, *Archaeologia, LXIV*, 1913

Stone, Laurence   The Building of Hatfield House, *Archaeological Journal, CXII*, 1955

Summerson, Sir John   Three Elizabethan Architects, *Bulletin of the John Rylands Library*, Vol. 40, 1957

Summerson, Sir John   The Building of Theobalds, 1564–85, *Archaeologia, XCVII*, 1959

Summerson, Sir John   John Thorpe and the Thorpes of Kingscliffe, *Architectural Review, CVI*, 1949

Williams, E. Carleton   *Bess of Hardwick*, 1959

Withington, Robert   *Elizabethan Pageantry*, 1918–20

Yates, Frances A.   Elizabethan Chivalry: the Romance of the Accession Day Tilts, *Journal of the Warburg and Courtauld Institutes*, 1958

THE SEVENTEENTH AND EIGHTEENTH CENTURIES

Adam, Robert and James   *Works*, 1773–8 and 1822

Ashley, Maurice   *England in the 17th Century*, 1952

Aubrey, J.   *Brief Lives and other Selected Writings*, ed. Anthony Powell, 1949

Brett-James, Norman G.   *The Growth of Stuart London*, 1935

Bolton, Arthur T.   *Robert and James Adam*, 1922

Bolton, Arthur T.   *The Works of Sir John Soane*, 1924

Campbell, C., Woolfe and Gandon   *Vitruvius Britannicus*, 5 vols, 1715–71

Carritt, E. F.   *A Calendar of British Taste, 1600–1800*, 1949

Chambers, Sir William   *Designs for Chinese Buildings*, 1757

Colvin, H. M.   Haunt Hill House, Weldon, *Studies in Building History*, ed. E. M. Jope, 1961

Curran, C. P.   Dublin Plasterwork, *Journal of the Royal Society of Antiquities of Ireland, LXX*, 1940

Dutton, Ralph   *The Age of Wren*, 1951

Field, H. and Bunney, M.   *English Domestic Architecture of the Seventeenth and Eighteenth Centuries*, 1928

Fiennes, Celia   *The Journeys of Celia Fiennes*, ed. Christopher Morris, 1947

Forrester, H.   *The Smaller Queen Anne and Georgian House*, 1964

Gerbier, Sir Balthazar   *A Brief Discourse concerning the three chief principles of magnificent Building*, 1662

Gerbier, Sir Balthazar   *Counsel and Advise to all Builders*, 1663

Gilpin, William   *Essays on Picturesque Beauty*, 1794

Gotch, J. A.   *The English House from Charles I to George IV*, 1919

Gotch, J. A.   *Inigo Jones*, 1928

Hill, Oliver and Cornforth, John   *English Country Houses: Caroline, 1625–86*, 1966

Hussey, C.   *English Country Houses, early Georgian, mid-Georgian and late Georgian*, 3 vols, 1955–8

Ison, W.   *Georgian Buildings of Bath*, 1948

Jones, Inigo   *Designs*. Published by W. Kent, 1770

Jourdain, Margaret and Ayscough, Anthony   *Country House Baroque*: Photographs of eighteenth century ornament, mostly stucco-work in English and Irish country houses and some Dublin houses, with a Foreword by Sacheverell Sitwell, 1940

Jourdain, Margaret   *English Decorative Plasterwork of the Renaissance*, 1926

Jourdain, Margaret   *The Work of William Kent*, 1948

Knight, Richard Payne   *Analytical Enquiry into the Principles of Taste*, 1808

Knoop, D. and Jones, G. P.   *The London Mason in the 17th Century*, 1935

Langley, Batty   *The City and Country Builder's and Workman's Treasury of Designs*, 1740

Langley, Batty   *The Builder's Jewel*, 1741

Lees-Milne, James   *The Age of Adam*, 1947

Lees-Milne, James   *The Age of Inigo Jones*, 1953

Lenygon, F.   The Chinese Taste of English Decoration, *Art Journal*, 1911

Maxwell, C.   *Country and Town in Ireland under the Georges*, 1940

Price, Sir Uvedale   *Essay on the Picturesque*, 1794

Ramsey, S. C.   *Small Houses of the late Georgian Period*, 1924

Reilly, P.   *An Introduction to Regency Architecture*, 1948

Repton, Humphrey   *Theory and Practice of Landscape Gardening*, 1803

Richardson, A. E.   *An Introduction to Georgian Architecture*, 1950

Richardson, A. E. and Eberlein, H. D.   *The Smaller English House of the Later Renaissance*, 1925

Rutter, John   *Delineations of Fonthill*, 1823

Scarfe, Norman   Little Haugh Hall, Suffolk, *Country Life*, June, 1958

Steegman, John   *The Rule of Taste*, 1936

Stroud, Dorothy   *Capability Brown*; with an Introduction by C. Hussey. Revised edn, 1957

Stroud, Dorothy   *The Architecture of Sir John Soane*; with an Introduction by H. R. Hitchcock, 1961

Stroud, Dorothy   *Humphrey Repton*, 1962

Stroud, Dorothy   *Henry Holland, his Life and Architecture*, 1966

Stutchbury, H. E.   *The Architecture of Colen Campbell*, 1967

Sugden and Edmondson   *History of English Wallpaper*, 1926

Summerson, Sir John   *John Nash, Architect to King George IV*, 1935

Summerson, Sir John   *Georgian London*, 1945

Swarbrick, John   *Robert Adam*, 1915

Trevelyan, G. M.   *England under the Stuarts*, 21st edn, 1963

Triggs, H. Inigo and Tanner, H.   *Architectural Works of Inigo Jones*, 1901

Ware, Isaac   *The Complete Body of Architecture*, 1624

Webb, Geoffrey   *Wren*, 1937

Whinney, Margaret and Millar, Oliver   *English Art 1625–1714*, 1957

Whistler, Laurence   *Sir John Vanbrugh*, 1938

Wood, John   *An Essay towards a Description of Bath*, 1742 and 1749

Wotton, H.   *The Elements of Architecture*, 1624

Youngson, A. J.   *The Making of Classical Edinburgh*, 1966

Index